WAR ON THE SAINTS

(Original unabridged edition)

Jessie Penn-Lewis
In collaboration with Evan Roberts

To THE READERS

As a key to a lock so is the truth in this book to need.
Evan Roberts

First published in 1912

This illustrated edition published 2025 by Cosmic Jive Publishing

ISBN 978-1-918219-35-7

And it was given unto him to make War with the saints, and to overcome them.
(Rev 8:7)

And some of them [the teachers, m] that be wise shall fall, to refine them and to purify them and to make them white, even to the time of the end.
(Dan: 11: 35)

FOREWORD TO 2025 PUBLICATION

There are books that every Christian should read. And this book is undoubtedly one of them. It's a classic, penned by people who were at the heart of the Great Welsh Revival. The book has changed the lives of many since first being published but its words of wisdom remain as revolutionary - and as challenging - as they ever were.

You may not agree with all of it - and that is fine - just as long as you *do* read it.

Blessings

Pastor Joe Lighthall,

Author of *'Angel Miracles'*

Vocabulary

Definitions of words used in this book:

Church: The spiritual and mystical body of Christ, joined to Him as Head
Communication: That which is understood
Communion: That which is to be felt
Counterfeit: an imitation or an exact copy and resemblance to Divine, human or Satanic things or workings
Deception: a wrong though admitted to the mind and believed to be truth
Evil spirits: spirit beings who are evil
Excuses: Incorrect reasons suggested to the mind by deceitful spirits to cover their workings
Experience: That which has been known, felt, proved, in contrast to mental knowledge only
'Ground": anything in a person whereby evil spirits gain
Impurity: That which is a mixture: not moral impurity, i.e purity of the mixture of soul and spirit, etc
Passivity: the non-use of will, or any of the faculties, or part of the whole being of man. It is practically the counterfeit of "surrender"
"Possession": .any hold which evil spirits have in or upon a person in any degree
"Refuse": the volitional act of the will, whereby a man expresses his choice. "Refusal "of "ground" is opposite to "giving".
Soul: this is never used for the person, but in the primary meaning of the "soul" person of the tripartite man,
Theory: speculation, apart from practice.

Scripture references are taken from the Revised Version, except where otherwise marked.

CONTENTS

Introductory Chapter	11
1. A Biblical Survey of Satanic Deception	15
2. The Satanic Confederacy of Wicked Spirits	34
3. Deception by Evil Spirits in Modern Times.	48
4. Passivity the Chief Basis of Possession	63
5. Deception and Possession	82
6. Counterfeits of the Divine	103
7. Ground and Symptoms of Possession	125
8. The Path to Freedom	144
9. The Volition and Spirit of Man	162
10. Victory in Conflict	177
11. War Upon the Powers of Darkness	199
12. Revival Dawn & the Baptism of the Spirit	218
SUPPLEMENTARY NOTES.	235

The True Workings of God & Counterfeits of Satan.
Summary of "Ground" -
Brief Notes
Appendix Note.

INTRODUCTORY CHAPTER

In common with the physical and mental realms of human experience, the spiritual sphere has its freaks and diseases; and this book is a "Text book on the work of deceiving spirits among the children of God, and the way of deliverance."

It is no more a book for the general reader than is either a medical work on cancer, or a text book on mental disorders. It should never be read for curiosity nor from mere academic interest. In her foreword to the first edition Mrs. Penn-Lewis wrote: "To the natural man; who has but a mental grasp of spiritual things, the language used may be meaningless, but Christians of all stages of growth in the spiritual life, who simply take what they can understand and leave the remainder for those who are in deeper need-and until they themselves are in deeper need-will obtain much light on matters within their horizon."

Its main appeal will be to two classes of readers. The first consists of those, who have become involved in some false system of religious teaching drawing its inspiration from satanic lies instead of from the sane balanced truth of the Word of God, and who have thus opened themselves to abnormal spiritual experiences which often result in demon possession. The suffering endured by these dupes of the powers of evil is intense; and since the first edition of this book was printed in 1912 there have been many testimonies to deliverance and help received through its pages from such readers. Eternity alone will reveal the ministry it has already exercised and will yet, by the mercy of God, fulfil in restoring such to hope, peace, and sanity.

The second type of reader, to whom this book is of immense value is the Christian worker who finds himself or herself faced with cases of spiritual abnormality, of which there seem to be an increasing number in these days of intense satanic activity. To such readers these pages will bring light and guidance, and it is perhaps striking that in recent months a magazine as well informed of Christian work in many lands as The Alliance Weekly of America, should feel it necessary to publish some very able articles by The Rev. J. A. Macmillan dealing with demon possession. A paragraph from one of these articles reads as follows: "Upon pastors and evangelists rests the greatest measure of responsibility for the instruction of the flock of God. It is in a special way theirs to discern the signs of enemy-working and to deliver their people. It is theirs also to teach and to warn of the perils which the threaten the spiritually minded. It must be realised that the "heavenlies," into which the saints are introduced by divine wisdom and grace, are in this present dispensation the habitat of "the power of the air." The believer who seeks the deepest experiences of the spiritual life may fall under deception unless he knows that "Satan himself is transformed into an angel of light" at times, and that the arch-enemy is at home in religious gatherings where earnest leaders are "ignorant of his devices."

Full "abandonment to God," unless guarded by the knowledge of the methods by which the Spirit of God reveals Himself, may open the life to the invasion of spirits of darkness. This statement should be pondered carefully in desiring gifts and manifestations. The distribution of such is strictly the function of the Holy Spirit, who divides "to each one severally (individually) AS HE WILL." The seeking believer should have his eyes upon the Throne, disregarding specific gifts (unless these are revealed as things which he should "covet"-1 Cor 12:31; 14:1). What the surrendered soul must pursue is the will of God as his chief and only aim, being watchful lest his mind be set on things which might promote carnality and be the issue of self-will. Many, many are the earnest souls who have unconsciously given themselves over through an unrecognised envy to grasp after what they have seen in the possession of others.

Demon possession is as a rule understood by the worker in heathen lands; and we must bear in mind that most civilised countries to-day have become strongholds of paganism. It is, therefore, not unreasonable to expect that spiritual phenomena usually associated with heathendom will manifest themselves more and more in the midst of the so-called culture, and pseudo-Christian paganism of our modem world.

In our mechanical age, in which liberty and private judgment are so often sacrificed, and in which dictatorship and mass propaganda have become such powerful forces, the chapter dealing with "passivity" should be read and re- read. "The powers of darkness" runs one passage from this chapter, "would make man a machine, a tool, an automaton, the God of holiness and love desires to make him a free, intelligent sovereign in his own sphere-a thinking, rational creature created after His own image (Eph. 4.24). Therefore, God never says to any faculty of man "Be thou idle." It does not seem possible to exaggerate the danger of slipshod thinking concerning spiritual things, and unreasoning abandonment to experiences not founded on a clear understanding of the broad principles of Scripture, and clear teaching along this line is necessary if a healthy advance is to be seen in the life of the Christian Church.

"War on the Saints" may well prove invaluable should God grant a true spiritual revival in answer to the many prayers which are going up from His children throughout the World. At such times satanic opposition stiffens, and many hidden workings of evil are brought out into the open. Then those, who have the responsibility of dealing with souls will need all the light they can obtain on the abnormalities caused by the hold of evil spirits gained either through acceptance of false doctrines, or by tampering with the supernatural.

A paragraph from a recent article by a medically qualified missionary working in China, and familiar with cases of possession by evil spirits, will be of value in maintaining a balanced view of this difficult subject. "A word of warning about mis-diagnosis and lack of balance in spiritual warfare. The exercise of our authority in CHRIST is not a cure for all ills. It has been said that "War is 99% waiting," and the soldier of JESUS CHRIST will not be required to spend his whole time in the front-line trenches. There were times when it was not for Moses to hold the rod of God aloft, but to get down to the hard toil of intercession, and times when his work was to trudge in the wilderness with his people. A Mrs. Yellow was brought by her heathen relatives day after day to the Mission compound because they said she was quieter there. (We took their word for it, but wondered whatever she was like at home!). We labeled her as demon- possessed, and took up our stand against the enemy with no effect whatsoever. It was months before we obtained a full history and found she had a common type of temporary insanity! To attribute troubles indiscriminately to the devil does not make for a healthy atmosphere. We do need balance, and, above all, we need to be so in touch with our Lord that He can give us spiritual perception."

Finally may we again quote from the foreword to the First Edition: "With the publication of the book six years of prayerful testing of the truth here given, and three years of toil in placing these truths in writing, in the face of unceasing attacks from the unseen realm, now draw to their close. The issue lies with God. He who has sustained, and given countless proofs of His protecting hand in a "thus far and no farther" to the attacking hosts of darkness, will carry through His purpose to the end. The light will reach those who need it. Let God fulfil His Will."

Those of us responsible for launching this 7th edition of War on the Saints, can only say "Amen" to that final prayer. We dare not withhold from publication a message which, as it has done in the past, will undoubtedly bring freedom from the torturing grip of the evil one to many in need. May the Spirit of God to whom "all hearts be open, all desires known, and from whom no secrets are hid" so guide, that every copy fall into the right hands, and may He also give all who read discernment to grasp the truth, which will meet need, without involving themselves and others in a maze of unnecessary complication.

CHAPTER 1
A Biblical Survey of Satanic Deception

Truth of every kind makes free, while lies bind up in bonds. Ignorance also binds up, because it gives ground to Satan. Man's ignorance is a primary and essential condition for deception by evil spirits. The ignorance of the people of God concerning the powers of darkness, has made it easy for the devil to carry out his work as deceiver. Unfallen man in his pure state was not perfect in knowledge. Eve was ignorant of "good and evil," and her ignorance was a condition which lent itself to the deception of the serpent.

The devil's great purpose, and for which he fights, is to keep the world in ignorance of himself, his ways, and his colleagues, and the Church is taking sides with him when siding with ignorance about him. Every man should keep an attitude of openness to all truth, and shun the false knowledge which has slain its tens of thousands, and kept the nations in the deception of the devil.

A SPECIAL ONSLAUGHT OF DECEIVING SPIRITS ON THE CHURCH

Today there is a special onslaught of deceiving spirits upon the Church of Christ, the fulfilment of the prophecy which the Holy Spirit expressly made known to the Church through the Apostle Paul, that a great deceptive onslaught would take place in the "later times." Since the utterance of the prophecy, more than eighteen hundred years have passed by, but the special manifestation of evil spirits in the deception of believers today, points unmistakably to the fact that we are at the close of the age.

The peril of the church at the close of this dispensation is foreshown to be especially from the supernatural realm, whence Satan would send forth an army of teaching spirits, to deceive all who would be open to teachings by spiritual revelation, and thus draw them away unwittingly from full allegiance to God.

Yet in face of this plain forecast of the peril in later times, we find the Church in almost entire ignorance of the workings of this army of evil spirits. The majority of believers too readily accept everything "supernatural" as of God, and supernatural experiences are indiscriminately accepted because all such experiences are thought to be Divine.

Through lack of knowledge, the majority of even the most spiritual people, do not carry out a full and perpetual war upon this army of wicked spirits; and many are shrinking from the subject, and the call to war against them, saying that if Christ is preached it is not necessary to give prominence to the existence of the devil, nor to enter into direct conflict with him, and his hosts. Yet large numbers of the children of God are becoming a prey to the enemy for lack of this very knowledge, and through the silence of teachers on this vital truth, the Church of Christ is passing on into the peril of the closing days of the age, unprepared to meet the onslaught of the foe.

On account of this, and in view of the plainly given prophetic warnings in the Scriptures; the already manifest influx of the evil hosts of Satan among the children of God; and the many signs that we are actually in the "later times" referred to by the Apostle; all believers should welcome such knowledge about the powers of darkness, as will enable them to pass through the fiery trial of these days, without being ensnared by the foe.

Apart from such knowledge, when thinking he is "fighting for truth," it is possible for a believer to fight for, defend, and protect evil spirits, and their works, believing he is thereby "defending" God, and His works; for if he thinks a thing Divine, he will protect and stand for it. It is possible for a man through ignorance to stand against God and to attack the very truth of God, and also defend the devil, and oppose God, unless he has knowledge.

KNOWLEDGE GAINED BY LETTER OF SCRIPTURE, & BY EXPERIENCE

The Bible throws much light upon the Satanic powers, which cannot fail to be discerned by all who search the Scriptures with open minds, but these will not obtain as much knowledge of the subject from the sacred record, as will those who have understanding by experience, interpreted by the Holy Spirit, and shown to be in line with the truth of the Word of God. The believer may have a direct witness in his spirit to the truth of the Divine Word, but through experience he gets a personal witness to the inspiration of Scripture, to its testimony concerning the existence of supernatural beings, and their works, and the way they deceive, and mislead the children of men.

THE WORK OF SATAN AS DECEIVER IN THE GARDEN OF EDEN

If all that the Bible contains on the subject of the supernatural powers of evil, could be exhaustively dealt with in this book, we should find that more knowledge is given of the workings of Satan, and his principalities and powers, than many have realised. From Genesis to Revelation the work of Satan as deceiver of the whole inhabited earth can be traced, until the climax is reached, and the full results of the deception in the Garden of Eden are unveiled in the Apocalypse.

In Genesis we have the simple story of the garden, with the guileless pair unaware of danger from evil beings in the unseen world. We find recorded there Satan's first work as deceiver, and the subtle form of his method of deception. We see him working upon an innocent creature's highest and purest desires, and cloaking his own purpose of ruin, under the guise of seeking to lead a human being nearer to God. We see him using the God-ward desires of Eve to bring about captivity, and bondage to himself. We see him using "good" to bring about evil; suggesting evil to bring about supposed good. Caught with the bait of being "wise," and "like God," Eve is blinded to the principle involved in obedience to God, and is deceived (1 Tim. 2: 14, A.V.).

Goodness is, therefore, no guarantee of protection from deception. The keenest way in which the devil deceives the world, and the Church, is when he comes in the guise of somebody, or something, which apparently causes them to go God-ward and good-ward. He said to Eve, "ye shall be as gods," but he did not say, "and ye shall be like demons."

Angels and men only knew evil when they fell into a state of evil. Satan did not tell Eve this, when he added "knowing good and evil." His true objective in deceiving Eve was to get her to disobey God, but his wile was, "ye shall be like God." Had she reasoned, she would have seen that the deceiver's suggestion exposed itself, for it crudely resolved itself into "disobey God" to be more like God!

THE CURSE OF GOD PRONOUNCED UPON THE DECEIVER

That a highly organsied monarchy of evil spirit-beings was in existence, is not made known in the story of the garden. Only a "serpent" is there; but the serpent is spoken to by God as an intelligent being, carrying out a deliberate purpose in the deception of the woman. The serpent-disguise of Satan is swept aside by Jehovah, as He makes known the decision of the Triune God in view of the catastrophe which had taken place. A "Seed" of the deceived woman, should eventually bruise the head of the supernatural being, who had used the form of the serpent to carry out his plan. Thenceforward the name of serpent is attached to him, the very name throughout the ages describing the climax action of his revolt against his Creator, in beguiling and deceiving the woman in Eden, and blasting the human race. Satan triumphed, but God overruled. The victim is made the vehicle for the advent of a Victor, who should ultimately destroy the works of the devil, and cleanse the heavens and the earth from every trace of his handiwork.

The serpent is cursed, but, in effect, the beguiled victim is blest, for through her will come the "Seed" which will triumph over the devil and his seed; and through her will arise a new race through the promised Seed (Gen. 3: 15), which will be antagonistic to the serpent to the end of time, through the enmity implanted by God.

Henceforth the story of the ages consists of the record of a war between these two seeds; the Seed of the woman--Christ and His redeemed--and the seed of the devil (See John 8: 44; 1 John 3: 10), right on to the furthermost point of the final committal of Satan to the lake of fire. Henceforth it is also war by Satan upon the womanhood of the world, in malignant revenge for the verdict of the garden. War by the trampling down of women in all lands where the deceiver reigns. War upon women in Christian lands, by the continuance of his Eden method of misinterpreting the Word of God; insinuating into men's minds throughout all succeeding ages, that God pronounced a "curse" upon the woman, when in truth she was pardoned and blessed; and instigating men of the fallen race to carry out the supposed curse, which was in truth a curse upon the deceiver, and not the deceived one (Gen. 3: 14).

"I will put enmity between thee and the woman," said God, as well as between "thy seed and her seed," and this vindictive enmity of the hierarchy of evil to woman, and to believers, has not lessened in its intensity from that day.

SATAN AS DECEIVER IN THE OLD TESTAMENT

When once we clearly apprehend the existence of an unseen host of evil spirit-beings, all actively engaged in deceiving and misleading men, Old Testament history will convey to us an open vision of their doings, hitherto hidden from our knowledge.

We can trace their operations in relation to the servants of God throughout all history, and discern the work of Satan as deceiver penetrating everywhere. We shall see that David was deceived by Satan into numbering Israel, because he failed to recognise the suggestion to his mind as from a Satanic source (1 Chron. 21: 1).

Job also was deceived, and the messengers that came to him, when he believed the report that the "fire" which had fallen from heaven was from God (Job. 1: 16); and that all the other calamities which befell him in the loss of wealth, home and children, came directly from the hand of God; whereas the early part of the book of Job clearly shows that Satan was the primary cause of all his troubles; as "prince of the power of the air" using the elements of nature, and the wickedness of men, to afflict the servant of God, in the hope that ultimately he could force Job into renouncing his faith in God, Who seemed to be unjustly punishing him without cause. That this was Satan's aim is suggested in the words of the wife of the patriarch, who became a tool for the Adversary, in urging the suffering man to "curse God and die," she, also, being deceived by the enemy into believing that God was the primary cause of all the trouble and the unmerited suffering which had come upon him.

In the history of Israel during the time of Moses, the veil is lifted more clearly from the Satanic powers, and we are shown the condition of the world as sunk in idolatry--which is said in the New Testament to be the direct work of Satan (1 Cor. 10: 20)--and actual dealing with evil spirits; the whole inhabited earth being thus in a state of deception, and held by the deceiver in his power. We also find numbers of God's own people, through contact with others under Satanic power, deceived into communicating with "familiar spirits," and into the using of "divination," and other kindred arts, inculcated by the powers of darkness, even though they knew the laws of God, and had seen His manifested judgments among them. (See Lev. 17: 7, R.V. margin "satyrs"; 19: 31; 20: 6, 27; Deut. 18: 10, 11).

In the book of Daniel, we find a still further stage of revelation reached concerning the hierarchy of evil powers, when in the tenth chapter we are shown the existence of the princes of Satan, actively opposing the messenger of God sent to Daniel to make His servant understand His counsels for His people.

There are also other references to the workings of Satan, his princes, and the hosts of wicked spirits, carrying out his will, scattered throughout the Old Testament, but on the whole the veil is kept upon their doings, until the great hour arrives, when the "Seed" of the woman, who was to bruise the head of the serpent, is manifested on earth in human form (Gal. 4: 4).

SATAN AS DECEIVER UNVEILED IN THE NEW TESTAMENT

With the advent of Christ, the veil which had hidden the active workings of the supernatural powers of evil, for centuries since the garden catastrophe, is still further removed, and their deception and power over man is clearly revealed, and the arch-deceiver himself appears in the wilderness conflict of the Lord, to challenge the "Seed of the woman," as it is not recorded that he appeared on earth since the time of the Fall. The wilderness of Judea, and the Garden of Eden, being parallel periods for the testing of the first and second Adam.

In both periods Satan worked as Deceiver, in the second instance wholly failing to deceive, and beguile the One who had come as his Conqueror. Traces of the characteristic work of Satan as deceiver can be discerned among the disciples of the Christ. He deceives Peter into speaking words of temptation to the Lord, suggesting His turning from the path of the Cross (Matt. 16: 22-23), and later on takes hold of the same disciple in the Judgment Hall (Luke 22: 31), prompting him to the lie, "I know not the Man," with the very purpose of deception (Matt. 26: 74). Further traces of the work of the deceiver may be seen in the epistles of Paul, in his references to the "false apostles," "deceitful workers," and Satan's workings as an "angel of light," and "his ministers as ministers of righteousness" among the people of God (2 Cor. 11: 13-15). In the messages to the Churches, also, given by the ascended Lord to His servant John, false apostles are spoken of, and false teachings of many kinds. A "synagogue of Satan" (Rev. 2: 9), consisting of deceived ones, is mentioned, and "deep things of Satan" are described as existing in the Church (Rev. 2: 24).

THE FULL REVELATION OF THE DECEIVER IN THE APOCALYPSE

THEN THE VEIL IS LIFTED AT LAST. The full revelation of the Satanic confederacy against God and His Christ, is given to the Apostle John. After the messages to the Churches, the worldwide work of the deceiver prince is fully disclosed to the Apostle, and he is bidden to write all that he is shown, that the Church of Christ might know the full meaning of the War with Satan in which the redeemed would be engaged, right on to the time when the Lord Jesus would be revealed from heaven, in judgment upon these vast, and terrible powers, full of cunning malignity, and hatred to His people, and as truly at work behind the world of men, from the days of the garden story to the end.

As we read the Apocalypse, it is important to remember that the organised forces of Satan described therein, were in existence at the time of the Fall of Eden, and only partially revealed to the people of God until the advent of the promised "Seed of the woman" Who was to bruise the serpent's head. When the fulness of time had come, God manifest in the flesh met the fallen archangel, and leader of the evil angelic host, in mortal combat at Calvary; and, putting them to open shame, shook off from Himself the vast masses of the hosts of darkness who gathered around the Cross, from the furthermost realms of the kingdom of Satan (Col. 2: 15).

The Scriptures teach us that God's unveilings of the truths concerning Himself, and all the things in the spiritual realm which we need to know, are always timed by Him to the strength of His people.

The full revelation of the Satanic powers disclosed in the Apocalypse was not given to the Church in its infancy, for some forty years passed after the Lord's ascension ere the Book of the Revelation was written. Possibly it was necessary, that the Church of Christ should first fully apprehend the fundamental truths revealed to Paul, and the other Apostles, ere she could safely be shown the extent of the war with supernatural powers of evil upon which she had entered.

THE LAST OF THE APOSTLES CHOSEN TO TRANSMIT THE REVELATION

Whatever the reason of the delay, it is striking that it was the last of the Apostles who was chosen to transmit, at the very end of his life, the full war- message to the Church, which would serve as a foreshadowing of the campaign until its close.

In the Revelation given to John, the name and character of the deceiver is more clearly made known, with the strength of his forces, and the extent of the war, and its final issues. It is shown that in the invisible realm there is war between the forces of evil, and the forces of light. John says that "the dragon warred, and his angels . . , " the dragon being explicitly described as the "serpent" from his guise in Eden--"called the Devil and Satan," the deceiver of the whole inhabited earth.

His worldwide work as deceiver is fully revealed, and the war in the earth realm caused by his deceiving of the nations, and the world-powers acting under his instigation and rule. The highly organised confederacy of principalities and powers, acknowledging the headship of Satan, is disclosed, and their "authority over every tribe and people and tongue and nation," all deceived by the supernatural and invisible forces of evil, and making "war with the saints" (Rev. 13: 7).

WORLD-WIDE DECEPTION DISCLOSED IN THE APOCALYPSE

War is the keyword of the Apocalypse; war on a scale undreamed of by mortal man; war between vast angelic powers of light and darkness; war by the dragon, and the deceived world-powers upon the saints; war by the same world-powers against the Lamb; war by the dragon upon the Church; war in many phases and forms, until the end when the Lamb overcomes, and they also overcome who are with Him, called and chosen and faithful (Rev. 17: 14).

The world is now drawing nearer to the "time of the end," characterised by the deception depicted in the Apocalypse as being world-wide; when there will be deception of nations, and individuals, on such a vast scale that the deceiver will practically have the whole earth under his control. Ere this climax is reached there will be preliminary stages of the deceiver's working, marked by the widespread deception of individuals, both within and without the Church, beyond the ordinary condition of deception in which the unregenerate world is lying.

To understand why the deceiver will be able to produce the world-wide deception depicted in the Apocalypse, which will permit the supernatural powers to carry out their will, and drive nations and men into active rebellion against God, we need clearly to grasp what the Scriptures say about unregenerate men in their normal condition, and the world in its fallen state.

If Satan is described in the Apocalypse as the deceiver of the whole earth, he has been so from the beginning. "The whole world lieth in the evil one" (1 John 5: 19), said the Apostle, to whom was given the Revelation, describing the world as already lying deep in darkness through the deception of the evil one, and blindly led by him through vast evil spirit hosts under his control.

THE WORD "DECEIVED" THE DESCRIPTION OF EVERY UNREGENERATE MAN

The word "deceived" is, according to the Scripture, the description of every unregenerate human being, without distinction of persons, race, culture, or sex. "We also were . . . deceived" (Titus 3: 3), said Paul the Apostle, although in his "deceived" condition he was a religious man, walking according to the righteousness of the law, blameless (Phil. 3: 6).

Every unregenerate man first of all is deceived by his own deceitful heart (Jer. 17: 9; Isa. 44: 20), and deceived by sin (Heb. 3: 13); the god of this world adding the "blinding of the mind" lest the light of the gospel of Christ should dispel the darkness (2 Cor. 4: 4). And the deception of the evil one does not end when the regenerating life of God reaches the man, for the blinding of the mind is only removed just so far as the deceptive lies of Satan are dislodged by the light of truth.

Even though the heart is renewed, and the will has turned to God, yet the deeply ingrained disposition to self-deception, and the presence, in some measure, of the blinding power of the deceiver on the mind, betrays itself in many forms, as the following statements from Scripture show :—

The man is deceived if he is a hearer, and not a doer of the Word of God (Jas. 1: 22).

He is deceived if he says he has no sin (1 John 1: 8).

He is deceived when he thinks himself to be "something" when he is nothing (Gal. 6: 3).

He is deceived when he thinks himself to be wise with the wisdom of this world. (1 Cor. 3: 18).

He is deceived by seeming to be religious, when an unbridled tongue reveals his true condition (Jas. 1: 26).

He is deceived, if he thinks he will sow, and not reap what he sows (Gal. 6: 7).

He is deceived, if he thinks the unrighteous will inherit the kingdom of God (1 Cor. 6: 9).

He is deceived , if he thinks that contact with sin will not have its effect (1 Cor. 15: 33) upon him.

DECEIVED! How the word repels, and how involuntarily every human being resents it as applied to himself, not knowing that the very repulsion is the work of the deceiver, for the purpose of keeping the deceived ones from knowing the truth, and being set free from deception. If men can be so easily deceived by the deception arising from their own fallen nature, how eagerly will the forces of Satan seek to add to it and not diminish it by one iota. How keenly will they work to keep men in bondage to the old creation, out of which will spring multitudinous forms of self-deception, enabling them the more readily to carry on their deceiving work. Their methods of deception are old and new, adapted to suit the nature, state, and circumstances of the victim. Instigated by hatred, malice, and bitter ill-will towards mankind and all goodness, the emissaries of Satan do not fail to execute their plans, with a perseverance worthy to be imitated by him who fain would reach his goal.

SATAN THE DECEIVER ALSO OF THE CHILDREN OF GOD

The arch-deceiver is not only the deceiver of the whole unregenerate world, but of the children of God also; with this difference, that in the deception he seeks to practise upon the saints, he changes his tactics, and works with acutest strategy, in wiles of error, and deception concerning the things of God (Matt. 24: 24; 2 Cor. 11: 3, 13, 14, 15).

The chief weapon which the deceiver-prince of darkness relies upon to keep the world in his power, is deception, and deception planned to beguile men at every stage of life; deception (1) of the unregenerate who are already deceived by sin; (2) deception suited to the carnal Christian; (3) and deception fitted to the spiritual believer, who has passed out of the preceding stages into a realm where he will be open to meet more subtle wiles. Let the deception be removed which holds the man in the earlier days of his unregenerate condition, and in the stage of the carnal Christian life; when he emerges into the heavenly places, described by Paul in the Epistle to the Ephesians, he will find himself in the very keenest workings of the wiles of the deceiver, where the deceiving spirits are actively at work attacking those who are united to the risen Lord.

THE DECEPTION PERIL OF THE LAST DAYS OF THE AGE

In the Apocalypse, we have the full unveiling of the Satanic confederacy in widespread control of the whole earth, and the war upon the saints as a whole; but the work of the deceiver among the foremost saints of God is especially depicted in the Ephesian letter of the apostle Paul, where, in Ephesians 6: 10- 18, we have the veil drawn aside from the Satanic powers, showing their war upon the Church of God, and the individual believer's armour and weapons for conquering the foe. From this passage we learn that in the plane of the believer's highest experience of union with the Lord, and in the "high places" of the spiritual maturity of the Church, will the keenest and closest battle be fought with the deceiver and his hosts.

Hence as the Church of Christ draws near to the time of the end, and is, by the inworking power of the Holy Spirit, being matured for translation, the full force of the deceiver and his hosts of lying spirits will be directed upon the living members of the Body of Christ. A glimpse into this onslaught of deceiving spirits upon the people of God in the close of the age, is given in the Gospel of Matthew, where the Lord uses the word deceived in describing some of the special marks of the latter days. He said: "Take heed that no man deceive you. For many shall come in My Name, saying, 'I am Christ:' and shall lead many astray" (Matt. 24: 4, 5, A.V. and R.V.); "and many false prophets shall arise, and shall deceive many" (Matt. 24: 11, A.V.). "There shall arise false christs, and false prophets, and shall show great signs and wonders, so as to lead astray [or "deceive" A.V.] if possible, even the elect" (Matt. 24: 24).

DECEPTION IN CONNECTION WITH THE SUPERNATURAL REALM

The special form of deception is said also to be in connection with spiritual, and not worldly, things; incidentally showing that the people of God, at the time of the end, will be expecting the coming of the Lord, and therefore be keenly awake to all movements from the supernatural world, in such a measure that deceiving spirits will be able to take advantage of it, and anticipate the Lord's appearing by "false Christs" and false signs and wonders; or mix their counterfeits with the true manifestations of the Spirit of God.

The Lord says that men will be deceived (1) concerning Christ and His parousia--or Coming; (2) concerning prophecy--or teaching from the spiritual world through inspired messengers; and (3) concerning the giving of proofs of the "teachings" being truly of God, by "signs" and "wonders" so Godlike, and therefore so exact a counterfeit of the working of God, as to be indistinguishable from the true by those described as His "elect"; who will need to possess some other test than the judging by appearances of a "sign" being from God, if they are to be able to discern the false from the true.

The Apostle Paul's words to Timothy, containing the special prophecy given to him by the Holy Spirit for the Church of Christ in the last days of the dispensation, exactly coincide with the words of the Lord recorded by Matthew.

The two letters of Paul to Timothy are the last epistles that he wrote ere his departure to be with Christ. Both were written in prison, and Paul's prison was to him what Patmos was to John, when he was "in spirit" (Rev. 1: 10 shown things to come. Paul was giving his last directions to Timothy for the ordering of the Church of God, right on to the end of her time on earth; giving "rules to guide," not only Timothy, but all God's servants, "in dealing with God's household." In the midst of all these detailed instructions, his keen seer's vision looks on to the "later times"; and by express command of the Spirit of God, he depicts in a few brief sentences, the peril of the Church in those times, in the same way that the Spirit of God gave the prophets of the Old Testament some pregnant prophecy, only to be fully understood after the events had come to pass.

The Apostle said: "The Spirit saith expressly, that in later times some shall fall away from the faith, giving heed to seducing spirits and doctrines of demons, through the hypocrisy of men that speak lies, seared in their own conscience as with a hot iron .. " (1 Tim. 4: 1, 2, R.V. m.).

PAUL'S STATEMENT IN 1 TIM. 4: 1, 2, THE ONLY SPECIFIC ONE SHOWING THE CAUSE OF THE PERIL

Paul's prophetic statement appears to be all that is foretold in specific words about the Church, and its history, at the close of the dispensation. The Lord spoke in general terms about the dangers which would encompass His people at the time of the end, and Paul wrote to the Thessalonians more fully about the apostasy, and the wicked deceptions of the Lawless one in the last days, but the passage in Timothy is the only one which explicitly shows the special cause of the peril of the Church in its closing days on earth, and how the wicked spirits of Satan would break in upon her members, and by deception beguile some away from their purity of faith in Christ.

The Holy Spirit, in the brief message given to Paul, describes the character and work of the evil spirits, recognising (1) their existence, (2) their efforts directed towards believers, to deceive them, and by deception draw them away from the path of simple faith in Christ, and all that is included in the "faith once for all delivered unto the saints" (Jude 3).

That the character of the spirits is described in 1 Tim. 4: 1-3, and not the men they somtimes use in the work of deception, may be understood from the Greek original

The peril of the Church at the close of the age, is therefore from supernatural beings who are "hypocrites," who pretend to be what they are not, who give "teachings" which appear to make for greater holiness, by producing ascetic severity to the "flesh," but who themselves are wicked and unclean, and bring in to those they deceive the foulness of their own presence. Where they deceive they gain possession; and whilst the deceived believer thinks he is more "holy," and more "sanctified," and more delivered from the desires of the flesh, these hypocritical spirits defile the deceived one by their presence, and under cover of sanctity hold their ground, and hide their workings.

THE PERIL OF DECEIVING SPIRITS AFFECTS EVERY CHILD OF GOD

The peril concerns every child of God, and no spiritual believer dare say he is exempt from peril. The prophecy of the Holy Spirit declares, that (1) "some" shall fall away from the faith; (2) the reason for the fall will be a giving heed to deceiving spirits, i.e., the nature of their working being not known evil, but deception, which is a covered working. The essence of deception is that the operation is looked upon as sincere and pure. (3) The nature of the deception will be in doctrines of demons, i.e., the deception will be in a doctrinal sphere. (4) The way of deception will be that the "doctrines" are delivered with "hypocrisy," i.e. spoken as if true. (5) Two instances of the effect of these evil spirit doctrines are given: (a) the forbidding of marriage, and (b) abstaining from meats; both, said Paul "created by God," Therefore their teaching is marked by opposition to God, even in His work as Creator.

THE SATANIC FORCES DESCRIBED IN EPHES. 6

Demoniacal "doctrines" have been generally tabulated as either belonging to the Church of Rome, because of the two marked results of demon teaching mentioned by Paul, which characterise that Church; or later "cults" of the twentieth century, with their omission of the fact of sin, and the need of the atoning sacrifice of Christ, and a Divine Saviour. But there is a vast realm of doctrinal deception by deceiving spirits, penetrating, and interpenetrating Evangelical Christendom, by which evil spirits, in more or less degree, influence the lives even of Christian men, and bring them under their power; even spiritual Christians being thus affected on the plane described by the Apostle, where believers united to the Risen Christ meet "spiritual wickedness" in "heavenly places." For the Satanic forces described in Eph. 6: 12, are shown to be divided into (1) "Principalities"--force and dominion dealing with nations and governments; (2) "Powers"--having authority and power of action in all the spheres open to them; (3) " World- rulers"-- governing the darkness, and blindness of the world at large; (4) "Wicked spirits" in the heavenly places--their forces being directed in, and upon the Church of Jesus Christ, in "wiles," "fiery darts," onslaughts, and every conceivable deception over "doctrines" which they are capable of planning.

The peril of the household of God is therefore not of a few, but all, for obviously none can "fall away from the faith" but those who arc actually in the faith to begin with. The peril is from an army of teaching spirits poured forth by Satan upon all who would be open to "teachings" from the spiritual world, and through ignorance of such a danger, be unable to detect the wiles of the enemy.

The peril assails the Church from the supernatural world, and comes from supernatural spirit-beings who are persons (Mark 1: 25) with intelligent power of planning (Matt. 12: 44, 45), with strategy (Eph. 6: 11) the deception of those who "give heed" to them.

The peril is supernatural. And those who are in peril are the spiritual children of God; who are not to be beguiled by the world or the flesh, but who are open to all they can learn of "spiritual" things, with sincere longing to be more "spiritual" and more advanced in the knowledge of God. For deception by doctrines would not concern the world so much as the Church. Evil spirits would not urge spiritual Christians to open sin, such as murder, drink, gambling, etc., but would plan deception in the form of "teaching" and "doctrines," the believer not knowing that deception on "teaching" and "doctrines" gives admission to evil spirits to "possess" the deceived one, as much as through sin.

HOW THE EVIL SPIRITS DECEIVE BY "DOCTRINES"

How the evil spirits as teachers get men to receive their teachings, may be summed up in three specific ways:

(1) By giving their doctrines, or teachings, as spiritual revelations, to those who accept everything supernatural as Divine because [it is] supernatural--a certain class unaccustomed to the spiritual realm, accepting all that is "supernatural" as from God. This form of "teaching" is direct to the person; in "flashes" of light on a text, "revelations" by visions of Christ, or streams of texts apparently from the Holy Spirit.

(2) By mixing their "teachings" with the man's own reasonings, so that he thinks he has come to his own conclusions. The teachings of the deceiving spirits in this form are so natural in appearance, that they seem to come from the man himself, as the fruit of his own mind, and reasoning. They counterfeit the working of the human brain, and inject thoughts and suggestions into the human mind; for they can directly communicate with the mind, apart from gaining possession (in any degree) of the mind or body.

Those who are thus deceived, believe that they have come to their own conclusions, by their own reasonings, ignorant that the deceiving spirits have incited them to "reason" without sufficient data, or on a wrong premise, and thus come to false conclusions. The teaching spirit has achieved his own end by putting a lie in the man's mind, through the instrumentality of a false reasoning.

(3) By the indirect means of deceived human teachers, supposed to be conveying undiluted Divine "truth," and implicitly believed because of a godly life and character, believers saying, "He is a good man, and a holy man, and I believe him." The life of the man is taken as a sufficient guarantee for his teaching, instead of judging the " teaching" by the Scriptures, apart from his personal character.

This has its foundation in the prevalent idea that everything that Satan and his evil spirits do is manifestly evil, the truth not being realised that they work under cover of light (2 Cor. 11: 14), i.e., if they can get a "good man" to accept some idea from them, and pass it on as "truth," he is a better instrument for deceptive purposes than a bad man who would not be believed.

FALSE AND DECEIVED TEACHERS

There is a difference between "false" teachers, and deceived ones. There are many deceived ones amongst the most devoted teachers to-day, because they do not recognise that an army of teaching spirits have come forth to deceive the people of God, and that the special peril of the spiritual section of the Church lies in the supernatural realm, from whence the deceiving spirits with "teachings" are whispering their lies to all who are "spiritual," i.e., open to spiritual things. The "teaching spirits" with "doctrines" will make special effort to deceive those who have to transmit "doctrine," and seek to mingle their "teachings" with truth, so as to get them accepted. Every believer must test all teachers to-day, for himself, by the Word of God, and their attitude to the atoning Cross of Christ, and other fundamental truths of the gospel, and not be misled into testing "teaching" by the character of the teacher. Good men can be deceived, and Satan needs good men to float his lies under the guise of truth.

THE EFFECT ON THE CONSCIENCE OF THE TEACHINGS BY EVIL SPIRITS

How teaching spirits teach, we find described by Paul, for he says they speak lies in hypocrisy, that is, speak lies as if they were truth. And the effect of their working is said to "cauterise" (Gr.) the conscience, i.e. , if a believer accepts the teachings of evil spirits as Divine, because they come to him "supernaturally," and he obeys, and follows those "teachings," "conscience" is unused, so that it practically becomes dulled and passive--or seared--and a man does things under the influence of supernatural "revelation" which an actively awakened "conscience" would keenly rebuke and condemn. Such believers "give heed"' to these spirits, by (1) listening to them, and then by (2) obeying them; for they are deceived by accepting wrong thoughts about God's presence, and about Divine love, and unknowingly give themselves up to the power of lying spirits. Working in the line of "teaching," deceiving spirits will insert their "lies" spoken in hypocrisy, into "holiness" teaching, and deceive believers about sin, themselves, and all other truths connected with the spiritual life.

Scripture is generally used as the basis of these teachings, and is skilfully woven together like a spider's web, so that they are caught in the snare. Single texts are wrenched from their context, and their place in the perspective of truth; sentences are taken from their correlative sentences, or texts are aptly picked out from over a wide field, and so netted together as to appear to give a full revelation of the mind of God; but the intervening passages, giving historical setting, actions and circumstances connected with the speaking of the words, and other elements which give light on each separate text, are skilfully dropped out.

A wide net is thus made for the unwary, or the untaught in the principles of Scripture exegesis, and many a life is side-tracked, and troubled by this false using of the Word of God. Because the experience of ordinary Christians in regard to the devil is limited to knowing him as a tempter, or as an accuser, they have no conception of the depths of his wickedness, and of the wickedness of evil spirits, and are under the impression that they will not quote Scripture, whereas they will quote the whole Book if they can but deceive one soul.

SOME WAYS OF "TEACHING" BY DECEIVING SPIRITS

The "teachings" of deceiving spirits now being promulgated by them, are too many in number to enumerate in a small compass. They are generally recognised only in "false religions," but the teaching spirits with their "doctrines," or religious ideas suggested to the minds of men are ceaselessly at work in every clime, seeking to play upon the religious instinct in men, and give a substitute for truth.

Therefore truth, alone, dispels the deceptive doctrines of the teaching spirits of Satan: the truth of God, not merely "views of truth." Truth concerning all the principles and laws of the God of Truth. "Doctrines of demons" simply consist of that which a man "thinks" and "believes" as the outcome of suggestions made to his mind by deceiving spirits. All "thought" and "belief" belongs to one of two realms--the realm of truth, or the realm of falsehood--each having its source in God or Satan. All truth comes from God, and all that is contrary to truth, from Satan. Even the "thoughts " that apparently originate in a man's own mind come from one of these two sources, for the mind itself is either darkened by Satan (2 Cor. 4: 4), and therefore fertile soil for his "teachings," or renewed by God (Ephes. 4: 23), and clarified from the veil of Satan, and made open to the reception and transmission of truth.

THE BASIC PRINCIPLE FOR TESTING TEACHINGS BY TEACHING SPIRITS

Since thought, or "belief," originates either from the God of Truth, or the father of lies (John 8: 44), there is but one basic principle for testing the source of all doctrines, or "thoughts" and "beliefs," held by believers, or unbelievers, i.e., the test of the revealed Word of God.

All "truth" is in harmony with the only channel of revealed truth in the world--the written Word of God. All "teachings" originating from deceiving spirits—

* Weaken the authority of the Scriptures;
* Distort the teaching in the Scriptures;
* Add to the Scriptures the thoughts of men; or
* Put the Scriptures entirely aside.

The ultimate object being to hide, distort, misuse, or put aside the revelation of God concerning the Cross of Calvary, where Satan was overthrown by the God-Man, and where freedom was obtained for all his captives.

The test of all "thought" and "belief" therefore is its

1. Harmony with the written Scriptures in its full body of truth
2. The attitude to the Cross, and sin.

In the Christianised world, some doctrines of demons, tested by these two primary principles, may be mentioned as in the heathen world:

In the Christian Church: Countless "thoughts" and "beliefs," which are opposed to the truth of God, are injected into the minds of Christians by teaching spirits, rendering them ineffective in the warfare with sin and Satan, and subject to the power of evil spirits, although they are saved for eternity through their faith in Christ, and accept the authority of the Scriptures, and know the power of the Cross. All "thoughts" and "beliefs" should therefore be tested by the truth of God revealed in the Scripture, not merely by "texts" or portions of the Word, but by the principles of truth revealed in the Word. Since Satan will endorse his teachings by "signs and wonders" (Matt. 24: 24; 2 Thess. 2: 9; Rev. 13: 13), "fire from heaven", "power" and "signs," are no proof of "teaching" being of God; nor is a "beautiful life" to be the infallible test, for Satan's "ministers" can be "ministers of righteousness" (2 Cor. 11: 13- 15).

THE CULMINATION OF THE FLOOD TIDE OF DECEIVING SPIRITS SHOWN IN 2 THESS. 2

The culmination of the flood tide of these deceiving spirits sweeping upon the Church, is described by the Apostle Paul in his letter to the Thessalonians, where he speaks of the manifestation of one, who will, eventually, have so deceived Christendom as to have gained an entrance into the very sanctuary of God; so that "he sitteth in the sanctuary of God, setting himself forth as God . . . " The "presence" of this one being a "Presence" like God, and yet "according to the working of Satan, with all power, and signs, and wonders, of falsehood, and with all deceit . ." (2 Thess. 2: 9, 10, R.V. See margin R.V.).

Confirmation of the Lord's words recorded by Matthew, is found in the revelation given by Him to John, on Patmos, that at the close of the age, the main weapon used by the deceiver for obtaining power over the people of the earth, will be supernatural signs from heaven, when a counterfeit "lamb" will do "great signs," and even "make fire come down out of heaven" to deceive the dwellers on the earth, and thereby exercise such control over the whole world, that "no man shall be able to buy or sell, save he that hath the mark of the beast" (Rev. 13:11-17). Through this supernatural deception, the full purpose of the deceiving hierarchy of Satan, thus reaches its consummation, in the foretold world-wide authority.

Deception of the world with deepening darkness; deception of the Church through "teachings," and "manifestations," will reach the highest flood-tide climax at the close of the age.

THE SPECIAL WARNING TO THE CHURCH BY THE WRITER OF THE APOCALYPSE

It is striking to note that the Apostle who was chosen to transmit the Apocalypse to the Church, in preparation for the last days of the Church militant, should be the one to write to the Christians of his day: "Believe not every spirit" (1 John 4: 1-6), and earnestly warn his "children" that the "spirit of anti-Christ," and the "spirit of error" (deception) was already actively at work among them. Their attitude was to be "believe not"--i.e., to doubt every supernatural "teaching" and "teacher," until proved to be of God. They were to prove the "teachings," lest they came from a "spirit of error," and be part of the deceiver's campaign as "anti- Christ," i.e., against Christ.

If this attitude of neutrality and doubt toward supernatural teachings was needed in the days of the Apostle John--some fifty-seven years after Pentecost-- how much more is it needed in the "later times" foretold by the Lord, and by the apostle Paul. Times which were to be characterised by a clamour of voices of "prophets," that is--in the language of the twentieth century--"speakers" and "teachers" using the sacred Name of the Lord; and when "teachings" received supernaturally from the spiritual realm, would abound. "Teachings" accompanied with such wonderful proofs of their "divine" origin, as to perplex even the most faithful of the Lord's people, and even, for a time, to deceive some of them.

DANIEL'S PROPHECY THAT "TEACHERS" SHOULD "FALL" AT THE TIME OF THE END

Daniel, in writing about this same "later time," said "Some of the teachers shall fall, to refine them, and to purify, and to make them white, even at the time of the end" (Dan. 11: 35, R.V. m.). Yes, the truth must be faced! The "elect" may be deceived, and, from Daniel's words, are apparently permitted to be deceived for a season, so that in the fire testing they may be "refined" (the word refers to the expulsion of dross by the smelting fire): "purified" (the removal of dross already expelled), and made "white" (the polishing and brightening of the metal after it has been freed from its impurities). Probably it is in connection with this solemn word, that one strange statement about the war at the close of the age is made, when it is said of the attack of the leopard-like beast, that "it was given unto him to make war with the saints, and to overcome them" (Rev. 13: 7).

Daniel also speaks of the same prevailing of the enemy for a season: The horn "made war with the saints, and prevailed against them" (Dan. 7: 21). Daniel adds: "Until the Ancient of Days came . . and the time came that the saints possessed the kingdom." It appears, therefore, that in the "time of the end," God will permit Satan to prevail for a season against His saints, even as he prevailed over Peter when he was handed over to him to be sifted (Luke 22: 31); as he apparently prevailed over the Son of God at Calvary, when "the hour and power of darkness" closed around Him at the Cross (Matt. 27: 38-46); and as he is shown to do over the "two witnesses" described in Rev. 11: 7, and in the last great manifestation of the dragon deceiver's triumph over the saints, and his power over the whole inhabited earth, in Revelation 13: 7-15.

All these instances have taken place at different periods of time in the history of Christ and His Church, and in the Apocalypse picture, the prevailing of the leopard-like beast may refer to the saints on the earth after the translation of the Church; but they show the principle that God's triumphs are ofttimes hidden in apparent defeat. The elect of God must therefore take heed, at all stages of the war with Satan as deceiver, not to be swayed, or moved by appearances; for the apparent triumph of supernatural powers which appear to be Divine, may prove to be Satanic; and appearances of outward defeat, which appear to be the devil's victory may prove to cover the triumph of God.

OUTWARD SUCCESS OR DEFEAT NO TRUE CRITERION FOR JUDGMENT

The enemy is a deceiver, and as a deceiver he will work and prevail in the later times. "Success" or "defeat" is no criterion of a work being of God or Satan. Calvary stands for ever as the revelation of God's way in working out His redemption purposes. Satan works for time, for he knows his time is short, but God works for eternity. Through death to life, through defeat to triumph, through suffering to joy, is God's way.

Knowledge of truth is the primary safeguard against deception. The "elect" must know, and they must learn to "prove" the "spirits" until they do know what is of God, and what is of Satan. The words of the Master, "Take heed, I have told you , " plainly implies that personal knowledge of danger is part of the Lord's way of guarding His own, and believers who blindly rely upon "the keeping power of God," without seeking to understand how to escape deception, when forewarned to "take heed" by the Lord, will surely find themselves entrapped by the subtle foe.

CHAPTER 2
The Satanic Confederacy of Wicked Spirits

A perspective view of the ages covered by the history in Bible records, shows that the rise and fall in spiritual power of the people of God, was marked by the recognition of the existence of the demoniacal hosts of evil. When the Church of God in the old and new dispensations was at the highest point of spiritual power, the leaders recognised, and drastically dealt with, the invisible forces of Satan; and when at the lowest they were ignored, or allowed to have free course among the people.

GOD LEGISLATING FOR DANGERS FROM EVIL SPIRITS

The reality of the existence of wicked spirits by whom Satan, their prince, carried out his work in the fallen world of men, cannot be more strongly proved, than by the fact that the statutes given by Jehovah to Moses in the fiery mount, embodied stringent measures for dealing with the attempts of evil spirit beings to find entry to the people of God.

Moses was instructed by Jehovah to keep the camp of Israel free from their inroads, by the drastic penalty of death for all who had dealings with them. The very fact of Jehovah thus giving statutes in connection with such a subject, and the extreme penalty enforced for disobedience to His law, shows in itself (1) the existence of evil spirits, (2) their wickedness, (3) their ability to communicate with, and influence human beings, and (4) the necessity for uncompromising hostility to them, and their works.

God would not legislate for dangers which had no real existence, nor would He command the extreme penalty of death, if the contact of the people with evil spirit beings of the unseen world, did not necessitate such drastic dealing. The severity of the penalty obviously implies, also, that the leaders of Israel must have been given acute "discerning of spirits," so sure and so clear, that they could have no doubt in deciding cases brought before them.

Whilst Moses and Joshua lived, and enforced the strong measures decreed by God to keep His people free from the inroads of Satanic power, Israel remained in allegiance to God, at the highest point of its history; but when these leaders died, the nation sank into darkness, brought about by evil spirit powers, drawing the people into idolatry and sin; the condition of the nation in after years, rising and falling (see Judges 2: 19, 1 Kings 14: 22-24; compare 2 Chron. 33: 2-5, 34: 2-7) into (1) allegiance to God, or (2) idolatrous worship of idols, and all the sins resulting from the substitution of the worship of Satan--which idolatry really meant-- in the place of Jehovah.

When the new dispensation opens with the advent of Christ, we find Him--the God-Man--recognising the existence of the Satanic powers of evil, and manifesting uncompromising hostility toward them, and their works--Moses in the Old Testament, Christ in the New. Moses, the man who knew God face to face. Christ, the Only Begotten Son of the Father, sent from God to the world of men. Each recognising the existence of Satan and the evil spirit beings; each drastically dealing with them as entering and possessing men, and each waging war against them, as actively opposed to God.

Taking a perspective view, from the time of Christ on throughout the early history of the Church, up to the giving of the Apocalypse, and the death of the Apostle John, the manifested power of God wrought (in varying degrees) among His people, and the leaders recognised and dealt with the spirits of evil--a period corresponding to the Mosaic period in the old dispensation.

THE CHURCH IN THE MIDDLE AGES

Then the forces of darkness gained, and, with intermittent intervals and exceptions, the Church of Christ sank down under their power, until, in the darkest hour, which we call the Middle Ages, all the sins having their rise through the deceptive workings of the evil spirits of Satan, were as rife as in the time of Moses, when he wrote by the command of God, "There shall not be found with thee . . one that useth divination, or that practiseth augury, or an enchanter, or a sorcerer, or a charmer, or a consulter with a familiar spirit, or a wizard, or a necromancer" (Deut. 18: 10-11).

Now, at the close of the dispensation, and on the eve of the millennial age, the Church of Christ will again arise, and reach God's purposed power, only when the leaders recognise, as Moses did in the Old Testament Church, and Christ and His apostles did in the New, the existence of evil spirit powers of darkness, and take towards them and their works, the same uncompromising attitude of hostility, and aggressive warfare.

THE CHURCH OF THE TWENTIETH CENTURY

Why the Church in the twentieth century has not recognised the existence, and workings, of evil supernatural forces, can only be attributed to its low condition of spiritual life and power. Even at the present time, when the existence of evil spirits is recognised by the heathen, it is generally looked upon by the missionary as "superstition" and ignorance; whereas the ignorance is often on the part of the missionary, who is blinded by the prince of the power of the air to the revelation given in the Scriptures, concerning the Satanic powers.

The "ignorance" on the part of the heathen is in their propitiatory attitude to evil spirits, because of their ignorance of the gospel message of a Deliverer and a Saviour sent to "proclaim release to the captives" (Luke 4: 18), and Who, when He was on earth, went about healing all who were "oppressed by the devil" (Acts 10: 38), and sent His messengers to open the eyes of the bound ones, that they might "turn from darkness to light, and from the power of Satan unto God" (Acts 26: 18).

If missionaries to the heathen recognised the existence of evil spirits, and that the darkness in heathen lands was caused by the prince of the power of the air (Eph. 2: 2; 4: 18 ; 1 John 5: 19; 2 Cor. 4: 4), and proclaimed to the heathen the message of deliverance from the evil hosts, they know so well to be real, and malignant, foes; as well as remission of sin, and victory over sin through the atoning sacrifice of Calvary; a vast change would come over the mission field in a few brief years. But the Holy Spirit is already at work, opening the eyes of the people of God, and many of the leaders in the Church are beginning to recognise the real existence of Satanic powers, and are seeking to know how to discern their workings, and how to deal with them in the power of God.

BELIEVERS MAY RECEIVE EQUIPMENT TO DEAL WITH SATANIC POWERS

The hour of need always brings the corresponding measure of power from God to meet that need. The Church of Christ must lay hold of the equipment of the apostolic period, for dealing with the influx of the evil spirit hosts among her members.

That all believers may receive the equipment of the Holy Spirit, whereby the authority of Christ over the demon hosts of Satan is manifested, is proved not only by the instance of Philip the deacon in the Acts of the Apostles, but also by the writings of the "Fathers" in the early centuries of the Christian era, which show that the Christians of that time (1) recognised the existence of evil spirits, (2) that they influenced, deceived and possessed men, and (3) that Christ gave His followers authority over them through His Name.

That this authority through the Name of Christ, wielded by the believer walking in living and vital union with Christ, is available for the servants of God at the close of the age, the Spirit of God is making known in many and divers ways.

God gives an object lesson, through a native Christian like Pastor Hsi, in China, who acted upon the Word of God in simple faith, without the questioning caused by the mental difficulties of Western Christendom; or He awakens the Church in the West, as in the Revival in Wales, by an outpouring of the Spirit of God; which not only manifested the power of the Holy Spirit at work in the twentieth century, as in the days of Pentecost; but also unveiled the reality of Satanic powers in active opposition to God and His people, and the need among the Spirit-filled children of God, for equipment for dealing with them.

Incidentally, too, the Revival in Wales threw light upon the Scripture records, showing that the highest points of God's manifested power among men, is invariably the occasion for concurrent manifestations of the working of Satan. It was so when the Son of God came forth from the wilderness conflict with the prince of darkness, and found the hidden demons in many lives aroused to malignant activity, so that from all parts of Palestine crowds of victims came to the Man, before whom the possessing spirits trembled in impotent rage.

The awakened part of the Church of today, has now no doubt of the real existence of the spirit beings of evil, and that there is an organised monarchy of supernatural powers, set up in opposition to Christ, and His kingdom, bent upon the eternal ruin of every member of the human race; and these believers know that God is calling them to seek the fullest equipment obtainable for withstanding, and resisting these enemies of Christ and His Church. In order to understand the working of the deceiver-prince of this power of the air, and become acute to discern his tactics, and his methods of deceiving men, such believers should search the

Scriptures thoroughly, to obtain a knowledge of his character, and how spirits of evil are able to possess, and use the bodies of men.

DISTINCTION BETWEEN SATAN AND EVIL SPIRITS

The distinction between the workings of Satan as prince of demons, and his evil spirits, should specially be noted, so as to understand their methods at the present day; for to many the adversary is merely a tempter, whilst they little dream of his power as a deceiver (Rev. 12: 9), hinderer (1 Thess. 2: 18), murderer (John 8: 44), liar (John 8: 44), accuser (Rev. 12: 10), and a false angel of light; and still less of the hosts of spirits under his command, constantly besetting their path, bent upon deceiving, hindering, and prompting to sin. A vast host wholly given up to wickedness (Matt. 12: 43-45), delighting to do evil, to slay (Mark 5: 2-5), to deceive, to destroy (Mark 9: 20); and having access to men of every grade, prompting them to all kinds of wickedness, and satisfied only when success accompanies their wicked plans to ruin the children of men (Matt. 27: 3-5).

SATAN'S CHALLENGE OF CHRIST IN THE WILDERNESS

This distinction between Satan, the prince of the demons (Matt. 9: 34), and his legion of wicked spirits, is clearly recognised by Christ, and may be noted in many parts of the Gospels (Matt. 25: 41).

We find Satan in person challenging the Lord in the wilderness temptation, and Christ answering him as a person, word for word, and thought for thought, until he retires, foiled by the keen recognition of his tactics, by the Son of God (Luke 4: 1-13).

We read of the Lord describing him as the "prince of the world" (John 14: 30); recognising him as ruling over a kingdom (Matt. 12: 26); using imperative language to him as a person, saying; "Get thee hence"; while to the Jews He describes his character as "sinning from the beginning," and being a "murderer," and a "liar," the "father of lies," who "abode not in the truth" (John 8: 44) which once he held as a great archangel of God. He is called, also, "that wicked one" (1 John 3: 12, A.V.), the "Adversary," and that "old serpent" (Rev. 12: 9).

In respect of his method of working, the Lord speaks of him as sowing "tares," which are "sons of the evil one," among the wheat-- the "sons" of God (Matt. 13: 38, 39); thus revealing the Adversary as possessing the skill of a master mind, directing, with executive ability, his work as "prince of the world," in the whole inhabited earth, and with power to place the men, who are called his "sons," wherever he wills.

We read also, of Satan watching to snatch away the seed of the Word of God from all who hear it, this again indicating his executive power in the world- wide direction of his agents, whom the Lord describes as "fowls of the air"; in His own interpretation of the parable (Matt. 13: 3, 4, 13, 19; Mark 4: 3, 4, 14, 15; Luke 8: 5, 11, 12); plainly saying that He meant by these "fowls" the "evil one" (Gr. Poneros, Matt. 13: 19); "Satan" (Gr. Satana, Mark 4: 15); or "Devil" (Gr. Diabolus, Luke 8: 12); whom we know, from the general teaching of other parts of the Scriptures, does his work through the wicked spirits he has at his command; Satan himself not being omnipresent, although able to transpose himself with lightning velocity to any part of his world-wide dominions.

THE LORD'S ATTITUDE TO & RECOGNITION OF SATAN

The Lord was always ready to meet the antagonist whom He had foiled in the wilderness, but who had only left Him "for a season" (Luke 4: 13). In Peter He quickly discerned Satan at work, and exposed him by one swift sentence, mentioning his name (Matt. 16: 23). In the Jews He stripped aside the mask of the hidden foe, and said, "Ye are of your father, the devil" (John 8: 44), and with keen-edged words spoke of him as the "murderer" and the "liar," prompting them to kill Him, and lying to them about Himself and His Father in heaven (John 8: 40-41).

On the lake in a storm, fast asleep, and awakened suddenly, He is alert to meet the foe, and stands with calm majesty to "rebuke" the storm, which the prince of the power of the air had roused against Him (Mark 4: 38, 39).

In brief, we find the Lord, right on from the wilderness victory, unveiling the powers of darkness, as He went forward in steady aggressive mastery over them. Behind what appeared "natural," He sometimes discerned a supernatural power which demands His rebuke. He "rebuked" the fever in Peter's wife's mother (Luke 4: 39), just as He "rebuked" the evil spirits in other, and more manifest forms, whilst in other instances He simply healed the sufferer by a word.

The difference between Satan's attitude to the Lord, and that of the spirits of evil, should also be noted. Satan, the prince, tempts Him, seeks to hinder Him, prompts the Pharisees to oppose Him, hides behind a disciple to divert Him, and finally takes hold of a disciple to betray Him, and then sways the multitude to put Him to death; but the spirits of evil bowed down before Him, beseeching Him to "let them alone," and not to command them to go into the abyss (Luke 8: 31).

The realm of this deceiver-prince is specifically mentioned by the Apostle Paul in his description of him as "prince of the power of the air" (Ephes. 2: 2), the aerial, or "heavenly places," being the special sphere of the activity of Satan, and his hierarchy of powers. The name Beelzebub, the prince of the demons, meaning the "god of flies," suggestively speaks of the aerial character of the powers of the air, as well as the word "darkness," describing their character, and their doings. The Lord's description of Satan's working through "fowls of the air" strikingly corresponds to these other statements, together with John's language about the "whole world lying in the evil one" (1 John 5: 19); the "air" being the place of the workings of these aerial spirits, the very atmosphere in which the whole human race moves, said to be "in the evil one."

EVIL SPIRITS IN THE GOSPEL RECORDS

The gospel record is full of reference to the workings of evil spirits, and shows that wherever the Lord moved, the emissaries of Satan sprang into active manifestation in the bodies, and minds, of those they indwelt; and that the ministry of Christ and His apostles was directed actively against them, so that again and again the record reads, "He went into their synagogues throughout all Galilee, preaching and casting out demons" (Mark 1: 39); He "cast out many demons, and He suffered not the demons to speak, because they knew Him" (Mark 1: 34); "Unclean spirits, whensoever they beheld Him, fell down before Him, and cried, saying, Thou art the Son of God" (Mark 3: 11). Then came the sending out of the twelve chosen disciples, when the spirits of evil again are taken into account, for "He gave them authority over unclean spirits" (Mark 6: 7). Later He appointed seventy other messengers, and as they went forward in their work, they, too, found the demons subject to them through His Name (Luke 10: 17).

Were Jerusalem, Capernaum, Galilee, and all Syria, then filled with people who were "insane" and "epileptic"? Or was the truth of evil spirit possession of people a common fact? In any case it is evident from the gospel records, that the Son of God dealt with the powers of darkness as the active, primary cause of the sin, and suffering of this world, and that the aggressive part of His, and His disciples' ministry, was directed persistently against them.

On the one hand He dealt with the deceiver of the world, and bound the "strong man," whilst on the other, He taught the truth about God to the people, to destroy the lies which the prince of darkness had placed in their minds (2 Cor. 4: 4) about His Father and Himself.

We find, too, that the Lord clearly recognised the devil behind the opposition of the Pharisees (John 8: 44), and the "hour and power of darkness" (Luke 22: 53) behind His persecutors at Calvary. He said that His mission was to "proclaim liberty to the captives" (Luke 4: 18), and who the captor was He revealed on the eve of Calvary, when He said, "Now is the judgment of this world, now shall the prince of this world be cast out" (John 12: 31); and later on that this "prince" would once more come to Him, but would find nothing in Him as ground for his power (John 14: 30).

CHRIST ALWAYS DEALING WITH THE INVISIBLE ENEMIES

It is striking to find that the Lord did not attempt to convince the Pharisees of His claims as the Messiah, nor take the opportunity of winning the Jews, by yielding to their desires for an earthly king. His one work in this world was manifestly to conquer the Satanic prince of the world by the death of the Cross (Heb. 2: 14); to deliver his captives from his control, and to deal with the invisible hosts of the prince of darkness working at the back of mankind (See 1 John 3: 8).

The commission He gave to the twelve, and to the seventy, was exactly in line with His own. He sent them forth, and "gave them authority over unclean spirits, to cast them out, and to preach the gospel" (Matt. 10: 1); to "first bind the strong man" (Mark 3: 27), and then to take his goods; to deal with the invisible hosts of Satan first, and then "preach the gospel."

From all this we learn that there is one Satan, one devil, one prince of the demons, directing all the opposition to Christ and His people; but myriads of wicked spirits called "demons," lying spirits, deceiving spirits, foul spirits, unclean spirits, subjectively at work in men. Who they are, and whence their origin, none can positively say. That they are spirit beings who are evil is alone beyond all doubt; and all who are undeceived and dispossessed from Satanic deception, become witnesses, from their own experience, to their existence, and power. They know that things were done to them by spirit beings, and that those things were evil; therefore they recognise that there are spirit beings who do evil, and know that the symptoms, effects and manifestations of demoniacal possession have active, personal agencies behind them. From experience they know that they are hindered by spirit beings, and therefore know that these things are done by evil spirits who are hinderers. Therefore, reasoning from experimental facts, as well as the testimony of Scripture, they know that these evil spirits are murderers, tempters, liars, accusers, counterfeiters, enemies, haters, and wicked beyond all the power of man to know.

The names of these evil spirits describe their characters, for they are called "foul," "lying," "unclean," "evil," and "deceiving" spirits, as they are wholly given up to every manner of wickedness, and deception, and lying works.

CHARACTERISTICS OF EVIL SPIRITS

What the characteristics of these wicked spirits are, and how they are able to dwell in the bodies and minds of human beings, will be seen by a careful examination of the specific cases mentioned in the Gospels; as well as their power to interfere with, mislead, and deceive, even servants of God, from references to them in other portions of the Word of God.

Evil spirits are generally looked upon as "influences," and not as intelligent beings, but their personality and entity, and difference in character as distinct intelligences, will be seen in the Lord's direct commands to them (Mark 1: 25; 5: 8; 3: 11, 12; 9: 25); their power of speech (Mark 3: 11); their replies to Him, couched in intelligent language (Matt. 8: 29); their sensibilities of fear (Luke 8: 31); their definite expression of desire (Matt. 8: 31); their need of a dwelling place of rest (Matt. 12: 43); their intelligent power of decision (Matt. 12: 44); their power of agreement with other spirits; their degrees of wickedness (Matt. 12: 45); their power of rage (Matt. 8: 28); their strength (Mark 5: 4); their ability to possess a human being, either as one (Mark 1: 26) or in a thousand (Mark 5: 9); their use of a human being as their medium for "divining," or foretelling the future (Acts 16: 16); or as a great miracle worker by their power (Acts 8: 11).

THE RAGE AND WICKEDNESS OF EVIL SPIRITS

When evil spirits act in a rage, they act as a combination of the maddest, and most wicked persons in existence, but all their evil is done with fullest intelligence, and purpose. They know what they do, they know it is evil, terribly evil, and they will to do it. They do it with rage, and with the full swing of malice, enmity and hatred. They act with fury and bestiality, like an enraged bull, as if they had no intelligence, and yet with fun intelligence they carry on their work, showing the wickedness of their wickedness. They act from an absolutely depraved nature, with diabolical fury, and with an undeviating perseverance. They act with determination, persistency, and with skilful methods, forcing themselves upon mankind, upon the Church, and still more upon the spiritual man.

VARIED MANIFESTATION OF EVIL SPIRITS THROUGH PERSONS

Their manifestations through the persons in whom they obtain footing, are varied in character, according to the degree and kind of ground they secure for possession. In one Biblical case the only manifestation of the evil spirit's presence was dumbness (Matt. 9: 32); the spirit possibly locating in the vocal organs; in another, the person held by the spirit was "deaf and dumb" (Mark 9: 25), and the symptoms included foaming at the mouth, grinding the teeth--all connected with the head--but the hold of the spirit was of such long standing (v. 21) that he could throw his victim down, and convulse the whole body (Mark 9: 20-22).

In other cases we find merely an "unclean spirit" in a man in a "synagogue," probably so hidden that none would know the man was thus possessed, until the spirit cried out with fear when he saw Christ, saying, "Art Thou come to destroy us?" (Mark 1: 24); or a "spirit of infirmity" (Luke 13: 11) in a woman of whom it might be said that she simply required "healing" of some disease, or that she was always tired, and only needed "rest," as some would say in the language of the twentieth century.

Again, we find a very advanced case in the man with the "legion," showing that the evil spirits' possession reached such a climax, as to make the person appear insane; for his own personality was so mastered by the malignant spirits in possession, as to cause him to lose all sense of decency, and self-control in the presence of others (Luke 8: 27). The unity of purpose in the spirits of evil to carry out the will of their prince, is especially shown in this case, as with one accord they besought to be allowed to enter the swine, and with one accord they rushed the whole herd into the sea.

DIFFERENT KINDS OF EVIL SPIRITS

That there are different kinds of spirits is evident from all the instances given in the gospel records. Their manifestation outside the gospel cases, may be seen in the story of the girl at Philippi, possessed by a "spirit of divination," and again in Simon the Sorcerer, who was so energised by Satanic power for the working of miracles, that he was considered to be "a great power of God" by the deceived people (Acts 8: 10).

Spiritists, to-day, are deceived, in so far as they really believe they are communicating with the spirits of the dead; for it is easy for spirits of evil to impersonate any of the dead, even the most devoted and saintly Christians. They have watched them (Acts 19: 15) all their lives, and can easily counterfeit their voices, or say anything about them, and their actions when on earth.

EVIL SPIRITS FORETELLING THROUGH MEDIUMS

In like manner as a "spirit of divination," deceiving spirits can use "palmists," and "fortune tellers," to deceive; for in their work of watching human beings, they inspire the mediums to foretell, not what they know about the future--for God alone has this knowledge--but things which they themselves intend to do; and if they can get the person, to whom these things are told, to co-operate with them, by accepting, or believing, their "fore-telling," they try eventually to bring them about; e.g., the medium says such and such a thing will happen, the person believes it, and by believing opens himself, or herself, to the evil spirit, to bring that thing to pass; or else admits the spirit, or gives free opportunity to one already in possession, to bring about the thing foretold. They cannot always succeed, and this is the reason why there is so much uncertainty about the response through mediums, because many things may hinder the workings of the evil spirit beings, particularly the prayers of friends, or intercessors in the Christian Church.

These are some of the "deep things of Satan" (Rev. 2: 24) mentioned by the Lord in His message to Thyatira, manifestly referring to far more subtle workings among the Christians of that time, than all that the Apostles had seen in the cases recorded in the gospels. "The mystery of lawlessness doth already work," wrote the Apostle Paul (2 Thess. 2: 7), showing that the deep laid schemes of deception through "doctrines" (1 Tim. 4: 1), foretold as reaching their full culmination in the last days, were already at work in the Church of God. Evil spirits are at work to-day, inside as well as outside the Church, and "spiritualism," in its meaning of dealing with evil spirits, may be found inside the Church, and among the most spiritual believers, apart from its true name. Christian men think they are free from spiritism because they have never been to a seance, not knowing that evil spirits attack, and deceive every human being, and they do not confine their working to the Church, or the world, but wherever they can find conditions fulfilled to enable them to manifest their power.

THE POWER OF EVIL SPIRITS OVER HUMAN BODIES

The control of the spirits over the bodies of those they possess is seen in the gospel cases. The man with the legion was not master over his own body or mind. The spirits would "seize him," "drive him" (Luke 8: 29), compel him to cut himself with stones (Mark 5: 5), strengthen him to burst every fetter and chain (v. 4), "cry out" aloud (v. 5), and fiercely attack others (Matt. 8: 28). The boy with the dumb spirit would be dashed to the ground (Luke 9: 42), and convulsed; the spirit forced him to cry out, and tore him, so that the body became bruised and sore (v. 39). Teeth, tongue, vocal organs, ears, eyes, nerves, muscles and breath, are seen to be affected and interfered with, by evil spirits in possession. Weakness and strength are both produced by their working, and men (Mark 1: 23), women (Luke 8: 2), boys (Mark 9: 17), and girls (Mark 7: 25), are equally open to their power.

That the Jews were familiar with the fact of evil spirit possession, is clear from their words, when they saw the Lord Christ cast out the blind and dumb spirit from a man (Matt. 12: 24). Also that there were men among them who knew some method of dealing with such cases (v. 27). "By whom do your sons cast them out?" said the Lord. That such dealing with evil spirits was not effective, may be gathered from some instances given, where it appears that alleviation of the sufferings from evil spirit possession, was the most that could be done; e.g. (1) the case of king Saul, who was soothed by the harp playing of David; (2) the sons of Sceva, who were professional exorcists, yet who recognised a power in the Name of Jesus which their exorcism did not possess. In both these cases the danger of attempted alleviation and exorcism, and the power of the evil spirits, is strikingly shown in contrast to the complete command manifested by Christ and His Apostles. David playing to Saul is suddenly aware of the javelin flung by the hand of the man he was seeking to soothe; and the sons of Sceva found the evil spirits upon them, and mastering them as they used the Name of Jesus, without the Divine co-working given to all who exercise personal faith in Him. Among the heathen, also, who know the venom of these wicked spirits, propitiation and soothing of their hate by obedience to them, is the most that they know.

THE EXORCISM OF EVIL SPIRITS CONTRASTED WITH CHRIST'S POWER OF WORD

How striking to contrast all this with the calm authority of Christ, who needed no adjuration, or methods of exorcism, and no prolonged preparation of Himself ere dealing with a spirit-possessed man. "He cast out the spirits by a word," "With authority and power He commandeth . . and they obey Him," was the wondering testimony of the awe-struck people; and the testimony, too, of the seventy sent forth by Him to use the authority of His Name, as they found the spirits subject to them, even as they were to their Lord (Luke 10: 17-20).

"'They' obey Him," said the people. "They"--the evil spirits whom the people knew to be real identities governed by Beelzebub, their prince (Matt. 12: 24- 27). The complete mastery of the Lord over the demons, compelled the leaders to find some way of explaining His authority over them, and so by that subtle influence of Satan--with which all who have had insight into his devices are familiar--they suddenly charge the Lord with having Satanic power Himself, by saying "He casteth out demons through Beelzebub, the prince of the demons," suggesting that Christ's authority over evil spirits was derived from their chief and prince.

The reference to the kingdom of Satan, and his kingship was left uncontradicted by the Lord, who simply declared the truth in the face of Satan's lie, that He cast out demons "by the finger of God," and that Satan's kingdom would soon fall were he to act against himself, and dislodge his emissaries from their place of retreat in human bodies, where alone they can achieve their greatest power, and do the greatest harm among men. That Satan does apparently fight against himself is true but when he does so, it is with the purpose of covering some scheme for greater advantage to his kingdom.

THE AUTHORITY OVER EVIL SPIRITS BY THE APOSTLES AFTER PENTECOST

That the Apostles after Pentecost recognised and dealt with the denizens of the invisible world, is evident from the records of the Acts of the Apostles, and other references in the Epistles. The disciples were prepared for Pentecost, and the opening of the supernatural world through the coming of the Holy Spirit, by their three years' training by the Lord. They had watched Him deal with the wicked spirits of Satan, and had themselves learned to deal with them, too, so that the power of the Holy Spirit could safely be given at Pentecost to men who already knew the workings of the foe. We see how quickly Peter recognised Satan's work in Ananias (Acts 5: 3), and how "unclean spirits" came out at his presence, as they did with his Lord (Acts 5: 16). Philip, too, found the evil hosts subservient (Acts 8: 7) to the word of his testimony, as he proclaimed Christ to the people, and Paul knew, also, the power of the Name of the Risen Lord (Acts 19: 11) in dealing with the powers of evil.

It is therefore clear in Bible history that the manifestation of the power of God invariably meant aggressive dealing with the Satanic hosts; that the manifestation of the power of God at Pentecost, and through the Apostles, meant again an aggressive attitude to the powers of darkness; and, ergo, that the growth and maturity of the Church of Christ at the end of the dispensation, will mean the same recognition, and the same attitude toward the Satanic hosts of the prince of the power of the air; with the same co-witness of the Holy Spirit to the authority of the Name of Jesus, as in the early Church. In brief, that the Church of Christ will reach its high water mark, when it is able to recognise and deal with demon-possession; when it knows how to "bind the strong man" by prayer; "command" the spirits of evil in the Name of Christ, and deliver men and women from their power.

THE CHURCH IN THE TWENTIETH CENTURY MUST RECOGNISE THE POWERS OF DARKNESS

For this the Christian Church must recognise that the existence of deceiving, lying spirits, is as real in the twentieth century as in the time of Christ, and their attitude to the human race unchanged. That their one ceaseless aim is to deceive every human being. That they are given up to wickedness all day long, and night long, and that they are ceaselessly, and actively pouring a stream of wickedness into the world, and are satisfied only when they succeed in their wicked plans to deceive, and ruin men.

Yet the servants of God have been concerned only to destroy their works; and to deal with sin; not recognising the need of using the power given by Christ, to resist by faith and prayer, and prayer and faith, this ever- flowing flood of Satanic power pouring in among men; so that men and women, young and old, and even Christian and non-Christian, become deceived and possessed through their guile, and because of ignorance about them, and their wiles.

These supernatural forces of Satan are the true hindrance to revival. The power of God which broke forth in Wales, with all the marks of the days of Pentecost, was checked and hindered from going on to its fullest purpose, by the same influx of evil spirits as met the Lord Christ on earth, and the Apostles of the early Church; with the difference that the inroad of the powers of darkness found the Christians of the twentieth century, with few exceptions, unable to recognise, and deal with them. Evil spirit possession has followed, and checked every similar revival throughout the centuries since Pentecost, and these things must now be understood, and dealt with, if the Church is to advance to maturity. Understood, not only in the degree of possession recorded in the gospels, but in the special forms of manifestations suited to the close of the dispensation, under the guise of the Holy Spirit, yet having some of the very characteristic marks in bodily symptoms, seen in the gospel records, when all who saw the manifestation knew that it was the work of the spirits of Satan.

CHAPTER 3
Deception by Evil Spirits in Modern Times

In the special onslaught of the deceiver, which will come upon the whole of the true Church of Christ at the close of the age, through the army of deceiving spirits, there are some more than others who are specially attacked by the powers of darkness, who need light upon his deceptive workings, so that they may pass through the trial of the Last Hour, and be counted worthy to escape that hour of greater trial, which is coming upon the earth (Luke 21: 34-36; Rev. 3: 10). For among those who are members of the Body of Christ, there are degrees of growth, and therefore degrees of testing, permitted by God, Who provides a way of escape for him who knows his need, and, by watching unto prayer, takes heed lest he fall (1 Cor. 10: 12, 13). He is the Sovereign Lord of the Universe, and Satan is set his limit with every redeemed believer (see Job 1: 12; 2: 6; Luke 22: 31).

Some of the members of Christ are yet in the stage of babyhood, and others do not even know the initial reception of the Holy Spirit. To such this book has not much to say, as they are among the weaker ones who need the "milk of the Word." But there are others, who may be described as the advance guard of the Church of Christ, who have been baptised with the Holy Ghost, or who are seeking that Baptism; honest and earnest believers, who sigh and cry over the powerlessness of the true Church of Christ, and who grieve that her witness is so ineffective; that Spiritism and Christian Science, and other "isms," are sweeping thousands into their deceptive errors, little thinking, that, as they themselves go forward into the spiritual realm, the deceiver, who has misled others, has special wiles prepared for them, so that he might render ineffective their aggressive power against him. These are the ones who are in danger of the special deception of the counterfeit "Christs," and false prophets, and the dazzling lure of "signs and wonders," and "fire out of heaven," planned to meet their longing for the mighty interposition of God in the darkness settling upon the earth, but who do not recognise that such workings of the spirits of evil are possible, and so are unprepared to meet them. These are the ones, also, who are recklessly ready to follow the Lord at any cost, and yet do not realise their unpreparedness for contest with the spiritual powers of the unseen world, as they press on into fuller spiritual things.

Believers who are full of mental conceptions wrought into them in earlier years, which hinder the Spirit of God from preparing them for all they will meet as they press on to their coveted goal; conceptions which also hinder others from giving them, out of the

Scriptures, much that they need to know of the spiritual world into which they are so blindly advancing. Conceptions which lull them into a false security, and give ground for, and even bring about, that very deception which enables the deceiver to find them an easy prey.

CAN "HONEST SOULS" BE DECEIVED?

One prevailing idea, which such believers have deeply embedded in their minds, is that "honest seekers after God" will not be allowed to be deceived. That this is one of Satan's lies, to lure such seekers into a false position of safety, is proved by the history of the Church during the past two thousand years, for every "wile of error" which has borne sad fruit throughout this period, first laid hold of devoted believers who were "honest souls."

The errors among groups of such believers, some well known to the present generation, all began among "honest" children of God, baptised with the Holy Ghost; and all so sure that, knowing the side-tracking of others before them, they would never be caught by the wiles of Satan. Yet they, too, have been deceived by lying spirits, counterfeiting the workings of God in the higher ranges of the spiritual life. Among such devoted believers, lying spirits have worked on their determination literally to obey the Scriptures, and by misuse of the letter of the written Word, have pushed them into phases of unbalanced truth, with resulting erroneous practices.

Many who have suffered for their adherence to these "Biblical commands," firmly believe that they are martyrs suffering for Christ. The world calls these devoted ones "cranks," and "fanatics," yet they give evidence of highest devotion and love to the Person of the Lord, and could be delivered, if they but understood why the powers of darkness deceived them, and the way of freedom from their power. T

he aftermath of the Revival in Wales, which was a true work of God, revealed numbers of "honest souls" swept off their feet by evil supernatural powers, which they were not able to discern from the true working of God. And later still than the Welsh Revival, there have been other "movements," with large numbers of earnest servants of God swept into deception, through the wiles of deceiving spirits counterfeiting the workings of God; all "honest souls," deceived by the subtle foe, and certain to be led on into still deeper deception, notwithstanding their honesty and earnestness, if they are not awakened to "return to soberness" and recovery out of the snare of the devil into which they have fallen (2 Tim. 2: 26).

FAITHFULNESS TO LIGHT NOT SUFFICIENT SAFEGUARD AGAINST DECEPTION

The children of God need to know that to be true in motive, and faithful up to light, is not sufficient safeguard against deception; and that it is not safe for them to rely upon their "honesty of purpose" as guaranteeing protection from the enemy's wiles, instead of taking heed to the warnings of God's Word, and watching unto prayer.

Christians who are true and faithful, and honest, can be deceived by Satan, and his deceiving spirits, for the following reasons:-

(a) When a man becomes a child of God, by the regenerating power of the Spirit, giving him new life as he trusts in the atoning work of Christ, he does not at the same time receive fulness of knowledge, either of God, himself, or the devil.

(b) The mind which by nature is darkened (Eph. 4: 18), and under a veil created by Satan (2 Cor. 4: 4) is only renewed, and the veil destroyed, up to the extent that the light of truth penetrates it, and according to the measure in which the man is able to apprehend it. (c) "Deception" has to do with the mind, and it means a wrong thought admitted to the mind, under the deception that it is truth. Since "deception" is based on ignorance, and not on the moral character; a Christian who is "true" and "faithful" up to the knowledge he has, must be open to deception in the sphere where he is ignorant of the "devices" of the devil (2 Cor. 2: 11), and what he is able to do. A "true" and "faithful" Christian is liable to be "deceived" by the devil because of his ignorance.

(d) The thought that God will protect a believer from being deceived if he is true and faithful, is in itself a "deception," because it throws a man off guard, and ignores the fact that there are conditions on the part of the believer which have to be fulfilled for God's working. God does not do anything instead of a man, but by the man's co-operation with Him; neither does He undertake to make up for a man's ignorance, when He has provided knowledge for him which will prevent him being deceived.

(e) Christ would not have warned His disciples "Take heed . . be not deceived" if there had been no danger of deception, or if God had undertaken to keep them from deception apart from their "taking heed," and their knowledge of such danger. The knowledge that it is possible to be deceived, keeps the mind open to truth, and light from God; and is one of the primary conditions for the keeping power of God; whereas a closed mind to light and truth, is a certain guarantee of deception by Satan at his earliest opportunity.

THE BAPTISM OF THE HOLY GHOST

As we glance back over the history of the Church, and watch the rise of various "heresies" or delusions--as they have sometimes been called--we can trace the period of deception as beginning with some great spiritual crisis, such as that which, in later years, we have termed "the Baptism of the Holy Ghost"; a crisis in which the man is brought to give himself up in full abandonment to the Holy Spirit, and in so doing thus opens himself to the supernatural powers of the invisible world.

The reason for the peril of this crisis, is, that up to this time, the believer used his reasoning faculties in judging right and wrong, and obeyed, what he believed to be, the will of God, from principle; but now, in his abandonment to the Holy Spirit, he begins to obey an unseen Person, and to submit his faculties, and his reasoning powers in blind obedience to that which he believes is of God.

What the Baptism of the Spirit means will be dealt with in a later chapter; at this point it is only necessary to say that it is a crisis in the life of a Christian, which none but those who have gone through it in experience, can fully understand. It means that the Spirit of God becomes so real to the man, that his supreme object in life is henceforth implicit "obedience to the Holy Ghost." The will is surrendered to carry out the Will of God at all costs, and the whole being is made subject to the powers of the unseen world; the believer, of course, purposing that it shall only be to the power of God, not taking into account that there are other powers in the spiritual realm, and that all that is "supernatural" is not all of God; and not realising that this absolute surrender of the whole being to invisible forces, without knowing how to discern between the contrary powers of God and Satan, must be of the gravest risk to the inexperienced believer.

The question whether this surrender to "obey the Spirit, " is one that is in accord with Scripture, should be examined in view of the way in which so many wholehearted believers have been misled, for it is strange that an attitude which is Scriptural should be so grievously the cause of danger, and often complete wreckage, to many devoted children of God.

IS THE PHRASE OBEYING "THE SPIRIT" SCRIPTURAL?

"The Holy Ghost, Whom God hath given to them that obey Him," is the principal phrase giving rise to the expression, "obey the Spirit." It was used by Peter before the Council at Jerusalem, but nowhere else in the Scriptures is the same thought given. The whole passage needs reading carefully to reach a clear conclusion. "We must obey GOD" (Acts 5: 29), Peter said to the Sanhedrin, for "we are witnesses . . and so is the Holy Ghost Whom God hath given to them that obey Him" (v. 32).

Does the Apostle mean "obey the Spirit," or "obey GOD," according to the first words of the passage? The distinction is important, and the setting of the words can only be rightly understood by the teaching of other parts of Scripture, that the Triune GOD in Heaven is to be obeyed, through the power of the indwelling Spirit of God. For to place the Holy Ghost as the object of obedience, rather than God the Father, through the Son, by the Holy Spirit, creates the danger of leading the believer to rely upon, or obey, a "Spirit" in, or around him, rather than God on the throne in heaven, Who is to be obeyed by the child of God united to His Son; the Holy Spirit being the media, or means, through Whom God is worshipped, and obeyed.

THE TRUE WORK OF THE HOLY SPIRIT IN THE BELIEVER

The Baptism of the Spirit, however, so brings the Holy Spirit as a Person into the range of the believer's consciousness, that for the time being, the other Persons of the Trinity, in heaven, may be eclipsed. The Holy Spirit becomes the centre and object of thought and worship, and is given a place which He Himself does not desire, and which it is not the purpose of the Father in heaven, that He should have, or occupy. "He shall not speak from Himself " (John 16: 13), said the Lord before Calvary, as He told of His coming at Pentecost. He should act as Teacher (John 14: 26), but teaching the words of Another, not His own; He should bear witness to Another, not to Himself (John 15: 26); He should glorify Another, not Himself (John 16: 14); He should only speak what was given Him to speak by Another (John 16: 13); in brief, His entire work would be to lead souls into union with the Son, and knowledge of the Father in heaven whilst He Himself directed, and worked in the background.

But the opening of the spiritual world, which takes place through the filling of the Spirit; and the work of the Spirit, which now occupies the attention of the believer, is just the opportunity for the arch-deceiver to commence his wiles under a new form.

If the man is untaught in the Scriptural statements of the work of the Triune God, to "obey the Spirit" is now his supreme purpose; and to counterfeit the guidance of the Spirit, and the Spirit Himself, is now the deceiver's scheme; for he must somehow regain power over this servant of God, so as to render him useless for aggressive warfare against the forces of darkness, drive him back into the world, or in some way side-track him from active service for God.

THE PERIL OF THE TIME OF THE BAPTISM OF THE SPIRIT

It is just here that the ignorance of the believer about (1) the spiritual world now opened to him, (2) the workings of evil powers in that realm, and (3) the conditions upon which God works in and through him, gives the enemy his opportunity. It is the time of greatest peril for every believer, unless he is instructed and prepared, as the disciples were for three whole years by the Lord.

The danger lies along the line of supernatural "guidance," through not knowing the condition of cooperation with the Holy Spirit, and how to discern the will of God; and counterfeit manifestations, through not knowing the "discerning of spirits" necessary to detect the workings of the false angel of light, who is able to bring about counterfeit gifts of prophesy, tongues, healings, and other spiritual experiences, connected with the work of the Holy Ghost.

Those who have their eyes opened to the opposing forces of the spiritual realm, understand that very few believers can guarantee that they are obeying God, and God only, in direct supernatural guidance, because there are so many factors liable to intervene, such as the believer's own mind, own spirit, own will, and the deceptive intrusion of the powers of darkness.

Since evil spirits can counterfeit God as Father, Son, or Holy Spirit, the believer needs also to know very clearly the principles upon which God works, so as to detect between the Divine and the Satanic workings.

There is a "discernment" which is a spiritual gift, enabling the believer to discern "spirits," but this also requires knowledge of "doctrine" (1 John 4: 1), so as to discern between doctrine which is of God, and doctrines, or teachings, of teaching spirits.

There is a detecting, by the gift of discerning of spirits, which spirit is at work; and a test of spirits, which is doctrinal. In the former a believer can tell by a spirit of discernment, that the lying spirits are at work in a meeting, or in a person, but he may not have the understanding needed for testing the "doctrines" set forth by a teacher. He needs knowledge in both cases; knowledge to read his spirit with assurance in the face of all contrary appearances, that the supernatural workings are "of God"; and knowledge to detect the subtlety of "teachings" bearing certain infallible indications that they emanate from the pit, while appearing to be from God.

In personal obedience to God, the believer can detect whether he is obeying God in some "command," by judging its fruits, and by knowledge of the character of God, such as the truth that (1) God has always a purpose in His commands, and (2) He will give no command out of harmony with His character and Word. Other factors needed for clear knowledge are dealt with later on.

WHY THE BAPTISM OF THE SPIRIT IS A SPECIAL TIME OF DANGER

Another question of grave importance arises just here. Why, after a Baptism of the Holy Spirit, the believer should be so specially open to the deceiver's workings, for the enemy must have ground to work upon, and with the Holy Spirit so manifestly in possession, how can "ground," be possible, or the believer be open to the deceiver's approach?

Possibly because in preceding years, through yielding to sin, an evil spirit may have obtained access to body or mind, and, hiding deeply in the structure of the man, never been detected, or dislodged. The manifestation of this evil spirit possibly being so apparently "natural," or so identified with the person's character, as to have had unhindered sway in his being; such as some peculiar idea in the mind being considered as part of the man's idiosyncrasy; some habit of body, as part of the upbringing of the man himself, therefore "put up with" by others, and looked upon by the believer as a lawful thing, or of trivial importance; or else this evil spirit had lodgement through some secret sin known only to the person, or through some disposition which gave him sway. [See also "Passivity," Chap. 4 and "obsession," Chap. 5].

In the Baptism of the Spirit, the sin will of necessity have been dealt with, that is, the "works of the devil," but the evil spirit manifested in the peculiar idiosyncrasy, is left undetected. The Baptism of the Spirit takes place, and the Holy Spirit fills the spirit of the man; the body and mind are "surrendered" to God, but hidden secretly in one, or both, is the evil spirit, or spirits, which obtained lodgement years before, but who now break forth into activity, and hide their "manifestations" under cover of the true workings of the Spirit of God, dwelling within the inner shrine of the spirit.

The result of this is, that for a time, the heart is filled with love; the spirit is full of light and joy; the tongue is loosed to witness, but ere long a "fanatical spirit" may be detected creeping in, or a subtle spirit of pride, or self-importance, and self-aggrandisement, concurrent with the other pure fruits of the Spirit, which are undeniably of God.

What the ground is upon which the deceiver works to carry out his schemes, and what these schemes are, and why in so many instances they succeed in ensnaring devoted believers, we shall deal with later on in this book. The fact to emphasise now, is, that "honest" and earnest believers can be deceived, and even "possessed" by deceiving spirits, so that for a period they go out of the main line into a bog of deception, or they are left deceived to the end, unless light for their deliverance reaches them.

THE NEED FOR EXAMINATION OF THEORIES

In the light of the working of deceiving spirits, and their methods of deception, it is also becoming clear that close examination is needed of the twentieth century theories, conceptions, and expressions, concerning things in connection with God, and His way of working in man; for only the truth of God, apart from "views" of truth, will avail for protection, or warfare, in the conflict with wicked spirits in the heavenly sphere.

All that is in any degree the outcome of the mind of the "natural man" (1 Cor. 2: 14) will prove to be but weapons of straw in this great battle, and if we rely upon others' "views of truth," or upon our own human conceptions of truth, Satan will use these very things to deceive us, even building us up in these theories and views, so that under cover of them he may accomplish his purposes.

We cannot therefore, at this time, over-estimate the importance of believers having open minds to "examine all things" they have thought, and taught, in connection with the things of God, and the spiritual realm. All the "truths" they have held; all the phrases and expressions they have used in "holiness teachings"; and all the "teachings" they have absorbed through others. For any wrong interpretation of truth, any theories and phrases which are man-conceived, and which we may build upon wrongly, will have perilous consequences to ourselves, and to others, in the conflict which the Church, and the individual believer, is now passing through. Since in the "later times" evil spirits will come to them with deceptions in doctrinal form, believers must examine carefully what they accept as "doctrine," lest it should be from the emissaries of the deceiver.

THE SPIRITUAL BELIEVER EXHORTED TO "JUDGE ALL THINGS"

The duty of this examination of spiritual things is strongly urged by the Apostle Paul, again and again. "He that is spiritual judgeth (margin, examineth, or, as in the Greek, investigates and decides), all things" (1 Cor. 2: 15). The "spiritual" believer is to use his "judgment," which is a renewed faculty if he is a "spiritual man," and this spiritual examination, or judging, is mentioned as operative in connection with "things of the Spirit of God" (1 Cor 2: 14), showing how God Himself honours the intelligent personality of the man He re-creates in Christ, by inviting the "judging" and "examining" of His own workings by His Spirit; so that even "the things of the Spirit" are not to be received as of Him, without being examined, and "spiritually discerned" as of God. When, therefore, it is said in connection with the supernatural, and abnormal manifestations of the present time, that it is not necessary, nor even according to the will of God, for believers to understand, or explain all the workings of God, it is out of accord with the Apostle's statement that, "he that is spiritual, judgeth all things," and consequently should reject all things which his spiritual judgment is unable to accept, until such a time as he is able to discern with clearness what are the things of God.

And not only is the believer to discern, or judge the things of the spirit--i.e., all things in the spiritual realm--but he is also to judge himself. For "if we discriminated ourselves"--the Greek word means a thorough investigation --we should not need the dealing of the Lord, to bring to light the things in ourselves which we have failed to discern by discrimination (1 Cor. 11: 31, m.).

"Brethren, be not children in mind, howbeit in malice be ye babes, but in MIND BE MEN" (Gr., of full, or mature age, 1 Cor. 14: 20), wrote the Apostle again to the Corinthians, as he explained to them the way of the working of the Spirit among them. The believer is in "mind" to be of "full age"; that is, able to examine, "bring to the proof" (Gr., to prove, demonstrate, examine, 2 Tim. 4: 2, R.V. m.), and "prove all things" (1 Thess. 5: 21). He is to abound in knowledge, and "all discernment," so as to "prove the things that differ," that he may be "sincere and void of offence" until the day of Christ (Phil. 1: 10, m.).

EXPRESSIONS, "VIEWS," DOCTRINES, NEED TO BE EXAMINED

In accordance with these directions of the Word of God, and in view of the critical time through which the Church of Christ is passing, every expression, "view," or theory, which we hold concerning things, should now be examined carefully, and brought to the proof, with open and honest desire to know the pure truth of God, as well as every statement that comes to our knowledge of the experience of others, which may throw light upon our own pathway. Every criticism--just or unjust--should be humbly received, and examined to discover its ground, apparent or real; and facts concerning spiritual verities from every section of the Church of God, should be analysed, independent of their pleasure, or pain, to us personally, either for our own enlightenment, or for our equipment in the service of God. For the knowledge of truth is the first essential for warfare with the lying spirits of Satan, and truth must be eagerly sought for, and faced with earnest and sincere desire to know it, and obey it in the light of God; truth concerning ourselves, discerned by unbiased discrimination; truth from the Scriptures, uncoloured, unstrained, unmutilated, undiluted; truth in facing facts of experience in all members of the Body of Christ, and not one section alone.

THE PLACE OF TRUTH IN DELIVERANCE

There is a fundamental principle involved in the freeing power of truth from the deceptions of the devil. Deliverance from believing lies must be by believing truth. Nothing can remove a lie but truth. "Ye shall know the truth, and the truth shall make you free" (John 8: 32), is applicable to every aspect of truth, as well as the special truth referred to by the Lord when He spoke the pregnant words.

In the very first stage of the Christian life the sinner must know the truth of the gospel, if he is to be saved. Christ is the Saviour, but He saves through, and not apart from instruments or means. If the believer needs freedom, he must ask the Son of God for it. How does the Son set free? By the Holy Spirit, and the Holy Spirit does it by the instrumentality of truth; or we may say, in brief, freedom is the gift of the Son, by the Holy Spirit working through truth.

There are three stages of apprehending truth :—

1. Perception of truth by the understanding.
2. Perception of truth for use, and personal application.
3. Perception of truth for teaching, and passing on to others.

Truth apparently not grasped may lie in the mind, and in the hour of need suddenly emerge into experience, and thus by experience become clear to the mind in which it has been lying dormant. It is only by continual application, and assimilation of truth in experience, that it becomes clarified in the mind in order to teach others.

The great need of all believers is that they should eagerly seek truth for their progressive liberation from all Satan's lies; for knowledge and truth alone can give victory over Satan as deceiver and liar. If the hearers of truth should resist it, or rebel against it, truth can well be left to the care of the Holy Spirit of Truth. Even in the case of resistance to truth it has at least reached the mind, and at any time may fructify into experience.

There are three attitudes of mind in regard to knowledge, i.e.,

1. Assumption of knowing a certain thing.
2. Neutrality toward it, i.e., "I do not know."
3. Certainty of real knowledge.

This is instanced in the life of Christ. Some said of Him, "He is a false prophet," with an assumption of knowledge; others said, "We do not know"- -taking a position of neutrality until they did know; but Peter said, "We know . . " and he had true knowledge.

THE SAFETY OF A NEUTRAL ATTITUDE TO ALL SUPERNATURAL MANIFESTATIONS

When believers first hear of the possibility of counterfeits of God, and Divine things, they almost invariably ask, "How are we to know which is which?" It is enough, first of all, for them to know that such counterfeits are possible; and then, as they mature, or seek light from God, they learn to know for themselves, as no human being can explain to them.

But they cry, "We do not know, and how can we know?" They should remain neutral to all supernatural workings until they do know. There is among many a wrong anxiety to know, as if knowledge alone would save them. They think that they must be either for, or against certain things, which they cannot decide are either from God, or from the devil; and want to know infallibly which is which, that they may declare their position: but believers can take the attitude of "for" or "against" without knowing whether the things they are in doubt about are Divine or Satanic; and maintain the wisdom and safety of the neutral position to the things themselves, until, by a means which cannot be fully described, they know what they have wanted to understand.

One effect of over-eagerness in desiring knowledge, is a feverish anxiety, and a restless impatience, worry and trouble, which causes a loss of moral poise and power. It is important in seeking one "blessing" not to destroy another. In seeking knowledge of spiritual things let not the believer lose patience, and calm quiet restfulness, and faith; let him watch himself, lest the enemy gain advantage, and rob him of moral power, whilst he is keen to get light and truth upon the way of victory over him.

MISTAKEN CONCEPTION ABOUT THE SHELTER OF THE BLOOD

Ere we pass on to deal with the ground for the working of deceiving spirits in believers, some misinterpretations of truth which are giving ground to the powers of darkness at this time, and which need examination to discover how far they are in accordance with Scripture, may briefly be referred to. (1) A mistaken conception concerning the "shelter of the Blood," claimed upon an assembly as a guarantee of absolute protection from the working of the powers of darkness.

The New Testament "proportion of truth" concerning the application of the Blood, by the Holy Spirit, may briefly be said to be as follows:--(1) The Blood of Jesus cleanses from sin, (a) "if we walk in the light," and (b) "if we confess our sins" (1 John 1: 7, 9). (2) The Blood of Jesus gives access to the Holiest of all; because of the cleansing power from sin (Hebrews 10: 19). (3) The Blood of Jesus is the ground of victory over Satan, because of its cleansing from every confessed sin, and because at Calvary, Satan was conquered (Rev. 12: 11), but we do not read that any can be put "under the Blood" apart from their own volition, and individual condition before God; e.g., if the "shelter of the Blood" is claimed over an assembly of people, and one present is giving ground for Satan, the "claiming of the Blood" does not avail to prevent Satan working on the ground which he has a right to in that person.

In gatherings of people at all stages of spiritual knowledge and experience, the actual effect of claiming the power of the Blood can only be upon the atmosphere where the evil spirits are; and the Holy Spirit bears witness to it there with immediate cleansing effect, as exampled in Rev. 12: 11, where the warfare spoken of is in the "heavens," with a spiritual foe, working as an accuser.

A misconception, therefore, about the protecting power of the Blood, is serious; for those who are present in a meeting where Satan is working as well as God, may believe they are personally safe from Satan's workings, apart from their individual condition and dealing with God; whilst through the ground they have given-- even unknowingly--to the adversary, they are open to his power.

MISTAKEN CONCEPTIONS CONCERNING "WAITING FOR THE SPIRIT"

(2) Mistaken conceptions concerning "waiting for the Spirit" to descend. Here again we find expressions and theories misleading, and opening the door to Satanic deceptions. "If we want a Pentecostal manifestation of the Spirit, we must 'tarry' as did the disciples before Pentecost," we have said the one to the other, and we have seized upon the text in Luke 24: 49, and Acts 1: 4, and passed the word along. "Yes, we must 'tarry,'" until, compelled by the inroads of the adversary in "waiting meetings," we have had to search the Scriptures once more, to discover that the Old Testament word of "wait on the Lord" so often used in the Psalms, has been strained beyond the New Testament proportion of truth, and exaggerated into a "waiting on God" for the outpouring of the Spirit, which has even gone beyond the "ten days" which preceded Pentecost, into four months, and even four years, and which, to our knowledge, has ended in an influx of deceiving spirits which has rudely awakened some of the waiting souls. The Scriptural truth concerning waiting for the Spirit" may be summed up as follows:

1. The disciples waited ten days, but we have no indication that they "waited" in any passive state, but rather in simple prayer, and supplication, until the fulness of time had come for the fulfilment of the promise of the Father.

2. The command to wait, given by the Lord (Acts 1: 4) was not carried forward into the Christian dispensation after the Holy Ghost had come, for in no single instance, either in the Acts or in the Epistles, do the Apostles bid the disciples "tarry" for the

gift of the Holy Spirit, but they use the word "receive" in every instance (Acts 19: 2).

It is true that at this time the Church is, as a whole, living experimentally on the wrong side of Pentecost, but in dealing with God individually for the reception of the Holy Spirit, this does not put the seekers back to the position of the disciples before the Holy Ghost had been given by the Ascended Lord. The Risen Lord poured forth the stream of the Spirit again and again after the day of Pentecost, but in each instance it was without "tarrying" as the disciples did at the first (see Acts. 4: 31). The Holy Spirit, Who proceeds from the Father through the Son to His people, is now among them, waiting to give Himself unceasingly to all who will appropriate, and receive Him (John 15: 26 ; Acts 2: 33, 38, 39). A " waiting for the Spirit" therefore is not in accord with the general tenor of the truth given in the Acts and the Epistles, which show rather the imperative call to the believer to put in his claim, not only to his identification with the Lord Jesus in His death, and union in life with Him in His resurrection, but also to the enduement for witnessing, which came to the disciples on the Day of Pentecost.

On the believer's side, we may say, however, that there is a waiting for God, whilst the Holy Spirit deals with, and prepares, the one who has put in his claim, until he is in the right attitude for the influx of the Holy Spirit into his spirit, but this is different from the "waiting for Him to come," which has opened the door so frequently to Satanic manifestations from the unseen world. The Lord does take the believer at his word when he puts in his claim for his share of the Pentecostal gift, but the "manifestation of the Spirit"--the evidence of His indwelling and outworking-- may not be according to any pre-conceptions of the seeker.

WHY WAITING MEETINGS ARE PROFITABLE TO EVIL SPIRITS

Why "waiting meetings"--that is, "waiting for the Spirit" until He descends in some manifested way--have been so profitable to deceiving spirits, is because they are not in accord with the written Word, where it is set forth that (1) The Holy Spirit is not to be prayed to, or asked to come, as He is the Gift of Another (see Luke 11: 13; John 14: 16). (2) The Holy Spirit is not to be "waited for," but to be taken, or received from the hand of the Risen Lord (John 20: 22; Eph. 5: 18); of Whom it is written, "He shall baptise you with the Holy Ghost and with fire" (Matt. 3: 11). [This is] out of line with the truth of the Scriptures, therefore prayer to the Spirit, "trust in the Spirit," "obeying the Spirit," "expecting the Spirit" to descend, may all become prayer, trust, and obedience to evil spirits, when they counterfeit the working of God, as we shall see later on.

Other mistaken conceptions of spiritual truth, centre around phrases, such as these: "God can do everything. If I trust Him He must keep me"; not understanding that God works according to laws, and conditions, and that those who trust Him, should seek to know the conditions upon which He can work in response to their trust. "If I were wrong, God would not use me"; not understanding that if a man is right in his will, God will use him to the fullest extent possible, but this being "used" of God is no guarantee that any man is absolutely right in all that he says and does .

"I have no sin," or "sin has been entirely removed"; not knowing how deeply the sinful life of Adam is ingrained in the fallen creation, and how the assumption that "sin" has been eliminated from the whole being, enables the enemy to keep the life of nature from being dealt with by the continual power of the Cross. "God, Who is Love, will not allow me to be deceived" is of itself a deception, based on ignorance of the depths of the Fall, and the misconception that God works irrespective of spiritual laws. "I do not believe it possible for a Christian to be deceived," is a shutting of the eyes to facts around us on every hand. "I have had too long an experience to need teaching" ; "I must be taught Of God direct, because it is written, 'Ye need not that any man teach you.' " is another misused passage of Scripture, which some believers interpret as meaning that they are to refuse all spiritual teaching through others. But that the Apostle's words, "Ye need not that any man teach you," did not preclude God teaching through anointed teachers, is shown in the inclusion of "teachers" in the list of gifted believers to the Church, for the "building up of the Body of Christ" through "that which every joint supplieth" (Eph. 4: 11-16). For God is sometimes able to teach His children more quickly by indirect means--that is, through others--than directly, because men are so slow in understanding the way of direct teaching by the Spirit of God.

Many other similar misconceptions of spiritual things by Christians of to- day, give opportunity to the deception of the enemy, because they cause believers to close their minds to (1) the statements of God's Word; (2) the facts of life; (3) and the help of others who could throw light upon the way (1 Pet. 1: 12).

THE DANGERS OF COINED PHRASES TO EXPRESS SPIRITUAL TRUTHS

Other dangers centre around the coining of phrases to describe some special experience, and words in familiar use amongst earnest children of God who attend Conventions; such as "possess," "control," "surrender," "let go," all containing truth in relation to God, but in the interpretation of them in the minds of many believers, liable to bring about conditions for the evil spirits of Satan to "possess" and "control" those who "surrender," and "let go" to the powers of the spiritual world, not knowing how to discern between the working of God and Satan.

Various preconceptions of the way God works, also give evil spirits their opportunity; such as, that when a believer is supernaturally compelled to act, it is a special evidence that God is guiding him, or that if God brings all things to our "remembrance" we need not use our memories at all.

Other thoughts which are liable to bring about the passive condition, which evil spirits need for their deceptive workings, may also be through the following misconceptions of truth:

- "Christ lives in me," i.e., I do not live now at all;
- "Christ lives in me," i.e., I have lost my personality, because Christ is now personally in me, based on Gal. 2: 20.
- "God worketh in me," i.e., I need not work, only surrender and obey, based on Phil. 2: 13.
- "God wills instead of me," i.e., I must not use my will at all;
- "God is the only one to judge," i.e., I must not use my judgment.
- "I have the mind of Christ," I must not have any mind of my own, based on 1 Cor. 2: 16.
- "God speaks to me," so I must not "think" or "reason," only "obey" what He tells me to do.
- "I wait on God," and "I must not act until He moves me."
- "God reveals His will to me by visions," so I do not need to decide, and use my reason and conscience.
- "I am crucified with Christ," therefore "I am dead," and must "practice" death, which I conceive to be passivity of feeling, thinking, etc.

To carry out in practice these various conceptions of truth, the believer quenches all personal action of mind, judgment, reason, will and activity, for the "Divine life to flow," through him, whereas God needs the fullest liberation of the faculties of the man, and his active and intelligent co-operation in will, for the working out of all these spiritual truths in experience.

What, then, is the condition of safety from the deception of evil spirits?

(1) Knowledge that they exist;
(2) that they can deceive the most honest believers (Gal. 2: 11-16);
(3) an understanding of the conditions and ground necessary for their working, so as to give them no place, and no opportunity of working; and, lastly, (
(4)) intelligent knowledge of God, and how to co-operate with Him in the power of the Holy Spirit. To make these points clear will be our purpose in succeeding pages

CHAPTER 4
Passivity the Chief Basis of Possession

That believers--true, fully surrendered children of God--can be deceived, and then up to the degree of deception, "possessed" by deceiving spirits, we have seen in the preceding chapters. The primary cause must now be made clear, and the conditions for deception and possession resulting therefrom; apart from the possession which is the outcome of yielding to sins of the flesh, or any sin which gives evil spirits a hold in the fallen nature.

It is first important to define the meaning of the word "possession": for it is generally thought to cover only cases of possession in the acute, and fully developed degree of the cases given in the gospel records. But even then it is overlooked that many degrees of possession are referred to in the gospels, such as the woman with the "spirit of infirmity"; the man who was apparently only deaf and dumb; the little girl with the demon which terribly vexed her; the boy who gnashed with his teeth, and was sometimes thrown on the fire, and the man with the legion, so wholly mastered by the powers of evil that he dwelt outside the abodes of men.

THE MEANING OF "POSSESSION" DEFINED

Such cases as these are known today, amongst even true believers in Europe, as well as in heathen China, but "possession" is much more wide-spread than is supposed, if the word "possession" is taken to mean just what it is, i.e., a hold of evil spirits on a man in any shade of degree; for an evil spirit "possesses" whatever spot he holds, even though it be in an infinitesimal degree, and from that one spot, as a spider finds his base ere he weaves his web, the intruder works to obtain further hold of the whole being.

Christians are as open to possession by evil spirits as other men, and become possessed because they have, in most cases, unwittingly fulfilled the conditions upon which evil spirits work, and, apart from the cause of will-full sin, given ground to deceiving spirits, through (1) accepting their counterfeits of the Divine workings, and (2) cultivating passivity, and non-use of the faculties; and this through misconception of the spiritual laws which govern Christian life.

It is this matter of ground given which is the crucial point of all. All believers acknowledge known sin to be ground given to the enemy, and even unknown sin in the life, but they do not realise that every thought suggested to the mind by wicked spirits, and accepted, is ground given to them; and every faculty unused invites their attempted use of it. The primary cause of deception and possession in surrendered believers may be condensed into one word, passivity; that is, a cessation of the active exercise of the will in control over spirit, soul and body, or either, as may be the case. It is, practically, a counterfeit of "surrender to God."

The believer who "surrenders" his "members"--or faculties--to God, and ceases to use them himself, thereby falls into "passivity" which enables evil spirits to deceive, and possess any part of his being which has become passive.

The deception over passive surrender may be exampled thus: a believer surrenders his "arm" to God. He permits it to hang passive, waiting for "God to use it." He is asked, "why do you not use your arm?" and he replies "I have surrendered it to God. I must not use it now; God must use it." But will God lift the arm for the man? Nay, the man himself must lift it, and use it, seeking to understand intelligently God's mind in doing so.

THE WORD "PASSIVITY" DESCRIBES OPPOSITE CONDITION TO ACTIVITY

The word "passivity" simply describes the opposite condition to activity; and in the experience of the believer it means, briefly, (1) loss of self-control--in the sense of the person himself controlling each, or all of the departments of his personal being; and (2) loss of freewill--in the sense of the person himself exercising his will as the guiding principle of personal control, in harmony with the will of God.

All the danger of "passivity" in the surrendered believer, lies in the advantage taken of the passive condition by the powers of darkness. Apart from these evil forces, and their workings through the passive person, "passivity" is merely inactivity, or idleness. In normal inactivity, that is, when the evil spirits have not taken hold, the inactive person is always holding himself ready for activity; whereas in "passivity" which has given place to the powers of darkness, the passive person is unable to act by his own volition.

The chief condition, therefore, for the working of evil spirits in a human being, apart from sin, is passivity, in exact opposition to the condition which God requires from His children for His working in them. Granted the surrender of the will to God, with active choice to do His will as it may be revealed to him, God requires co-operation with His Spirit, and the full use of every faculty of the whole man.

In brief, the powers of darkness aim at obtaining a passive slave, or captive to their will; whilst God desires a regenerated man, intelligently and actively willing, and choosing, and doing His will in liberation of spirit, soul and body from slavery.

The powers of darkness would make a man a machine, a tool,

an automaton; the God of holiness and love desires to make him a free, intelligent sovereign in his own sphere--a thinking, rational, renewed creation created after His own image (Eph. 4: 24). Therefore, God never says to any faculty of man, "Be thou idle." God does not need, nor demand non-activity in the believer, for His working in, and through him; but evil spirits demand the utmost non-activity and passivity. God asks for intelligent action (Rom. 12: 1-2, "Your reasonable service,") in co-operation with Him.

Satan demands passivity as a condition for his compulsory action, and in order to compulsorily subject men to his will and purpose. God requires the cessation of the evil actions of believers, primarily because they are sinful, and secondly because they hinder co-operation with His Spirit.

Passivity must not be confused with quietness, or the meek and quiet spirit," which, in the sight of God, is of great price. Quietness of spirit, of heart, of mind, of manner, voice and expression, may be co-existent with the most effective activity in the will of God (1 Thess. 4: 11, Gr. "Ambitious to be quiet.").

THE CLASS OF BELIEVERS WHO ARE OPEN TO PASSIVITY

The persons open to "passivity," of whom the evil spirits take advantage as ground for their activity, are those who become fully surrendered to God, and are brought into direct contact with the supernatural world by receiving the Baptism of the Holy Ghost.

There are some who use the word "surrender," and think they are surrendered fully to carry out the will of God, but are only so in sentiment and purpose, for actually they walk by the reason and judgment of the natural man; although they submit all their plans to God, and because of this submittal sincerely believe they are carrying out His will. But those who are really "surrendered," give themselves up to implicitly obey, and carry out at all costs, what is revealed to them supernaturally as from God, and not what they themselves plan and reason out to be the will of God. Believers who surrender their wills, and all they have and are to God, yet who WALK BY THE USE OF THEIR NATURAL MINDS, are not the ones who are open to the "passivity" which gives ground to evil spirits, although they may, and do, give ground to them in other ways. These we may call Class No. 1, as shown in the following table.

THREE CLASSES AMONG BELIEVERS

1. Unsurrendered. These use the word "surrender," but do not really know it, and act it out in practice.

2. Surrendered, Deceived, Possessed. These seem more "foolish"

than those in Class 1, but in reality are more advanced

3. Surrendered but Undeceived, Dispossessed and Victorious. The mind is liberated, and all the faculties are operating. Believers in this stage are more reasonable than those in No. 2, because their faculties have not been yielded into passivity. These believers call those in the next class "cranks," "faddists," .. "extremists," etc.

In order to understand the actions of No. 2, it is needful to read them from their inner standpoint, for to them all that they do seems right. These are open to both Divine and Satanic power. Are liable to be "puffed up." These are open to light and all that is Divine, but they seek watchfully to close themselves to all that is Satanic.

No. 3 can read Nos. 1 and 2 intelligently. Class No. 1 are "surrendered" in will, but not surrendered in fact, in the sense of being ready to carry out "obedience to the Holy Ghost" at all costs. They consequently know little of conflict, and nothing of the devil, excepting as a tempter or accuser. They do not understand those who speak of the "onslaughts of Satan," for, they say, they are not "attacked" in this way. But the devil does not always attack when he can. He reserves his attack until it suits him. If the devil does not attack a man, it does not prove that he could not.

Another class among believers--Class No. 2--are those who are surrendered in such a measure of abandonment that they are ready to obey the Spirit of God at all costs, with the result that they become open to a passivity which gives ground for the deception and possession of evil spirits. These surrendered believers (Class No. 2) fall into passivity after the Baptism of the Holy Ghost, (1) because of their determination to carry out their "surrender" at all costs; (2) their relationship with the spiritual world, which opens to them supernatural communications, which they believe to be all of God; (3) their "surrender" leading them to submit, subdue and make all things subservient to this supernatural plane.

The origin of the evil passivity which gives the evil spirits opportunity to deceive, and then possess, is generally a wrong interpretation of Scripture, or wrong thoughts or beliefs about Divine things. Some of these interpretations of Scripture, or wrong conceptions, which cause the believer to give way to the passive condition, we have already referred to in a previous chapter. The passivity may affect the whole man, in spirit, soul and body, when it has become very deep, and is of many years' standing. The progress is generally very gradual, and insidious in growth, and consequently the release from it is gradual and slow.

PASSIVITY OF THE WILL

There is a passivity of the will; the "will" being the helm, so to speak, of the ship. This originates from a wrong conception of what full surrender to God means. Thinking that a "surrendered will" to God means no use of the will at all, the believer ceases to (1) choose, (2) determine, and (3) act of his own volition.

The serious effect of this, he is not allowed by the powers of darkness to discover, for at first the consequences are trivial, and scarcely noticeable. In fact, at first it appears to be most glorifying to God. The "strong-willed" person suddenly becomes passively yielding. He thinks that God is "will"-ing for him in circumstances, and through people, and so he becomes passively helpless in action. After a time no "choice" can be got from him in matters of daily life; no "decision," or initiative in matters demanding action; he is afraid to express a wish, much less a decision. Others must choose, act, lead, decide, while this one drifts as a cork upon the waters. Later on, the powers of darkness begin to make capital out of this "surrendered" believer, and to work around him evil of various kinds, which entangle him through his passivity of will. He has now no power of will to protest, or resist. Obvious wrong in his environment, which this believer alone has a right to deal with, flourishes, and grows strong and blatant.

The powers of darkness have slowly gained, both personally and in circumstances, upon the ground of passivity of the will, which at first was merely passive submission to environment, under the idea that God was "will"-ing for him in all things around him. The text that such believers misinterpret is Phil. 2: 13, "It is God which worketh in you, both to will, and to work, for His good pleasure." The "passive" person reads it, ". . . God which worketh in me the willing, and the doing," i.e., "willeth instead of me."

The first means God working in the soul up to the point of the action of the will, and the second assumes His actually "will"-ing instead of, and "working" instead of the believer. This wrong interpretation gives ground for not using the will, because of the conclusion "God wills instead of me"; thus bringing about passivity of will.

GOD DOES NOT WILL INSTEAD OF MAN

The truth to be emphasised is that God never "wills" instead of man, and whatever a man does, he is himself responsible for his actions.

The believer whose "will" has become passive, finds, after a time, the greatest difficulty in making decisions of any kind, and he looks outside, and all around him for something to help him to decide the smallest matters. When he has become conscious of his passive condition, he has a painful sense of being unable to meet some of the situations of ordinary life. If spoken to, he knows he cannot will to listen till a sentence is completed; if asked to judge a matter, he knows he cannot do it; if he is required to "remember" or use his imagination, he knows he is unable to, and becomes terrified at any proposed course of action where these demands may come upon him.

The tactics of the enemy now may be to drive him into situations where these demands may be made, and thus torture or embarrass him before others. Little does the believer know that in this condition be may, unknowingly, rely upon the assistance of evil spirits, who have brought about the passivity for this very object.

The faculty unused lies dormant and dead in their grip, but if used it is an occasion for them to manifest themselves through it. They are too ready to "will" instead of the man, and they will put within his reach many "supernatural" props to help him in "decision," especially in the way of "texts" used apart from their context, and supernaturally given, which the believer, seeking so longingly to do the will of God, seizes upon, and firmly grasps as a drowning man a rope, blinded, by the apparently given Divine help, to the principle that God only works through the active volition of a man, and not for him in matters requiring his action.

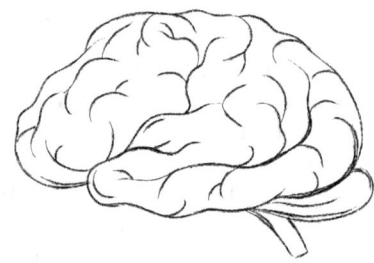

PASSIVITY OF THE MIND

Passivity of the mind is engendered by a wrong conception of the place of the mind in the life of surrender to God, and obedience to Him in the Holy Spirit. Christ's call of fishermen is used as an excuse for passivity of brain, for some believers say, God has no need for the use of the brain, and can do without it! But the choice of Paul who had the greatest intellect of his age, shows that when God sought for a man through whom He could lay the foundations of the Church, He chose one with a mind capable of vast and intelligent thinking. The greater the brain power, the greater the use God can make of it, provided it is submissive to truth.

The cause of passivity of mind, sometimes lies in the thought that the working of the brain is a hindrance to the development of the Divine life in the believer. But the truth is, that (1) the non-working of the brain hinders, (2) the evil working of the brain hinders, (3) but the normal and pure working of the brain is essential, and helpful for cooperation with God. This is dealt with fully in Chapter 6, where the various tactics of the powers of darkness are shown in their efforts to get the mind into a condition of passivity, and hence incapable of action to discern their wiles.

The effects of passivity of the mind may be seen in inactivity, when there should be action; or else over activity beyond control, as if a suddenly released instrument broke forth into ungovernable action; hesitation, or rashness; indecision (as also from a passive will); unwatchfulness; lack of concentration; lack of judgment; bad memory.

Passivity does not change the nature of a faculty, but it hinders its normal operation. In the case of passivity hindering the memory, the person will be found looking outside himself for every possible "aid to memory," until he becomes a veritable slave to note book, and helps, which fail at a critical moment.

With this is also passivity of the imagination, which places the imagination outside personal control, and at the mercy of evil spirits who flash to it what they please. One danger is to take these visions, and call them "imaginations." The passive state can be produced without crystal gazing, i.e., if a person gazes at any object for a prolonged period the natural vision is dulled, and the deceiving spirits can then present anything to the mind. In pure inactivity of the mind, the mind can be used at the will of the person, but in evil passivity of the mind, the person is helpless, and he "can't think!" He feels as if his mind were bound, and held by an iron band, or by a weight or pressure on his head.

PASSIVITY OF JUDGMENT AND REASON

Passivity of judgment and reason, which means that the man in this condition has closed the mind to all arguments, and statements upon which he has come to settled conclusions, and all effort to give him further truth and light is regarded as interference, and the person attempting it as ignorant, or intrusive. The believer in this stage of passivity lapses into a state of evil positiveness, and infallibility; from which nothing can release the "judgment," but the rude shock of seeing that he has been deceived, and possessed by evil spirits. To undermine the deception of a believer in this condition, almost means the re-laying of the very foundations of his spiritual life. Hence the few--called "fanatics" and "cranks" by the world--who have been saved out of this degree of the deception of the enemy.

PASSIVITY OF THE CONSCIENCE

As for the passivity of the reasoning powers, when such believers have taken words spoken to them supernaturally, as God's expressed will, they become law to them, so that they cannot be induced to reason over them. If they receive a "commandment" (supernaturally) about anything, they will not examine it, or reason or think upon that point, and they steadfastly determine to close themselves absolutely to any further light in this particular direction. This brings about, what may be described as, passivity of the conscience. The conscience becomes passive through non-use, when believers think that they are being guided by a higher law of being told to do this, or that, directly from God; that is, by direct guidance through voices, and texts.

When believers sink into passivity of conscience, there is a manifestation of moral degradation in some, and in others stagnation, or retrogression in life or service. Instead of using their mind, or conscience in deciding what is good and evil, and right and wrong, they walk, as they believe, according to the "voice of God," which they make the deciding factor in all their decisions. When this takes place, they will not listen to their reason, or conscience, or the words of others, and having come to decision through the supposed direction of God, their minds become as a closed and sealed book on the matter in question.

Ceasing to use their true reasoning powers, they become open to all kinds of suggestions from evil spirits, and false "reasonings"; for example, in regard to the coming of Christ, some have falsely reasoned that because Christ is coming soon, they do not need to carry on their usual work, overlooking the words of the Lord on this very matter: "Who then is the faithful and wise servant, whom his lord hath set over his household, to give them their food in due season? Blessed is that servant, whom his lord, when he cometh, shall find so doing."

Because of what he will gain through it, therefore, the devil will do anything to engender passivity in any form whatsoever, in spirit, or mind or body.

PASSIVITY OF THE SPIRIT

Passivity of the spirit is closely associated with passivity of mind, because there is a close relationship between mind and spirit; a wrong thought generally means a wrong spirit, and a wrong spirit a wrong thought.

The human "spirit" is often spoken of in the Scriptures as having activities, and is described as being in various conditions. It can be moved, or be inactive, it can be "loosed," bound, depressed, faint, free, and moved from three sources: God, the devil, or the man himself. It can be pure, or "filthy" (2 Cor. 7: 1, A.V.), or in a mixed condition, in the sense of being pure up to a degree, with other degrees of impurity to be dealt with.

By the cleansing power of the Blood of Christ (1 John 1: 9), and the indwelling of the Holy Spirit, the spirit is brought into union with Christ (1 Cor. 6: 17), and should actively dominate the man in full co-operation with the Holy Spirit. But passivity of spirit can be brought about by so many causes, that believers may be scarcely conscious of having any "spirit" at all, or else, through the Baptism of the Holy Spirit, which releases the human spirit into freedom and buoyancy, the man may become acutely conscious of the spirit life for a season, and afterwards sink into passivity of spirit, unknowingly. This, then, means absolute powerlessness in the warfare with the powers of darkness; for full liberty, and usage of the spirit in co-working with the indwelling Holy Spirit, is a supreme essential for personal victory, and wielding the authority of Christ over the powers of evil. (See example of Paul in Acts 13: 9, 10).

CAUSES OF PASSIVITY OF SPIRIT

Passivity of spirit generally follows the Baptism of the Spirit, by the will and the mind becoming passive through lack of use; and the believer then wonders why he has lost the buoyant light and liberty of his joyous experience. It may come about through:

(1) Ignorance of the laws of the spirit, and how to keep in the freedom of the spirit.

(2) Wrong mental conclusions, or wrong thoughts Mixing up feelings, such as physical, soulish and spiritual, not knowing which is which, i.e., (1) putting the spiritual down to soulish and physical, or (2) attributing to the spiritual that which is natural and physical.

(3) A drawing upon of the soulish life instead of the spirit, through lack of knowledge of the difference between them; also by quenching the spirit through ignoring the spiritual sense;for the mind should be able to read the sense of the spirit, as clearly as it does the sense of seeing, hearing, smelling, and all the senses of the body. There is a knowledge of the mind, and a knowledge in the spirit, hence a "sense" of the spirit which we should learn to understand. It should be read, used, cultivated, and when there is a weight on the spirit of the believer, he should be able to recognise it, and know how to get rid of it.

(4) Drainage and exhaustion of the body or mind, by constant activity of the mind in excessive use. In short, the mind and body must be released from strain, before the spirit can be fully operative. (Compare experience of Elijah in 1 Kings 19: 4, 5, 8, 9).

Worry, or trouble over the past, or future, checks the free action of the spirit, by making the outer man and outer affairs dominant, instead of the inner man being at liberty for the will of God in the moment.

The result of all these causes is that the spirit becomes locked up, so to speak, so that it cannot act, or fight against the powers of darkness, either in their indirect attacks through environment, or in aggressive warfare against them. The rapidity with which a believer can sink into passivity, at any moment when the resisting attitude ceases, may be likened to the sinking of a stone in water.

PASSIVITY OF THE BODY

When passivity of body takes place, it practically means a cessation of consciousness, through the passivity affecting sight, hearing, smell, taste, feeling, etc. Assuming the person to be in normal health, he should be able to focus his eyes on any object he chooses, either for vision or work, and he should have the same control over all the other senses, as avenues of knowledge to his mind and spirit. But with all, or some of these senses in a passive condition, the consciousness becomes dulled or deadened. The believer is "unconscious," of what he should be keenly alive to, and automatic in his actions. "Unconscious" habits, repulsive or peculiar, are manifested. It is easier for persons in this condition to see these things in others, than to know what is going on in themselves; whilst they may be hyper-conscious of external things touching their own personality.

When the passive condition brought about by evil spirits reaches its climax, passivity of other parts of the body may result, such as stiff fingers, lost elasticity of the frame in walking, lethargy, heaviness, stooping of the back and spine The handshake is flabby, and passive; the eyes will not look straight into the eyes of others, but move from side to side; all indicating passivity, brought about by deepening interference of the powers of darkness with the whole man, resulting from the first passive condition of the will and mind, in which the man gave up (1) his self-control, and (2) use of his will.

PASSIVITY OF THE WHOLE MAN

At this stage every department of the whole being is affected. The man acts without using, or using fully, the mind, will, imagination, reason; that is, without thinking (volitionally), deciding, imagining, reasoning. The affections seem dormant, as well as all the faculties of mind and body. In some cases the bodily needs are also dormant, or else the man suppresses them, and deprives himself of food, sleep and bodily comfort at the dictation of the spirits in control; thus carrying out a "severity to the body" which is not of any real value against the indulgence of the flesh (Col. 2: 23). The animal part of the man may also be awakened, and whilst stoical in sensibilities and feeling, be gluttonous in the demand for supply of bodily needs; that is, the machinery of the bodily frame goes on working independently of the control of mind or will, for the body now dominates spirit and soul. Men may live in the (1) human spirit, (2) in the soul, or in the (3) body; for example, the glutton lives in, or after, the body; the student in mind, or soul, the spiritual man "in the spirit." "Spiritists" are not really "spiritual," or true men of spirit, for they live in the sense realm generally, and only have to do with "spirit" through their dealing with the evil spiritual forces, through understanding the laws for their workings, and fulfilling them.

THE SPIRIT SENSE LOST IN SENSATIONS OF THE BODY

When the believer is in any degree possessed by evil spirits, he is liable to live in the body, give way to the sensuous, and to be dominated by the physical realm. This can become the case through "spiritual" experiences felt in the physical frame, but which are not really spiritual, because not from the spirit. A sense of "fire" in the body, "glow," "thrills," and all exquisite bodily sensations from apparently "spiritual" causes, really feed the senses; and, unconsciously to themselves, whilst they have these experiences, believers live in the sense-realm, practically walking "after the flesh," though they call themselves "spiritual." For this reason "I keep under my body" (1 Cor. 9: 27), is practically impossible in demon-possession, even in its most refined, or weakest degree; because the sense-life is aroused in all kinds of ways, and the sensations of the body are forced upon the consciousness of the man. The spirit sense is practically lost in the acute realisation of all the sensations in the bodily consciousness. A man, for example, in normal health, is oblivious of the physical action of breathing going on in his physical frame. In like manner, a believer under the domination of the spirit, ceases to register his bodily sensations, but the opposite is the case when evil spirits have gained a footing, and awakened the sense-life to abnormal action, either by beautiful experiences, or the contrary

The cultivation of this condition of passivity may be ignorantly, and sedulously, carried out for years by the surrendered believer, so that it deepens its hold upon him to an incredible extent; until, when it reaches its consummation, the man may become so under the bondage of it as to awaken to his state; and then he thinks that "natural causes" alone explain his condition, or else that in some unaccountable way, his acute sensitiveness to God, and Divine things, has become dulled beyond power of restoration or renewal. The physical feelings become deadened, or atrophied, and the affections seem petrified, and stoical. This is the time when deceiving spirits suggest that he has grieved God beyond repair, and a man goes through agonies of seeking the Presence he thinks he has grieved away.

The cultivation of passivity may come about from reliance upon the many helps, contrived, (unknowingly), by the person to counteract, or obviate the inconvenience of the passive state, such as the provision of, and dependence upon, outward helps to the eye for assisting the passive memory; utterance in speech to assist the "thinking" of the passive mind; and, what may be termed "crutches" of all kinds, known only to the individual; elaborately constructed, and multiplied to meet his different needs, but all keeping him from recognising his true condition, even if he has the knowledge for doing so.

MANIFESTATIONS OF INFLUENCE OF EVIL SPIRITS CALLED NATURAL IDIOSYNCRASIES

But this truth about the working of evil spirits among believers, and the causes and symptoms of their power upon mind or body, has been so veiled in ignorance, that multitudes of children of God are held in bondage to their power without knowing it. The manifestations are generally taken as natural idiosyncrasies, or infirmities. The Lord's work is put on one side, or even never taken up, because the believer is "over strained," or else "without gifts" for doing it. He is "nervous," "timid," has no "gift of speech, " no "power of thought," where the service of God is concerned; but in the social sphere these "deficiencies" are forgotten, and the "timid" ones shine out at their best. It does not occur to them to ask why it is that only in God's service are they thus incapable? But it is only in respect to such a service that the hidden workings of Satan interfere.

THE SHOCK WHEN THE BELIEVER APPREHENDS THE TRUTH

The shock is great when the believer first apprehends the truth of deception and possession as possible in himself, but as the ultimate issue is realised, the joy of the one who sets himself to understand, and fight through to full deliverance, is more than words can tell. Light pours in upon the unsolved problems of years; both in the personal experience, and in the perplexities of environment; as well as on conditions in the Church and in the world.

As he seeks for light from God, the subtle inroads of the deceiving spirits into his life, slowly become clear to the open minded believer; and their many devices to deceive him stand revealed, as the searchlight of truth goes far back into the past, revealing the cause of unaccountable difficulties in experience and life, and many mysterious happenings which had been accepted as "the inscrutable will of God."

Passivity! How many have fallen into it, little knowing their state! Through the passivity of their faculties much time is lost in dependence upon the help of outward circumstances, and environment. In the lives of so many there is much "doing," with so little accomplished, many beginnings, and few endings. How familiar we are with the words "Yes, I can do that," and the impulse is moved, but by the time the need for action has come, the passive man has lost his momentary interest. This is the key to much of the lamented "apathy," and the dulled sympathy of Christians to really spiritual things, whilst they are keenly alive to the social, or worldly elements around them. The worldling can be stirred in acutest feeling for the sufferings of others, but many of the children of God have, unknowingly, opened themselves to a supernatural power which has dulled them in thought, and mind and sympathy. Ever craving for comfort and happiness and peace in spiritual things, they have sung themselves into a "passivity"--i.e., a passive state of "rest," "peace" and "joy"--which has given opportunity to the powers of darkness to lock them up in the prison of themselves, and thus make them almost incapable of acutely understanding the needs of a suffering world.

PASSIVITY OCCASIONED BY WRONG INTERPRETATIONS OF THE TRUTH OF "DEATH"

This condition of passivity may come about by wrong interpretations of truth, even the truth of "death with Christ" as set forth in Romans 6 and Galatians 2: 20, when it is carried beyond the true balance of the Word of God. God calls upon true believers to "reckon" themselves "dead indeed unto sin," and also to the evil self-life, even in a religious or "holiness" form; that is, the life which came from the first Adam, the old creation; but this does not mean a death to the human personality, for Paul said "Yet I live," although "Christ liveth in me!" There is a retention of the personal being, the ego, the will, the personality, which is to be dominated by the Spirit of God, as He energises the man's individuality, held by him in "self-control" (Gal. 5: 23, m.).

In the light of the misconception of the truth of "death with Christ" as conceived to mean passivity, and suppression of the actions of the personality of the man, it is now easy to see why the apprehension of the truths connected with Romans 6: 6, and Galatians 2: 20, have been the prelude, in some cases, to supernatural manifestations of the powers of darkness. The believer through the misconception of these truths, actually fulfilling the primary conditions for the working of evil spirits; the very conditions understood by spiritist mediums to be necessary for obtaining the manifestations they desire. In such cases it may be said that truth is the devil's fulcrum for launching his lies.

So far as Romans 6 is understood to be a momentary declaration of an attitude to sin; and Galatians 2: 20 another declaration of an attitude to God; and 2 Cor. 4: 10- 12 and Phil. 3: 10 the out-working of the Spirit of God in bringing the believer into actual conformity to the death of Christ as he maintains his declared attitude; the powers of darkness are defeated; for the momentary declared attitude demands active volition, and active co-operation with the Risen Lord, and active acceptance of the path of the Cross. But when these truths are interpreted to mean

(1) a loss of personality; (2) an absence of volition and self-control, and (3) the passive letting go of the "I myself" into a condition of machine-like, mechanical, automatic "obedience," with "deadness" and heaviness which the believer thinks is "mortification" or "the working of death" in him; it makes the truth of death with Christ a fulfilling of conditions for evil spirits to work, and an absence of conditions upon which God can alone work; so that "supernatural manifestations" taking place on the basis of passivity, can have no other source than the lying spirits, however beautiful and God-like they may be.

This counterfeit of spiritual "death" may take place in regard to spirit, soul or body. How the truth of death with Christ can be misconstrued, and made the occasion for evil spirits to obtain the ground of passivity, may be exampled in some of the following ways:--

MISCONCEPTION OF SELF-EFFACEMENT

1. Passivity caused by misconception of self-effacement: Under the conception of surrender of self to God, as meaning self-effacement, self-renunciation, and, practically, self-annihilation, the believer aimed at unconsciousness of (1) personality, (2) personal needs, (3) personal states, feelings, desires, external appearance, circumstances, discomforts, opinions of others, etc., so as to be "conscious" of God only moving, working, acting, through him. To this end he gave over his "self-consciousness" to "death," and prayed that he might have no consciousness of anything in the world, but the presence of God; then to carry out this absolute surrender of self to death, and this entire self-effacement, he consistently, in practice, "yields to death" every trace of the movement of "self" he becomes aware of, and sets his will steadily to renounce all consciousness of personal wishes, desires, tastes, needs, feelings, etc. All this appearing to be so "self-sacrificing" and "spiritual," but which results in an entire suppression of personality, and the giving of ground to evil spirits in a passivity of the whole being. This permits the powers of darkness to work, and bring about an "unconsciousness" which becomes in time a deadness and dullness of the sensibilities, and an inability to feel; not only for himself, but for others, so as not to know when they suffer, and when he himself causes suffering.

MISCONCEPTION OF TRUTH PART OF "TEACHINGS" OF DECEIVING SPIRITS

As this conception of self-effacement, and loss of self-consciousness is contrary to the believer's full use of the faculties, which the Spirit of God requires for co-operation with Him, evil spirits gain ground on the basis of this deception about "death."

The misconception of what death means in practice, was really part of their "teachings," subtly suggested, and received by the man who was ignorant of the possibility of deception, over, what looked like, devoted, whole-hearted surrender to God. The "teachings of demons" can, therefore, be based on truth, under the guise of misconception, or misinterpretation of the truth, whilst the believer is honestly holding the truth itself.

The effect of the deception on the believer is, in due time, an "unconsciousness" produced by evil spirits, which is hard to break. In his state of unconsciousness, he has no ability to discern, recognise, feel or know things around him, or in himself. He is "unconscious" of his actions, ways and manners, together with a hyper-self-consciousness which he is unconscious of, and which makes him easily hurt, but "unconscious" of his own hurting of others. He has practically become stoical, and unable to see the effect of his actions in putting others into suffering. He acts "unconsciously," without volitional thinking, reasoning, imagining, deciding, what be says and does. His actions are consequently mechanical and automatic. He is "unconscious" of sometimes being a channel for the transmission of words, thoughts, feelings which pass through him apart from the action of his will and his knowledge of the source.

"Unconsciousness" as the effect of demon-possession, becomes a formidable stumbling block in the way of deliverance, for the evil spirits may hold, hinder, attack, divert, suggest, impress, draw, or do any other equally offensive, and injurious thing, in or through the person, whilst he is "unconscious" of their workings.

PASSIVITY CAUSED BY WRONG ACCEPTANCE OF SUFFERING

2. Passivity caused by wrong acceptance of suffering. The believer consents to accept "suffering with Christ" in the "way of the Cross," and in fulfilment of this surrender to suffering, from this time on passively yields to suffering in whatever form it may come, believing that "suffering with Christ" means (a) reward, and (b) fruitfulness. He does not know that evil spirits can give counterfeit "suffering," and that he may accept suffering from them, believing it to be from the hand of God, and, by thus doing, give ground to them for possession. Possession interprets both sin in the life which cannot be got rid of, and suffering in the life which cannot be explained. By understanding the truth of possession, the first can be got rid of, and the latter explained. Suffering is a great weapon to control and compel a person into a certain course, and is a great weapon for evil spirits to control men, as by suffering they can drive a man to do what he would not do, apart from its compulsion.

Not knowing these things the believer may entirely misinterpret the suffering he goes through. Believers are often deceived over what they think to be "vicarious" suffering in themselves for others, or for the Church. They look upon themselves as martyrs, when they are really victims, not knowing that "suffering" is one of the chief symptoms of possession. By putting a man into suffering, the evil spirits ease themselves of their enmity, and hatred to man.

MARKS OF SUFFERING CAUSED BY EVIL SPIRITS

Suffering directly caused by evil spirits may be discriminated from the true fellowship of Christ's sufferings, by a complete absence of result, either in fruit, victory, or ripening in Spiritual growth. If carefully observed, it will be seen to be entirely purposeless. On the other hand, God does nothing without a definite object. He does not delight in causing suffering for the sake of suffering, but the devil does. Suffering caused by evil spirits is acute and fiendish in its character, and there is no inward witness of the Spirit which tells the suffering believer that it is from the hand of God. To a discriminating eye it can be as clearly diagnosed when from an evil spirit, as any physical pain can be discriminated from a mental one, by a skillful physician.

The suffering caused by evil spirits can be (1) spiritual, by causing acute suffering in the spirit, injecting "feelings" to the spirit, repugnant or poignant; (2) soulish, by acute darkness, confusion, chaos, horror in the mind; anguished, knife-like pain in the heart, or other innermost vital parts of the being; or (3) physical, in any part of the body.

The ground given for the evil spirits to produce counterfeit suffering in such an acute degree as this, may be traced back to the time when the believer, in his absolute surrender to God for the "way of the Cross," deliberately willed to accept suffering from Him. Then afterwards, in fulfilment of this surrender, he gave ground to the enemy, by accepting some specific suffering as from God, which really came from the spirits of evil , thus opening the door to them, by (1) the reception of their lie, (2) the admittance of their actual power manifested in the suffering--continuing still further to give more ground by believing their interpretation of the suffering--and (3) as "the will of God"; until the whole life became one prolonged "yielding to suffering," which seemed unreasonable, unaccountable in its origin, and purposeless in its results. God's character is thus often maligned to His children, and the deceiving spirits do their utmost to arouse rebellion against Him for what they themselves are doing.

PASSIVITY THRU' WRONG IDEAS OF HUMILITY

3. Passivity caused by wrong ideas of humility and self-abasement. The believer consents in accepting "death," to let it be carried out in a "nothingness" and a "self-effacement" which gives

him no place for proper and true self-estimation whatsoever (compare 2 Cor. 10: 12-18). If the believer accepts the self-depreciation, suggested to him and created by evil spirits, it brings an atmosphere of hopelessness and weakness about him, and he conveys to others a spirit of darkness and heaviness, sadness and grief. His spirit is easily crushed, wounded and depressed. He may attribute the cause to "sin," without being aware of any specific sin in his life; or may even look upon his "suffering" experience as "vicarious" suffering for the Church; whereas an abnormal sense of suffering is one of the chief symptoms of possession.

In the counterfeit of the true elimination of "pride," and all the forms of sin arising from it, the counterfeit caused by possession may be recognised by (1) the believer obtruding his self-depreciation at moments most inopportune, with painful perplexity to those who hear it; (2) a shrinking back from service for God, with inability to recognise the interests of the kingdom of Christ; (3) a laborious effort to keep "I" out of sight, both in conversation and action, and yet which forces the "I" more into view in an objectionable form; (4) a deprecatory, apologising manner, which gives opportunity to the "world-rulers of the darkness of this world," to instigate their subjects to crush, and put aside this "not I" person, in moments of strategic importance to the kingdom of God; (5) an atmosphere around such an one of weakness, darkness, sadness, grief, lack of hope, easily wounded touchiness--all of which may be the result of the believer "will"-ing, in some moment of "surrender to death," to accept an effacement of the true personality, which God requires as a vessel for the manifestation of the Spirit of Christ, in a life of fullest co-operation with the Spirit of God. The believer, by his wrong belief, and submission to evil spirits, suppressed into passivity a personality which could not, and was not meant to "die"; and by this passivity opened the door to the powers of darkness to gain ground for possession.

PASSIVITY CAUSED BY WRONG THOUGHT ABOUT WEAKNESS

4. Passivity caused by a wrong thought about weakness. The believer consents to a perpetual condition of weakness, under a misconception of its being a necessary state for the manifestation of Divine life and strength. This is generally based upon Paul's words "When I am weak, then am I strong," the believer not apprehending that this was a statement made by the Apostle of a simple fact that when he was weak, he found God's strength sufficient for all His will; and that it is not an exhortation to God's children deliberately to will to be weak, and hence unfit for service in many ways, instead of saying "I can do all things through Christ which strengtheneth me." That the "will" to be weak, so as to have a claim on Christ's strength, is a wrong thought, can be seen

practically in many lives, where "weakness" is passively accepted, with a burden and care to others, which is no evidence of such an attitude being in accordance with God's plan and provision. The "will" to be weak actually hinders God's strengthening, and by this subtle deception of the enemy in the minds of many, God is robbed of much active service for Him.

PASSIVITY WITH SATANIC ACTIVITY

It does not mean that "passivity" in its full extent, means no "activity"; for once the man becomes passive in volition and mind, he is held by deceiving spirits without power to act, or is driven into Satanic activity; that is, uncontrollable activity of thought, restlessness of body, and wild, unbalanced action of all degrees. The actions are spasmodic and intermittent, the person sometimes dashing ahead, and at other times sluggish and slow; like a machine in a factory, with the wheels whirring aimlessly, because the switch of the centre control is out of hand of the master. The man cannot work, even when he sees so much to be done, and is feverish because he cannot do it. During the time of passivity he appeared to be content, but when he is driven into Satanic activity, he is restless, and out of accord with all things around him. When his environment should lead to a state of full content, yet something (may it not be "somebody"?) makes it impossible for him to be in harmony with his external circumstances, however pleasant they may be. He is conscious of a restlessness and activity which is painfully feverish; or of passivity and weight; of a doing of "work," and yet no work. All the manifestations of a demoniacal destruction of his peace.

DELIVERANCE FROM PASSIVITY

The believer needing deliverance from the condition of passivity, must first seek to understand what should be his normal or right condition; and then test, or examine himself in the light of it, to discern if evil spirits have been interfering. To do this, let him recollect a moment in his life, which he would call his "best," either in spirit, soul and body, or in his whole being; and then let him look upon this as his normal condition, which he should expect as possible to be maintained, and never rest satisfied below it.

As the passivity has come about gradually, it can only end gradually, as it is detected, and destroyed. The full co-operation of the man is necessary for its removal, and is the cause of the long period needed for his deliverance. Deception and passivity can only be removed as the man understands, and co-operates by the use of his volition in the refusal of the ground, and the deception which came through it. This is also the reason why, in this aspect of "possession," evil spirits cannot be "cast out," because the cause which gave them admittance is a factor in their expulsion.

An important point in deliverance from passivity is to keep perpetually in the mind, the standard of the normal condition, and if at any time the believer drops below it to find out the cause, so as to have it removed. Whatever faculty, or part of the being, has been surrendered into passivity, and therefore lost for use, must be retaken by the active exercise of the will, and brought back into personal control. The "ground" given which caused any faculty to fall into bondage to the enemy, must be found out, and given up; and then refused persistently, in a steady resistance to the spirits of evil in their hold of it, remembering that the powers of darkness fight against the loss of any part of their kingdom in man, as much as any earthly government would fight to protect its own territory and subjects. The "Stronger than he" is the Conqueror, and strengthens the believer for the battle, and to recover all the spoil.

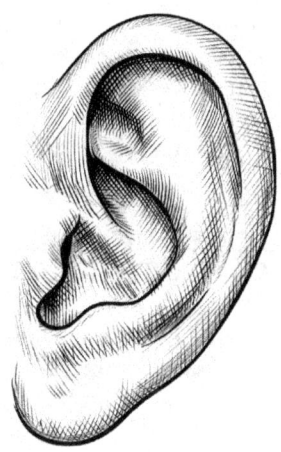

CHAPTER 5
Deception and Possession

To be deceived by lying spirits does not mean that the believer is necessarily possessed by an evil spirit; and a person may be "possessed" without having been deceived. For instance, a believer may be misled in guidance, or be deceived by counterfeit visions and manifestations, without these deceptions leading on into possession; and where there is yielding to sin, either known or unknown, even by a believer, an evil spirit may take possession of the mind, or body, without there being any experience of deception (1 Cor. 5: 5).

The faculties may become severally held, or possessed, by evil-spirits, by (1) yielding to the sin of passivity--passivity is the sin of omission, for God does not give a faculty either for misuse, or nonuse, or (2) yielding to sins of action, e.g., if the tongue lends itself to slander or foul language, it lends itself to sin; and becomes liable to possession. And so with the eyes, ears and other parts of the body; the lust of the eyes in seeing, and looking at vile things; the ears by wrong listening-eaves-dropping is lending the ears to the emissaries of Satan--or, on the other hand, evil spirits may take hold of the nerves of the ear, so that the person cannot hear what he should, yet is permitted to be alert enough in bearing all that he should not hear.

DEGREE OF GROUND NEEDED FOR, EVIL SPIRIT TO POSSESS CANNOT BE DEFINED

The needed degree of ground given to an evil spirit in order to possess, cannot be clearly defined, but that there is (1) sin without evil spirit possession; (2) sin which opens the door to possession; and (3) sin which is unmistakably the result of Satanic possession (John 13: 2) is beyond question.

If the man, be he unbeliever or believer, sins so as to admit an evil spirit, the ground given may be deepened without measure. (1) the ground given admits the demon, (2) the "manifestation" of the evil spirit takes place, (3) then the misinterpretation of the manifestation again gives further ground, because he believes, and admits still more of the lies of the evil one.

It is possible, also, for deception and possession to come about, and pass away without the man being conscious of either. He may yield to sin which gives access to an evil spirit, and then take the position of death (Rom. 6: 6, 11) to the sin or its ground, when, unconsciously to himself, the possession passes away.

Multitudes of believers are "possessed" in various degrees but do not know it, as they attribute the "manifestations" to "natural" causes, or to "self" or "sin," and they put them down to these causes because they do not appear to bear the characteristics of demoniacal possession.

There is also a degree of deception by deceiving spirits, in connection with counterfeits of God and Divine things, which leads on to possession; and this too, depends upon the extent of the counterfeits which have been accepted by the believer.

Through "possession" by accepting the counterfeit of the workings of the Holy Spirit, believers can, unknowingly, be brought to (1) put their trust in evil spirits, (2) rely on them, (3) surrender to them, (4) be guided by them, (5) pray to them, (6) listen to them, (7) obey them, (8) receive messages from them, (9) receive Scripture texts from them, (10) help them in their desires and working, (11) stand by them, and (12) work for them; believing they are in these attitudes towards God, and doing these things for God.

In some cases, the counterfeit manifestations have been accepted with such reckless abandonment, that deception has quickly developed into possession in a most acute, yet subtle, and highly refined form; giving no apparent trace of the presence of evil, yet the peculiar double personality, characteristic of fully developed "demon possession," is easily recognisable to trained spiritual discernment; although it may be hidden under the of the most beautiful "angel of light" manifestation, with all the fascinating attraction of "glory light" upon the face, exquisite music in song, and a powerful effect in speech.

THE DUAL PERSONALITY OF DEMON POSSESSION

The dual personality of fully developed demon possession is generally only recognised when it takes the form of objectionable manifestations; such as when a distinct other-intelligence obscures the personality of the possessed one, and speaks through the vocal organs, in a distinctly separate or altered voice, expressing thoughts or words unintended, or only partially volitioned by the subject; the victim is compelled to act in ways contrary to his natural character, and the body is manipulated by a foreign power, and nerves and muscles are twisted in contortions, and convulsions, such as are described in the Scripture records (Luke 9: 39).

A characteristic of the dual-personality of demon possession also is that the manifestations are usually periodical, and the victim is comparatively natural, and normal, between what are described as "attacks," but which are really periods of manifestations of the intruding power.

DUAL PERSONALITY OF EVIL SPIRIT POSSESSION IN CHRISTIANS

Evidences are now available, proving that this dual-personality of possession in its fullest degree, has taken place in believers who are not disobedient to light, or yielding to any known sin; but who have become possessed through deception in their abandonment to supernatural power, which they believed to be of God; such cases having all the symptoms and manifestations described in the gospel records.

The demon answering questions in his own voice, and speaking words of blasphemy against God through the person, whilst he is, in spirit, in peace and fellowship with God; thus evidencing (1) the Holy Spirit to be in the spirit, and (2) the demon, or demons, in the body, using the tongue, and throwing the body about at their will.

This same "dual-personality," under entirely different manifestations , is easily recognisable by any who have the "discerning of spirits." At times the environment of the subject is more favourable than others for the spirit manifestations, and then they can be detected in both beautiful and objectionable forms.

The fact of the demon possession of Christians destroys the theory that only people in "heathen countries," or persons deep in sin, can be "possessed" by evil spirits. This unexamined, unproved theory in the minds of believers, serves the devil well as a cover for his workings to gain possession of the minds and bodies, of Christians in the present time. But the veil is being stripped off the eyes of the children of God by the hard path of experience; and the knowledge is dawning upon the awakened section of the Church that a believer baptised in the Holy Ghost, and indwelt by God in the inner shrine of the spirit can be deceived into admitting evil spirits into his being; and be possessed, in varying degrees, by demons, even whilst in the centre he is a sanctuary of the Spirit of God; God working in, and through his spirit, and the evil spirits in, or through, mind, or body, or both.

DUAL STREAMS OF POWER

From such possessed believers there can proceed, at intervals, streams from the two sources of power; one from the Spirit of God in the centre, and the other from an evil spirit in the outer man; and with the two parallel results to those who come in contact with the two streams of power.

In preaching, all the truth spoken by such a believer may be of God, and according to the Scriptures, correct and full of light--the spirit of the man right--whilst evil spirits working in mind or body, make use of the cover of the truth to insert their manifestations, so as to find acceptance with both speaker and hearers. That is to say, there may pour through a believer at one moment, a stream of truth from the Word, giving light and love and blessing to receptive ones among the listeners; and the next moment, a foreign spirit, hidden in mind or body, may send forth a streamlet through the soulish or physical part of the man, producing corresponding effects in soul or body among the listeners, who respond in their soulish or physical part to the Satanic stream, either by emotional or physical manifestations, or in nervous or muscular actions.

One or the other of the "streams" of power from the Holy Spirit in his spirit, or from the deceiving spirit in mind or body, may predominate at different times, thus making the same man appear dual in character, with short intervals, at different periods of time. "See how he speaks! How he seeks to glorify God! How sane and reasonable he is! What a passion he has for souls!" may be said with truth of a worker, until some moments later some peculiar change is seen in him, and in the meeting.

A strange element comes in, possibly only recognisable to some with keen spiritual vision, or else plainly obvious to all. Perhaps the speaker begins to pray quietly, and calmly, with a pure spirit, but suddenly the voice is raised, it sounds "hollow," or has a metallic tone; the tension of the meeting increases; an overwhelming, overmastering "power" falls upon it; and no one thinks of "resisting" what appears to be such a "manifestation of God!"

MIXED MANIFESTATIONS

The majority of those present may have no idea of the mixture which has crept in. Some fall upon the ground unable to bear the strained emotion, or effect upon the mind; and some are thrown down by some supernatural power; others cry out in ecstasy; the speaker leaves the platform, passes by a young man, who becomes conscious of a feeling of intoxication upon him, which does not leave his senses for some time. Others laugh with the exuberance of the intoxicating joy. Some have had real spiritual help and blessing through the Word of God being expounded ere this climax came, and during the pure outflow of the Holy Spirit; consequently they accept these strange workings as from God, because in the first stage of the meeting, their needs have been truly met by Him; and they cannot discern the two separate "manifestations" coming through the same channel!

If they doubt the latter part of the meeting, they fear they are untrue to their inner conviction that the earlier part was "of God." Others are conscious that the "manifestations" are contrary to their spiritual vision, and judgment; but on account of the blessing of the earlier part they stifle their doubts, and say "We cannot understand the 'physical' manifestations, but we must not expect to understand all that God does. We only know that the wonderful outpouring of truth and love and light at the beginning of the meeting was from God, and met our need. No one can mistake the [sincerity, the pure motive of the speaker . . therefore, although I cannot understand, or say I 'like' the physical manifestations, yet--it must be all of God . . "

TRUE AND COUNTERFEIT ACCEPTED TOGETHER

Briefly put, this is a glimpse into the mixed "manifestations" which have come upon the Church of God, since the Revival in Wales; for, almost without exception, in every land where revival has since broken forth, within a very brief period of time the counterfeit stream has mingled with the true; and almost without exception, true and false have been accepted together, because of the workers being ignorant of the possibility of concurrent streams; or else have been rejected together by those who could not detect the one from the other; or it has been believed that there was no "true" at all, because the majority of believers fail to understand that there can be mixed workings of the (1) Divine and Satanic, (2) Divine and human, (3) Satanic and human, (4) soul and spirit, (5) soul and body, (6) body and spirit; the three latter in the way of feelings and consciousness, and the three former in the way of source and power.

There must be more than one quantity to make a mixture; at least two. The devil mixes his lies with the truth, for he must use a truth to carry his lies. The believer must therefore discriminate, and judge all things. He must be able to see so much to be impure, and so much that he can accept. Satan is a "mixer." If in anything he finds ninety-nine percent pure, he tries to insert one percent of his poisonous stream, and this grows, if undetected, until the proportions are reversed. Where there is mixture acknowledged to be in meetings where supernatural manifestations take place, if believers are unable to discriminate, they should keep away from these "mixtures" until they are able to discern.

In accepting the counterfeits of Satan, the believer thinks, and believes, he is complying with Divine conditions in order to ascend to a higher life; whereas he complies with conditions for Satanic workings in his life, and thereby descends into a pit of deception and suffering, with his spirit and motive pure.

How evil spirits gain access to the believer, is the next question we need to consider; and here we give in column form, six concise lists of (1) how they deceive; (2) the ground given for deception; (3) where they enter; (4) the excuses the spirit makes to hide the ground, and keep the believer in ignorance of his presence and the ground he holds; (5) the effect on the man thus deceived; and (6) the symptoms of the possession.

HOW EVIL SPIRITS DECEIVE

We shall see how subtly the evil spirit works, first to deceive, and then to gain access to the mind or body, or both, of the believer. One principle governs the working of God, and the working of Satan in seeking access to a man. In the creation of a human being with a free will, God, Who is Sovereign Lord of the Universe, and of all angelic powers, has limited Himself in that He does not violate man's freedom in obtaining his allegiance; neither can Satan's evil spirits enter, and obtain possession of any part of the man apart from his consent, given either consciously, or unconsciously. Just as a man "wills" a good thing, and God makes it fact, so when the man "wills" an evil thing, evil spirits make it fact. Both God and Satan need the will of man for working in man.

In the unregenerate man the will is enslaved to Satan, but in the man who has been regenerated, and delivered from the power of sin, the will is liberated to choose the things of God. In one who has thus been brought into fellowship with God, Satan can only gain ground by stratagem, or, in Bible terms, by "wiles"; for he knows he will never get from a believer deliberate consent to the entry, and control of evil spirits. The Deceiver can only hope to obtain that consent by guile: i.e., by feigning to be God Himself, or a messenger from Him. He knows, too, that such a believer is determined to obey God at all costs, and covets the knowledge of God above all else on earth.

There is, therefore, no other way to deceive this one, but by counterfeiting God Himself, His presence and His workings; and under pretence of being God, to obtain the co-operation of the man's will in accepting further deceptions; so as eventually to lead to "possession" of some part of the believer's mind or body, and thus injure or hinder his usefulness to God, as well as that of others who will be affected by him.

DISTINCTION BETWEEN THE PERSON AND THE PRESENCE OF GOD

The counterfeit of God in and with the believer, is the basis on which is built the whole after structure of possession through deception. Believers desire and expect God to be with, and in them. They expect God's presence with them, and this is counterfeited. They expect God to be in them as a Person, and evil spirits to counterfeit the three Persons of the Trinity.

In order to understand the counterfeiting methods of evil spirits, we must distinguish between the Presence and the Person of God. The "Presence" as giving forth an influence, and the Person manifested as Father, Son, or Holy Spirit. Crudely put, it may be described as the difference between God as Light, and having light from God. God as Love, and having love from God. The one is the Person Himself in His nature, and the other the outshining, or giving forth of what He is.

The thought with many is that the Person of Christ is in them, but in truth, Christ as a Person is in no man. He dwells in believers by His Spirit--the Spirit of Christ (Rom. 8: 9), as they receive the "supply of the Spirit of Jesus" (Phil. 1: 19; Acts 16: 7 R.V.).

It is necessary also, to understand the teaching of the Scriptures on the Trinity, and the different attributes and work of each Person of the Trinity, to discern the counterfeiting work of the deceiver.

God the Father, as a Person, is in the highest heaven. His presence is manifested in men as the "Spirit of the Father." Christ the Son is in heaven as a Person, His presence in men is by His Spirit. The Holy Spirit, as the Spirit of the Father, and of the Son, is on earth in the Church, which is the Body of Christ; and manifests the Father or the Son, in, and to believers, as they are taught by Him to apprehend the Triune God. Hence Christ said "I will manifest Myself," to those who loved and obeyed Him; and later "We will come, and make our abode with him" (John 14: 23) i.e., by the Holy Spirit to be given on the Day of Pentecost.

THE PERSON OF GOD IN HEAVEN, HIS PRESENCE ON EARTH BY HIS SPIRIT

The Person of God is in heaven, but the presence is manifested on earth, in and with believers; through and by the Holy Spirit; in, and to the human spirit, as the organ of the Holy Spirit for the manifested presence of God.

The believer's misconceptions of the manner in which God can be in, and with him, and his ignorance that evil spirits can counterfeit God and divine things, form the ground upon which he can be deceived into accepting the counterfeit workings of evil spirits, and give them access into, and possession, and control of his inner being.

If God, Who is Spirit, can be in and with a man, evil spirits can also be in and with men, if they can obtain access by consent. Their aim and desire is possession and control. These are terms which are often used of God's work in believers, but which are not really Scriptural, in the meanings which are given to the words in the present day, i.e., God "possesses" a man in the sense of ownership, and then He asks for co-operation, not " control". The believer is to control himself, by co-operation in his spirit with the Spirit of God; but never does God "control" the man as a machine is controlled by another, or by some dynamic force.

DISTINCTION BETWEEN GOD AND DIVINE THINGS

We must also make a distinction between God and Divine things, i.e., all that is Divine is not God Himself, just as all that is Satanic is not Satan himself, and all that is human is not the man himself; Divine, Satanic and human things, being those which emanate from God, Satan, and man respectively.

These three sources must always be taken into account in everything, e.g., Guidance can be (1) divine, (2) satanic, or (3) human. Obedience may be rendered to (1) God, (2) Satan, or (3) men. Visions may have their source in (1) God, (2) evil spirits, or (3) the man himself. Dreams can come from (1) God, (2) evil spirits, or (3) the man's own condition. Writing in its source may be from (1) God, (2) evil spirits, or (3) the man's own thoughts. Counterfeits by evil spirits may therefore be (1) of God, and divine things, (2) of Satan and satanic things, or (3) the human and human things.

To obtain possession, and control of believers, who will not be attracted by sin, the deceiving spirits must first counterfeit the manifestation of the presence of God, so that under cover of this "presence" they can get their suggestions into the mind, and their counterfeits accepted without question. This is their first, and sometimes their long piece of labour. It is not always an easy task, especially when the soul has been well grounded in the Scriptures, and learnt to walk by faith upon the Word of God, nor is it easy when the mind is acute in usage, and well guarded in thought, and healthily occupied.

THE COUNTERFEIT OF THE PRESENCE OF GOD

From the counterfeit presence, comes the influence which causes the counterfeit to be accepted. Evil spirits must make something to imitate the presence of God, as their "presence" does not, and cannot be a counterfeit of it. The counterfeit presence is a work of theirs, made by them, but is not the manifestation of their own persons, e.g., they give sweet or soothing feelings, or feelings of peace, love, etc., with the whispered suggestion, adapted to the ideal of the victim, that these indicate the presence of God.

When a counterfeit presence, or influence, is accepted, then they go on to counterfeit a "Person," as one of the Persons of the Trinity, again adapted to the ideals or desires of the victim. If the believer is drawn to one more than another of the Persons of the Holy Trinity, the counterfeit will be of the One he is attached to most. The Father, to those who are drawn to Him; the Son to those who think of Him as "Bridegroom" and crave love; and the Holy Spirit to those who crave for power.

The counterfeit "Presence," as an influence, precedes the counterfeit of the "Person" of God, through which much ground is gained.

The period of danger is, as already shown in Chapter 3, at the time of seeking the Baptism of the Holy Spirit, when much has been said by others about manifestations of God to the consciousness, or some "coming upon" of the Spirit, felt by the senses. This is the opportunity for the watching spirits.

What believer is there that does not long for the "conscious" presence of God, and would not give up all to obtain it? How difficult it is to walk by "faith," when passing through the dark places of life! If the "conscious presence" is to be obtained by the Baptism of the Spirit, and there can be supernatural effects upon the senses, so that God is really felt to be at hand--then who would not be tempted to seek it? It looks to be an absolutely necessary equipment for service, and it appears from the Bible story of Pentecost, as if the believers then must have had this conscious presence, felt by them physically and actually.

SATAN'S WORKING UPON THE SENSES

Here lies the danger point which first opens the door to Satan. The working upon the senses in the religious realm, has long been Satan's special mode of deceiving men throughout the whole world, of which he is the god and prince. He knows how to soothe, and move, and work upon the senses in every possible way, and, in every form of religion ever known, deceiving unregenerate men with the form of godliness whilst denying the power. Among the truly converted, and even sanctified believers, the senses are still his way of approach. Let the soul admit a craving for beautiful emotions, happy feelings, overwhelming joy, and the conception that manifestations, or "signs," are necessary to prove the presence of God, especially in the Baptism of the Spirit, and the way is open for Satan's lying spirits to deceive.

THE TRUE MANIFESTATION OF CHRIST

The Lord said, on the eve of His Cross, concerning the coming of the Holy Spirit to the believer, "I will . . manifest Myself unto him" (John 14: 21), but He did not say how He would fulfil His promise. To the woman at the well He said "God is spirit," and "they that worship Him must worship Him in spirit and in truth." The manifestation of Christ is, therefore, to the spirit, and not in the realm of the senses, or animal soul. Hence the craving for sense-manifestation opens the door to deceiving spirits to counterfeit the real presence of Christ; but the consent and co-operation of the will to their control must be obtained, and this they seek to get under the guise of an "angel of light"; as a messenger of God apparently clothed with light, not darkness, for light is the very nature and character of God.

The basis of this deception of the believer is his ignorance of the principles on which God works in man, and the true conditions for His manifested presence in the man's spirit; and his ignorance of the conditions upon which evil spirits work, in a passive surrender of the will, mind and body to supernatural power. In his ignorance of the true working of God, the believer expects Him to move on the physical being, so that He is manifested to the senses, and to use his faculties apart from him, as a proof of His presence and "control," whereas God only moves in, and through the man himself by the active co-operation of his will--the will being the ego, or centre of the man. Neither does God use the faculties of the man apart from conjunction with the man, i.e., through his will. Not instead of the man, but with him (2 Cor. 6: 1).

THE COUNTERFEIT PRESENCE IS AN INFLUENCE UPON THE BELIEVER

The counterfeit presence is an influence from outside upon the believer; and can begin in some cases, not only at the time of the Baptism of the Spirit, but by a "practice" of the "Presence of God," if the believer means by that a sense consciousness of "God," who is to be known and recognised by the sense of the spirit, not the senses of the body. The true presence of God is not felt by the physical senses, but in the spirit, and the same is true of "feeling" the presence of evil spirits, or Satan. The spirit sense alone can discern the presence of God, or Satan; and the body only feels indirectly.

It is important clearly to recognise the distinction between the "obsession," or influence of the counterfeit presence; and the "possession," or access obtained, which follows the acceptance of the obsession, or influence from without.

The distinction and the characteristics may be briefly described as follows:--(1) Obsession: an influence from outside; a counterfeit presence of God as an influence upon the person, to which he opens himself in mind and body.

(2) Possession: the counterfeit of a person within (after obtaining a footing), generally as love. Absolute abandonment to this of the affections and will. Exquisite feelings in physical and soulish realm, with spirit untouched. The man thinks all is "spiritual," when it is really the sensuous life in a spiritual form.

The word obsession has been exaggerated in modern use, and

symptoms, or manifestations truly belonging to possession, are frequently put down to it.

OBSESSION AND ITS CAUSE

"Obsession" means an evil spirit, or spirits, hovering around, and influencing a man with the object of obtaining a footing in him, and gaining possession, in however small a degree. If these influences are yielded to, it must result in possession, e.g., if an evil spirit counterfeits the presence of God, and comes upon the man as an influence only, it may be described as obsession; but when a footing is gained in him, it is "possession," because the obsessing spirits have gained access, and possess the ground they hold, up to the extent of the ground given.

The meaning of the word obsession as given in the dictionary bears this out. It means "to besiege," and it is described as "persistent attack, especially of an evil spirit upon a person; and "the state of being molested from without, as opposed to 'possession' or control by an evil spirit from within." According to this description of obsession, it is evident that it is a very common form of attack by the powers of darkness upon the children of God; not to speak of the unregenerate who are already, according to the Scriptures (Eph. 2: 2), controlled from within, i.e., "the spirit that now worketh in the children of disobedience" (A.v.).

EXTERIOR MANIFESTATIONS OF THE CHARACTER OF OBSESSION

Evil spirits "obsess," or persistently molest, and besiege the man, to gain possession. They obsess his mind with some dominating idea which destroys his peace, and clouds his life; or they counterfeit some Divine experience, which seems to come from God, and which the believer accepts without question. This is one dangerous form of obsession in the present day, when evil spirits seek to gain admittance to a believer by counterfeiting some exterior manifestation of God, such as a "Presence" filling the room, and felt by the physical senses; "waves" of "power" pouring upon, and through the physical being; or a feeling of wind, air, or a breathing upon the outer man, apparently from Divine sources. In brief, all exterior manifestations to the believer, coming from without upon the body, have the characteristics of "obsession," because they may come from deceiving spirits seeking access to mind or body.

The deliverance of persons under obsession of any kind, or degree, is by truth, such as:—

1. Giving them knowledge how to detect what is of God or the devil, by understanding the principles distinguishing the working of the Holy Spirit, and evil spirits.

2. Showing them that they should accept nothing from without either in suggestions to the mind, or influence of any kind coming upon the body; as God the Holy Spirit works from within the spirit of the man, illuminating and renewing his mind, and bringing the body under the believer's own control.

3. Teaching them how to stand in Christ, and resist all besieging attacks of the powers of darkness.

For the deliverance of souls under the bondage of evil spirits in possession, i.e., when they have, after obsession, gained admittance in any degree; much knowledge of God and of spiritual things is needed.

It is generally thought that "casting out" the spirit or spirits, is the only method of dealing with them, but since the ground they obtained to gain entrance, and abide in, cannot be "cast out," it is obvious that although the "casting out" may avail in some cases, it is not the only means of deliverance.

SOME WAYS OF DELIVERANCE FROM POSSESSION

Much depends upon the cause of the possession. In China, among the heathen, demons are cast out immediately after the simple prayer of faith by the Christians. In Germany, an evangelist of ripe experience, speaks of men delivered from demon-possession after one prayer, but others who were "weeks, months, years, before they got free," and this only after much wrestling in prayer by men of God, mighty in faith.

But for believers who have become possessed by evil spirits as a result of deception, the main principle of deliverance is them being undeceived . To deal with "possession" which is the fruit of deception, by commanding the spirits to depart, is to deal with the effect, rather than the cause; and to bring about only temporary, if any, relief, with the danger of the evil spirit returning quickly to his "house," i.e., the ground which gave him lodgement.

Believers who discover themselves to be possessed through deception, should therefore seek light upon the ground through which the evil spirits entered, and give it up. It is by ground given that they obtain access, and it is by ground removed that they depart. It is for this reason that emphasis is placed in this book upon the understanding of truth, rather than upon the aspect of the casting out of demons, as it is written for the deliverance of believers deceived and possessed through accepting counterfeits of the working of God.

Deceived and possessed believers should also be taught the fundamental principle of the attitude of the human will in relation to God, and Satan, and his deceiving spirits. The Scriptures are full of this truth. "If any man willeth to do His will, he shall know . ." (John 7: 17); "he that will, let him take . ." (Rev. 22: 17).

Let it be emphasised again: deceiving spirits are obliged to get the consent of the man's will ere they can enter, and as to how far they enter. This they do by counterfeit and deception. They can only obtain the believer's surrender to their power, by feigning to be God. In fact, obsession, and possession, in all cases, both of regenerate and unregenerate, is based upon deception and guile; for it is not until a man is very fully under the power of Satan that he willfully, and knowingly, yields himself up to him.

Deliverance, therefore, requires the active exercise of the will, which must, in reliance upon the strength of God, and in the face of all beguilements, and suffering, be kept steadily set against the powers of darkness, to nullify previous consent to their working.

Deceiving spirits also counterfeit God in His holiness, and in His righteousness. The effect in such a case is to make the believer afraid of God, and to shrink away from, and loathe all spiritual things. They try to terrorise those who are timid and fearful; to influence those who yearn for power; or to draw into their control those who are open to the attraction of love and happiness.

PHYSICAL SENSES SHOULD NOT FEEL GOD'S PRESENCE

It may be said deliberately, that it is never safe in any case to feel God's presence with the physical senses, for it is almost beyond doubt a counterfeit "presence"--a subtle snare of the enemy to gain a footing in the man. This is one reason why some who have urged upon other believers their need of a "realisation of God"--meaning a felt presence in the atmosphere, or within them--have, to their grief and dismay, lost the "realisation" they themselves had, and sunk into darkness, and numbness of feeling. These believers not knowing this to be the direct result--either quickly or at some distant period--of all supernatural manifestations to the senses; the victim looking for the cause of the breakdown, or "deadness" to spiritual things, in "overstrain" or "sin," and not to the realisation experience he rejoiced in.

The normal condition of the faculties for use, is plainly to be seen in all Bible records of men in direct communication with God. Paul in a "trance" (Acts 22: 18), had full possession of his faculties, and intelligent use of mind and tongue. Especially so is this recognisable in John on Patmos. His physical being was prostrate from the weakness of the natural man in the unveiled presence of the glorified Lord; but after the quickening touch of the Master, his full intelligence was in use, and his mind clearly at work, in power to grasp and retain all that was being said and shown to him (Rev. 1: 10-19).

The difference between the Bible records of the revelations of God, and the conditions of the men to whom they were given; and the records of many of the supernatural manifestations to-day, lies in a principle which reveals the distinction, in striking contrast, between the pure Divine working, and the Satanic counterfeits of God: i.e., the contrasting principles of,

1. The retention of the use of the will, and faculties;
2. The loss of personal control through passivity.

We may take as example what is called "clairvoyance" and "clairaudience"; i.e., the power to see and the power to hear: the first meaning the seeing of supernatural things, and the second the hearing of supernatural words. There is a true seeing and hearing, and a false seeing and hearing of supernatural things; and they result either from a Divine gift, which is the true (Rev. 1: 10-12); or an evil passive state, which admits the counterfeit.

CLAIRVOYANCE AND CLAIRAUDIENCE AND THEIR CAUSE

It is said that clairvoyance and clairaudience powers are "natural gifts," but they are really the result of an evil state, in which evil spirits are able to manifest their power and presence. Crystal gazing is also merely a means of inducing this passive state, and so with all the various methods in vogue in the East and elsewhere, to bring about the manifestations and workings of supernatural powers. The principle is the same. The key to all these, and other Satanic workings in the human frame, is the need of the suspension of the mental activity; whereas in all Divine revelations, the mental faculties and powers are unchecked, and in full operation.

The people at the foot of Mount Sinai "saw God," yet they were not "passive." Vision--whether mental or physical--is really active and not passive, that is, separated from volition and personal action; and "visions" may be either physical, mental or spiritual.

SUPERNATURAL WRITING AND SPEAKING

In writing under the control of evil spirits the same principle is manifested, i.e., the suspension of volitional and mental action:—
1. The person writes what he hears dictated audibly in a supernatural way.
2. He writes what he sees presented to his mind supernaturally, sometimes with rapidity as if compelled.
3. He writes automatically, as his hand is moved, without any mental, or volitional action.

In descriptive writing, or writing from what is supernaturally presented to the mind, the words may pass before the mental vision as clearly as if they were seen by the physical eye, sometimes in letters of fire, or light. The same may take place in public speaking, when the speaker may describe what is presented to the mental vision--that is, if his mind is in a passive state--thinking that all is "illumination by the Holy Spirit."

This may take place in some, in such a refined degree, that the man is deceived into thinking that it comes from a "brilliant mind," "gifts of imagination," "delicate power of poetic description," whilst none of it is the real product of his own mind; for it is not the outcome of thought , but the seizing of subtly presented "pictures" given at the moment when writing or speaking. It can be tested by its fruits; being (1) empty of tangible results, and sometimes (2) mischievous in suggestion; certain sentences intermingled with words of truth, being subversive of the pure gospel; whilst the whole has no spiritual substance at the back of the beautiful words, or any permanent result in the salvation of the unregenerate, or the building up of believers.

PREACHING FROM MENTAL PRESENTATIONS

It is possible that this may be the hidden cause of the evanescent character of Missions carried out on a wide scale, which seem at the time to be fruitful, but which pass away like the morning cloud in a few brief weeks. The speakers gave the truths of the gospel, but may have preached from mental presentations, and not from the source of the spirit in co-operate action with the Holy Spirit. The powers of darkness have nothing to fear from words--even words of gospel truth--if there is no fructifying life in them from the source of the Spirit of God; and that there are spurious conversions on a wide scale permitted, if not brought about, by the spirits of evil, is now beyond question. It is easy for them to, apparently, let go their captives when it suits their plans to deceive the people of God, and there is much in the religious movements of to-day which absorbs the energy of Christians, and appears to extend the Kingdom of God, but leaves undisturbed the kingdom of the spirits of the air.

In automatic writing, and in the more refined presentations referred to, the mind is passive in greater or lesser degree; and the man writes, or speaks, not what comes from the normal action of the mind, but what he sees presented to him.

Ignorant of the existence of evil spirits, and their unceasing schemes to deceive every child of God; and equally ignorant of the danger of fulfilling the conditions for their working; a great number of believers do not know that in the ordinary circumstances of life they can be opening themselves to the deceptions of supernatural beings, who are keenly watching to gain admittance, and to use the servants of God, e.g., a public speaker who seeks to depend on "supernatural help," and does not keenly use his brain in alert spiritual "thinking," practically cultivates a passive condition which the enemy may make use of to the fullest degree; and thus unknowingly gain an influence in his life, which is manifested in unaccountable attacks of all kinds, with, apparently, no ground given by him in life or action.

The same may be true of an author, who in some way, unknown to himself, has become passive--or bluntly put, mediumistic --in some faculty, or part of his inner life, and thereby has opened himself to the supernatural "presentations" of evil spirits, for his speaking or writing, which he thinks is illumination from God.

TRUE WRITING UNDER THE HAND OF GOD

In writing under Divine guidance, three factors are required:
1. A spirit indwelt by, and moved by the Holy Spirit (2 Peter 1: 21).
2. An alert and renewed mind, acute in active power of apprehension and intelligent thinking (See 1 Cor. 14: 20).
3. A body under the complete control of the spirit and volition of the man (See 1 Cor. 9: 27).

In writing or speaking under the control of evil spirits, a man is not truly "spiritual," for his spirit is not in use; what appears "spiritual" being the work of supernatural powers manifesting their spirit power on, and through, the passive mind of the man, apart from his spirit. But in writing under the guidance of God; since it is not given by dictation, as to an automaton, but by the movement of the Holy Spirit in the man's spirit; the man must be truly spiritual, the source being in the spirit, and not in the mind, as it is when men write the products of their own thoughts. The Scriptures bear the marks of their having been written in this way. "Holy men of God spake as they were moved by the Holy Ghost (2 Pet. 1: 21). They spake from God," but as men they received and uttered, or wrote the truth given in the spirit, but transmitted through the full use of their divinely enlightened faculties.

Paul's writings all show the fulfillment of the three requirements mentioned; of his spirit being open to the movement of the Holy Spirit, his mind in full use, and his body an obedient instrument under the control of the spirit; his letters also revealing the capacity of the renewed mind for apprehending the deep things of God.

PAUL'S POWER OF SPIRITUAL DISCERNMENT

In Paul, too, we see the clear discrimination possessed by a spiritual man, able to recognise what came from God in his spirit, and what was the product of his own thought in the exercise of his judgment as a servant of God.

The records of most "supernatural revelations" today, almost entirely show (1) the absence of the requirements for true Divine manifestations; and (2) of having fulfilled the law for the workings of evil spirits; i.e., the suspension of the use of the mental faculties, with the consequent emptiness, and sometimes childish folly, of the words said to have been "spoken by God," and the purposelessness of the "visions," and other manifestations.

Let the conditions necessary for evil spirits to work in the human frame be fulfilled, and then no experience of the past, no dignity of position, no intellectual training, or knowledge, will protect the believer from their counterfeit manifestations. Consequently, the deceiver will do anything and everything to engender passivity in the children of God, in any form whatsoever, either in spirit, soul or body; for he knows that sooner or later he will gain the ground then given. It can therefore be said unhesitatingly, that if the law for evil spirits to work is fulfilled, in the non-use of the mind and faculties, evil spirits will work and deceive the very elect of God.

WHY EVIL SPIRITS WANT THE BODY

It may be asked why evil spirits want the body, and why they so persistently work to gain access and possession?

1. Because in it they find "rest" (Matt. 12: 43), and seem to find some relief for themselves in some way we do not know. But still more than this:
2. Because the body is the outlet of the soul and spirit; and if they can control the exterior, they can thereby control the inner man at the centre by hindering his freedom of action manward, although they may not do so God-ward.

In the case of the believer, they do not destroy the life at the centre, but they can imprison it, so that the inner man, indwelt by the Holy Spirit, is unable to attack and destroy their kingdom and works. When the evil spirits gain possession of a believer's body and mind in any degree, all previous spiritual growth is practically of no service value. In the spiritual section of the Church of Christ, a great number of believers need light for liberation of their circumference. Their spiritual growth is checked and hindered by the dulling of their faculties, the clog of misconceptions and deceptions in their minds, or weakness and disease in their bodies. These conditions also checking the outflow of the Holy Spirit indwelling the spirit, so that the life of Jesus cannot be manifested through them, in the using of the mind for the transmission of truth, or in the strengthening and using of the body in active effective service.

Therefore, when the outer man becomes dispossessed, it does not bring the centre life into existence, but into freedom of operation. All this may be in various degrees, for all believers are not in the same degree of bondage. There are degrees of (1) inner spiritual growth; of (2) mixture in the life, of workings of God from the spirit, and evil spirits in the outer man; of (3) passivity of the man in spirit, soul and body, resulting in (4) degrees of "possession."

The moment ground is given, in any degree, to evil spirits, the faculties are dulled by them, or become passive through non-use. Their aim then is to substitute themselves for the person in all his actions, and so to gain entrance to him, over the rails, so to speak, of his passive faculties, will, etc., as to intertwine themselves in the innermost structure of his being, and thus to control him and use him for their own purposes; the man meanwhile believing that he is admitting Divine substitutions for himself--that is, God working, and acting instead of himself--and thus he is becoming "God-possessed."

Believers in such a degree of possession by deceiving spirits then have "supernatural power", and can, in a supernatural way, get from the spirits in control of them, and give forth from them as their transmitters, many supernatural workings, or manifestations such as:--

The getting and transmitting of "Revelations." The power of "Prophecy."
The power of divination.The receiving and giving of impressions, supernaturally. The getting of specific "guidance," supernaturally.
The foretelling of events.
The power of writing automatically, or otherwise. The receiving and giving of information.
The receiving of interpretations.
The getting of visions.
Such a possessed believer may also obtain power:--
Of listening to spirit beings.
Of concentration necessary for listening.
Of getting knowledge, supernaturally.
Of holding communication and communion supernaturally.
Of translating, criticising, correcting, judging.
Of getting and giving suggestions.
Of getting and giving messages.
Of dealing with obstacles, supernaturally.
Of receiving and giving "meanings" to facts and imaginations.
Of giving supernatural meanings to natural facts; and natural meanings to supernatural facts.
Of being led and controlled.

Many of these manifested workings of the evil spirits in possession of the believer, appear to be the working of the man himself; but of which actions he is incapable naturally; e.g., he may have no "natural" power of "translating, criticising," etc. Yet the spirits in possession can give him power for so doing, thus creating a false personality in the eyes of others, who think him possessed of such and such "gifts" (naturally), and are disappointed when he will not use them; not knowing that he is unable to "manifest" or use such supposed "gifts," except at the will of the spirits in control of him. Also that when the deceived believer discovers such manifestations to be the fruit of possession, and refuses any longer to be the slave of the lying spirits of Satan, such "gifts" cease to exist. This is the time when the undeceived man is persecuted by the revengeful spirits of evil, through their suggestions to others that he has "lost his power," or "retrograded" in his spiritual life, when in truth he is being liberated from the effects of their wicked and fiendish workings.

EVIL SPIRITS SUBSTITUTE FOR GOD

The following examples show how the deceiving spirits may substitute themselves, and their own working in the believer's life, through his misconceptions of spiritual truth.

1. Substitution in speaking. Text: "It is not ye that speak . . ." (Matt. 10: 20). Believers think that this means Divine substitution for their speaking. That God will speak through them. The man says, "I must not speak, God is to do so," and he "surrenders" his mouth to God to be His mouthpiece, bringing about passivity of the lips and vocal organs, which are abandoned for usage to the supernatural power which he thinks isGod.

Result: (a) The man himself does not speak; (b) God does not speak, because He makes no man an automaton; (c) evil spirits speak, as the condition of passivity is fulfilled for their doing so. The outcome is the substitution of evil spirits in possession and control of the believer, particularly in the form of supernatural "messages"n which increasingly demand his passive obedience, and in due time bring about a mediumistic condition wholly unforeseen by him.

2. Substitution in memory. Text: "Shall bring all things to your remembrance" (John 14: 26). Believers think this means that they need not use the memory. God will bring all things to their mind.
Result: (a) the man himself does not use his memory; and (b) God does not use it, because He will not do so apart from the believer's

co-action; (c) evil spirits use it, and substitute their workings in the place of the believer's volitional use of his memory.

3. Substitution of conscience. Text: "Shall hear a word behind thee saying, this is the way . . " (Isa. 30: 21). Believers look upon supernatural guidance in a voice or text directing them, as a higher form of guidance than through conscience. The man then thinks that he does not need to reason or think, but simply "obey." He follows this so-called "higher guidance," which he substitutes for his conscience. Result: (a) he does not use his conscience; (b) God does not speak to him for automatic obedience; (c) evil spirits take the opportunity, and supernatural voices are substituted for the action of the conscience. The outcome is the substitution of evil spirit guidance in his life.

From this time the man is not influenced by what he feels or sees, or by what others say, and he closes himself to all questions, and will not reason. This substitution of supernatural guidance for the action of the conscience explains the deterioration of the moral standard in persons with supernatural experiences, because they have really substituted the direction of evil spirits for their conscience. They are quite unconscious that their moral standard is lowered, but their conscience has become seared by deliberately ceasing to heed its voice; and by listening to the voices of the teaching spirits, in matters which should be decided by the conscience in respect to their being right or wrong, good or evil.

4. Substitution in decision. Text: "It is God that worketh in you to will . . . " The believer thinks this to mean that he is not to use his own will, for God is to will through him. Result: (a) the man himself does not exercise his will; (b) God does not either, or he would cease to be a free agent; (c) evil spirits seize upon the passive will, and either hold it in a paralysed condition of inability to act, or else make it domineering and strong. The apparent "Divine substitution" of God's will in the place of the man's will, turns out to be a Satanic substitution, and thus the emissaries of Satan gain a hold of the very centre of the life; eventually making the believer a victim to indecision and weakness in will-action, or else energising the will to a force of mastery, even over others, which is fraught with disastrous results.

EVIL SPIRITS SUBSTITUTE FOR SELF

In like manner, evil spirits will not only endeavour to substitute their own workings in a man's life in the place of God, on the ground of the believer's misconception of the true way of co-acting with God; but they will also seek to substitute their workings for all the mental faculties of the man, i.e., the mind, the reason, the memory, the imagination, the judgment. This is a counterfeit of self through substitution. The person thinks it is himself all the time.

This substitution by evil spirits of themselves on the ground of the passive surrender to non-use of any part of the inner, or outer, life of the believer, is the basis of deep deception and possession among the most "surrendered" children of God; the deception and possession taking an entirely spiritual form at first, such as the man having an exaggerated sense of his importance in the Church, his "world-wide ministry," his lofty position of influence arising out of his "divine commission," his abnormal height of spirituality, and definite and almost unprecedented "experience," which makes him feel he has been placed far above other men. But a tremendous and inevitable fall awaits such an one. He ascends his pinnacle, pushed by the enemy, without any power whatsoever to control the inevitable descent, which must follow when he is undeceived, a crash being the result, shaking the things that can be shaken. Then he experiences awful darkness, and the effects of possession in its true results. The effect of demon possession in its fullest climax is darkness; nothing but darkness; darkness within, darkness without; intense darkness; darkness over the past; darkness enveloping the future. Darkness surrounding God and all His ways.

Here many sink under the horror that they have committed the "unpardonable sin." Some, however, discover that their bitter experience may be turned into light for the Church in its fight with sin and Satan, and as those who have been in the camp of the enemy and heard all his secrets, they become a terror to the forces of evil on their emergence to liberty, with the result that they are assailed with intensified malignity on account of their knowledge of the foe.

CHAPTER 6
Counterfeits of the Divine

In seeking to obtain full control of the believer, the first great effort of evil spirits is directed toward getting the man to accept their suggestions, and workings, as the speaking, working, or leading of God. Their initial device is to counterfeit a "Divine Presence," under cover of which they can mislead their victim as they will. The word counterfeit meaning the substitution of the false for the true.

The condition on the part of the believer, which gives the deceiving spirits their opportunity, and the basis of this counterfeit, is the mistaken location of God; either (1) in them (consciously); (2) or around them (consciously). When they pray they think of, or pray to God in themselves, or else to God around them, in the room, or atmosphere. They use their imagination, and try to "realise" His presence, and they desire to "feel" His presence in them, or upon them.

THE LOCATION OF GOD BY BELIEVERS

This locating of God, in, or around the believer, usually comes about at the time of the Baptism of the Holy Ghost; for up to that time of crisis in his life, he lived more by the acceptance of facts declared in the Scriptures, as understood by his intelligence; but with the Baptism of the Spirit he becomes more conscious of the presence of God by the Spirit, and in the spirit, and so begins to locate the Person of God as in, around, or upon him. Then he turns inward, and begins to pray to God as within him, which in time, really results in prayer to evil spirits, if they succeed in gaining admittance under counterfeit.

The logical sequence of prayer to God as located within, can be pressed to absurdity, i.e., if the soul prays to God in himself, why not pray to God in another elsewhere? The limitation of God as a Person within, and all the possible dangers arising from this misconception of truth are obvious.

Some believers so live inwardly in communion, worship and vision, as to become spiritually introverted, and cramped and narrowed in their outlook; with the result that their spiritual capacity and mental powers become dwarfed and powerless. Others become victims to the "inner voice," and the introverted attitude of listening to it, which is the ultimate result of the location of God as a Person within, so that eventually the mind becomes fixed in the introverted condition with no out-going action at all.

In fact, all turning inwards to a subjective location of God as indwelling, speaking, communing, and guiding, in a materialistic, or conscious sense, is open to gravest danger; for upon this thought and belief, sedulously cultivated by the powers of darkness, the most serious deceptions, and final out-workings of deceiving spirits have taken place.

THE ULTIMATE RESULT OF MISTAKEN LOCATION OF GOD

Upon this principle of the mistaken location of God; used by evil spirits as the ground work for manifestations to support and deepen this belief; has come about the delusions of believers during past ages, and of recent years, who assert themselves to be "Christ." On the same principle will come about the great deceptions at the end of the age, foretold by the Lord in Matthew 24: 24, of the "false Christs" and false prophets; and the "I am the Christ" of the leaders of groups of sidetracked believers; and the thousand others who have been sent to asylums, although they are not monomaniacs at all.

The devil's richest harvest is from the effects of his counterfeits; and unwittingly, many sober and faithful teachers of "holiness" have aided him in his deceptions, through the using of language which gives a materialistic idea of spiritual things, and which is eagerly laid hold of by the natural mind.

Those who locate God personally, and wholly in themselves, make themselves, by their assertions, practically, "divine" persons. God is not wholly in any man. He dwells in those who receive Him, by His own Spirit communicated to them. "God is Spirit," and mind or body cannot hold communion with spirit. Sensuous feelings, or "conscious" physical enjoyment of some supposed spiritual presence is not true communion of spirit with spirit, such as the Father seeks from those who worship Him (John 4: 24). God is in heaven. Christ the Glorified Man is in heaven. The location of the God we worship is of supreme importance. If we think of our God as in us, and around us, for our worship, and for our "enjoyment" (?) we unwittingly open the door to the evil spirits in the atmosphere which surrounds us; instead of our penetrating in spirit through the lower heavens (see Heb. 4: 14; 9: 24; 10: 19, 20) to the throne of God, which is in the highest heaven, "above principality and power, and every name that is named, not only in this world, but in that which is to come" (Eph. 1: 21, A.V.).

THE TRUE LOCATION OF GOD

The Word of God is very clear on this point, and we need only ponder such passages as Heb. 1: 3; 2: 9; 4: 14-16; 9: 24; and many others, to see it. The God we worship, the Christ we love, is in heaven; and it is as we approach Him there, and by faith apprehend our union with Him in spirit there, we, too, are raised with Him and seated with Him, above the plane of the lower heavens where the powers of darkness reign, and seated with Him, see them under His feet (Eph. 1: 20-23; 2: 6).

The Lord's words recorded in the gospel of John, chapters 14, 15 and 16, give the truth very clearly concerning His indwelling in the believer. The "in Me" of being with Him, and in Him, in His heavenly position (John 14: 20), being the fact for the believer's faith, and apprehension; and the "I in you"-spoken to the company of disciples, and hence to the Body of Christ as a whole--following as a result in the individual life of the believer. The union with the Person in the glory, resulting in the inflow and outflow of His Spirit and life, through the believer on earth (see Phil. 1: 19).

In other words, the "subjective" is the result of the "objective." The "object" of Christ in heaven, being the basis of faith for the subjective inflow of His life and power, by the Holy Spirit of God.

CHRIST AS A PERSON IN HEAVEN

The Lord said "If ye abide in Me (i.e., in the glory), and My words abide in you, ye shall ask what ye will. . ." (John 15: 7). Christ abides in us by His Spirit, and through His words, but He Himself, as a Person, is in heaven, and it is only as we abide in Him there, that His Spirit, and His life, through His Word, can be manifested in us here.

"Abiding" means an attitude of trust, and dependence on a Person in heaven; but if the attitude is changed into a trust and dependence upon a Christ within, it is really a resting upon an inward experience, and a turning from the Christ in heaven, which actually blocks the avenue for the inflow of His life, and disassociates the believer from co-operation with Him by the Spirit.

Any manifestation therefore of a "presence" within, cannot be a true "manifestation" from God, if it uncentres the believer from his right attitude toward the Christ in heaven. There is a true knowledge of the presence of God, but it is in the spirit, when joined to Him Who is within the veil; a knowledge of spiritual union and fellowship with Him which lifts the believer, so to speak, out of himself to abide with Christ in God.

The counterfeit "presence" of God is nearly always manifested as love, to which the believer opens himself without hesitation, and finds it fill and satiate his innermost being, but the deceived one does not know that he has opened himself to evil spirits in the deepest need of his inner life.

COUNTERFEIT PRESENCE OF GOD

How the powers of darkness counterfeit the presence of God to those ignorant of his devices may be somewhat as follows. At some moment when the believer is yearning for the sense of God's presence, either alone, or in a meeting, and certain conditions are fulfilled, the subtle foe approaches, and wrapping the senses round with a soothing, lulling feeling--sometimes filling the room with light, or causing what is apparently a "breath from God" by a movement of the air--either whispers "This is the presence you have longed for," or leads the believer to infer that it is what he has desired.

Then, off his guard, and lulled into security that Satan is far away, some thoughts are suggested to the mind, accompanied by manifestations which appear to be Divine; a sweet voice speaks, or a vision is given, which is at once received as "Divine guidance," given in the "Divine presence," and hence beyond question as from God.

If accepted as from God, when from the spirits of evil, the first ground is gained. The man is now so sure that God has bidden him do this or that. He is filled with the thought that he has been highly favoured of God, and chosen for some high place in His Kingdom. The deeply hidden self-love is fed and strengthened by this, and he is able to endure all things by the power of this secret strength. He has been spoken to by God! He has been singled out for special favour! His support is now within upon his experience, rather than upon God Himself, and the written Word. Through this secret confidence that God has specially spoken to him, the man becomes unteachable and unyielding, with a positiveness trending on infallibility. He cannot listen to others now, for they have not had this "direct" revelation from God. He is in direct, special, personal communion with God, and to question any "direction" given to him, becomes the height of sin. Obey he must, even though the direction given is contrary to all enlightened judgment, and the action commanded opposed to the spirit of the Word of God.

In brief, when the man at this stage believes he has a

"command" from God, he will not use his reason, because he thinks it would be "carnal" to do so "common-sense" is lack of faith, and therefore sin--and "conscience" for the time being, has ceased to speak.

Some of the suggestions made to the believer by deceiving spirits at this time, may be: (1) "You are a special instrument for God," working to feed self-love; (2) "You are more advanced than others" working to blind the soul to sober knowledge of itself; (3) "You are different from others," working to make him think he needs special dealing by God; (4) "You must take a separate path," a suggestion made to feed the independent spirit; (5) "You must give up your occupation, and live by faith," aiming at causing the believer to launch out on false guidance, which may result in the ruin of his home, and sometimes the work for God in which he is engaged.

All these suggestions are made to give the man a false conception of his spiritual state; for he is made to believe he is more advanced than he actually is, so that he may act beyond his measure of faith and knowledge (Rom. 12: 3), and consequently be more open to the deceptions of the beguiling foe.

Upon the basis of the supposed revelation of God, and the special manifestation of His presence, and the consequent full possession of the believer by Him, the lying spirits afterwards build their counterfeits.

THE COUNTERFEIT "PRESENCE" IS SENSUOUS

Counterfeits of the Father, the Son, and the Holy Spirit, are recognisable by the manifestations being given to the senses; i.e., in the physical realm; for the true indwelling of God is in the shrine of the spirit alone; and the soul vessel, or personality of the believer, is purely a vehicle for the expression of Christ, Who is enthroned within by His Spirit; whilst the body, quickened by the same Spirit, is governed by God from the central depths of the human spirit, through the self-control of the man; acting by his renewed will.

The counterfeit presence of God is given by deceiving spirits working upon the physical frame, or within the bodily frame, upon the senses. We have seen the beginning of this, and how the first ground is gained.

It is deepened by these sense-manifestations being repeated, so gently, that the man goes on yielding to them, thinking this is truly "communion with God"--for believers too often look upon "communion with God" as a thing of sense, and not of spirit--and here he commences praying to evil spirits under the belief that he is praying to God. The self-control is not yet lost, but as the believer responds to, or gives himself up to these "conscious" manifestations, he does not know that his will-power is being slowly undermined.

At last through these subtle, delicious experiences, the faith is established that God Himself is consciously in possession of the body, quickening it with felt thrills of life, or filling it with warmth and heat, or even with "agonies" which seem like fellowship with the sufferings of Christ, and travail for souls, or the experience of death with Christ in the consciousness of nails being driven into the bodily frame, etc.

From this point the lying spirits can work as they will, and there is no limit as to what they may do to a believer deceived to this extent.

COUNTERFEIT MANIFESTATIONS OF DIVINE WORKINGS IN THE BODY

Counterfeit manifestations of the Divine life in various ways now follow quickly; movements in the body, pleasant thrills, touches, a glow as of fire in different parts of the body; or sensations of cold, or shakings, and tremblings; all accepted by the believer as from God, but showing what a full entry the deceiving spirit has obtained to the bodily frame; for there is a distinction between the manifestations of evil spirits "with" and "in" the body and mind of the believer; although when they are really inside, they can also make it appear as if they were outside, both in influence and action.

When evil spirits are really outside, and desirous of entry, they work by sudden suggestion, which is not the ordinary working of the mind, but suggestions which come from without; "flashes of memory," again not the ordinary working of the memory, but coming from without; touches and twitches of the nerves; feelings of draught and sensations of wind blowing on the circumference, etc.

EFFECTS OF EVIL SPIRIT ENTRY TO THE BODILY FRAME

When the evil spirits are inside, the whole frame is affected, at times with the pleasant sensations referred to, but at others with pains in the head and body which have no physical cause, or else so working with the "natural" that the supernatural cannot easily be distinguished from it; such as accelerating the heartbeat so as to appear palpitation, and in other ways working with the physical causes, so that part has natural ground, and part is from the accentuating force of evil.

Depression then ensues in proportion to the previous exhilaration; exhaustion and fatigue in reaction from the demand upon the nervous system in the hours of ecstasy; or else a sense of drainage of strength without any visible cause; grief and joy, heat and cold, laughter and tears, all succeed each other in rapid changes, and varied degrees--in brief, the emotional sensibilities seem to have full play.

The "senses" are aroused, and are in full mastery of the person, apart from the man's volition; or they may be apparently under control, so that the evil spirit's presence may be hidden from the knowledge of the believer, his workings being carefully measured to suit the victim he has studied so well; for he knows he must not go a shade too far, lest he awaken suspicion of the cause of the abnormal movements of the emotions, and of the sensitive parts of the bodily frame.

It can easily be seen that in time the health of the deceived one must be affected by this play upon mind and body; hence the "breakdown" that so often follows experiences of an abnormal kind, or else a snapping of the tension, by a sudden stoppage of all conscious feelings, and the apparent withdrawal of the "conscious presence of God;" followed by an entire change of tactics by the deceiving spirits in the body, who may now turn upon their victim with terrible accusations; and charges of having committed the "unpardonable sin," producing as acute anguish and real suffering, as he once experienced of the bliss of heaven.

COMPULSORY "CONFESSIONS" OF SIN

Here the evil spirits may push the man to "confessions" of all kinds, however public and painful, which he hopes may result in regaining the "experience" apparently lost; but all in vain.

These confessions instigated by deceiving spirits may be recognised by their compulsory character. The man is forced to "confess" sin, and ofttimes sins which have no existence, but in the accusations of the enemy. As it does not dawn upon him that evil spirits will push a man to do what looks like the most meritorious thing, and which the Scriptures declare is the one condition for obtaining forgiveness, he yields to the drive upon him, simply to get relief.

Herein lies the danger of widespread "confessions of sin" during times of Revival, when almost a "wave" of "confession" passes over a community, and the depths of sinful lives are exposed to the gaze of others; through this enabling the lying spirits to disseminate the very poison of the pit into the atmosphere, and into the minds of the listeners.

TRUE CONFESSION OF SIN

True confession of sin should come from deep conviction and not compulsion, and should, be made only to God, if the sin is one only known by God; to man personally, and in private, when the sin is against man; and to the public only when the sin is against the public. "Confession" should never be made under the impulse of any compulsory emotion, but should be the deliberate act of the volition; choosing the right, and the putting things right, according to the will of God.

That Satan's kingdom gains by public "confessions" is evident by the devices of the enemy used to push men into them. Evil spirits drive a man into sin, and then compel that man publicly to confess the sin which they forced him to commit--contrary to his true character--in order to make the sin which they forced him into, a stigma upon him for the remainder of his life.

Ofttimes the "sins" confessed have their rise in the believer, from the insertion by wicked spirits, of feelings as consciously abhorrent and loathsome, as were the former "conscious" feelings of heavenly purity and love; when the man who experienced them, declared that he knew of no "sin to confess to God," or "no rising of an evil impulse" whatever; leading him to believe in the complete elimination of all sin from his being.

In short, the counterfeit manifestations of the Divine presence in the body, in agreeable and heavenly feelings, can be followed by counterfeit feelings of sinful things, wholly repugnant to the volition and central purity of the believer--who is as faithful to God now in his hatred to sin, as in the days when he reveled in the sense of purity given consciously to his bodily frame.

The deceiving spirit in possession of the body, may now reveal his malignity in attacks of apparent disease, or acute pain without physical cause, counterfeiting or producing (1) consumption, (2) fever, (3) nerve breakdown, and other illnesses, under which the life of the victim may be lost, unless the workings of the "murderers" acting under Satan are discerned, and dealt with by prayer against them, as well as the bodily frame cared for in the natural way.

COUNTERFEIT GUIDANCE

Counterfeit guidance is one of the fruits of the possession of the body which the deceiver obtains through guile. Many believers think the "guidance" or "leading" of God, to be only by a voice saying "Do this," or "Do that;" or by a compulsory movement or impulse, apart from the action or volition of the man. They point to the expression used about the Lord, "the Spirit driveth Him into the wilderness"; but this was abnormal in the life of Christ, for the statement implies intense spirit conflict wherein the Holy Spirit departed from His ordinary guidance. We have a glimpse into a similar intense movement in the Spirit of the Lord Jesus, in John 11: 38, when "groaning with indignation in His spirit" He moved to the grave of Lazarus. In both instances He was moving forward to direct conflict with Satan--in the case of Lazarus, with Satan as the prince of death. The Gethsemane agony was of the same character.

But normally the Lord was guided, or led, in simple fellowship with the Father; deciding, acting, reasoning, thinking, as One who knew the will of God, and intelligently--speaking reverently--carried it out. The "voice" from heaven was rare, and, as the Lord Himself said, was for the sake of others, and not for Himself. He knew the Father's will, and with every faculty of His being as Man, He did it. (See John 12: 30, 5: 30, 6: 38).

As Christ was a pattern or example for His followers, guidance or "leading" in its perfect and true form is shown in His life, and believers can only expect the co-working of the Holy Spirit when they walk after the pattern of their Example. Out of line with the Pattern they cease to have the working of the Holy Spirit, and become open to the deceptive counterfeit workings of evil spirits.

If the believer ceases to use mind, reason, will, and all his other faculties as a person, and depends upon voices, and impulses for guidance in every detail of life, he will be "led" or guided by evil spirits, feigning to be God.

COUNTERFEIT "INWARD" DRAWINGS

At first, after the Baptism of the Spirit, the believer knows to a great extent the true guidance of the Spirit of God. He knows true inward constraint to act, and restraint from action in like manner; such as when to speak to another about his soul, when to rise and testify in a meeting, etc., but after a time he ceases to watch for this pure inward moving of the Spirit; often through ignorance of how to read the monitions of his spirit; and begins to wait for some other incentive or manifestation to guide him in action. This is the time for which the deceiving spirits have been watching. Because at this point the believer has ceased, unknown to himself, to co-operate with the inward spirit action; to use his volition, and to decide for himself, he is now watching for some other supernatural indication of the way to go, or the course to take. Hence he must have "guidance" somehow, some "text," some "indication," some "providential circumstance," etc., etc. This is the moment of opportunity for a deceiving spirit to gain his faith and confidence: and so some word or words are whispered softly, that are exactly in accordance with the inward drawing that he has had, but which he has not recognised as from another source than the Holy Spirit, Who acted by the deep inner constraining and restraining of the spirit .The soft whisper of the deceiving spirit is so delicate and gentle, that the believer listens to, and receives the words without question, and begins to obey this soft whisper, yielding more and more to it, without any thought of exercising mind, judgment, reason, or volition.

The "feelings" are now in the body, but the believer is unconscious that he is ceasing to act from his spirit, and by the pure unfettered action of his will and his mind, which, under the illumination of the Spirit, is always in accord with the spirit. This is a time of great danger if the believer fails to discriminate the source of his "drawing" feelings, and yields to them before finding out their source. He should examine his basic principle of decision, especially when it has to do with feeling, lest he should be led away by any feeling without being able to say where it comes from, or whether it is safe for him to go by it. He should know there are physical feelings, soulish feelings, and feelings in the spirit, either of which can be Divine or Satanic in their source, therefore reliance on "feelings"--feeling drawn, etc.--is a source of great mischief in the Christian life.

From this point deceiving spirits can increase their control, for the believer has begun the listening attitude, which can be developed acutely, until he is always watching for an "inner voice," or a voice in the ear, which is an exact counterfeit of the voice of God in the spirit; and thus the believer moves, and acts as a passive slave to "supernatural guidance."

THE COUNTERFEIT VOICE OF GOD

Evil spirits are able to counterfeit the voice of God, because of the ignorance of believers that they can do so, and of the true principle of God's way of communication with His children. The Lord said: "My sheep know My voice . . " i.e., My way of speaking to My sheep. He did not say this voice was an audible voice; nor a voice giving directions which were to be obeyed apart from the intelligence of the believer, but, on the contrary, the word "know," indicates the use of the mind, for although there is knowledge in the spirit, it must reach the intelligence of the man, so that spirit and mind become of one accord.

The question whether God now speaks by his direct voice audibly to men, needs consideration at this point. A careful study of the epistles of Paul--which contain an exhaustive epitome of

God's will for the Church, the Body of Christ, as the books of Moses contained God's will and laws for Israel--seems to make it clear that God, having "spoken to us in His Son," no longer speaks by His own direct voice to His people. Nor does it appear that since the coming of the Holy Spirit to guide the Church of Christ into all truth, does He frequently employ angels to speak, or to guide His children.

THE MINISTRY OF ANGELS

The angels are "sent forth to minister to the heirs of salvation" (Heb. 1: 14), but not to take the place of Christ or the Holy Spirit. The Apocalypse seems to show that this ministration of angels to the saints on earth, is a ministration of war in the spiritual realm, against the forces of Satan; but there is little indication given of ministry in any other way. After the first Advent, when there was great angelic activity over the wondrous event of the Father bringing the "Firstborn" of the new race (Rom. 8: 29) into the inhabited earth (Heb. 1: 6, R.V.); and again at the Advent of the Holy Spirit on the Day of Pentecost to begin His work of forming a Body like unto the Risen Head--and during the early years of the Church--the employment of angels in direct and visible communication with believers, seems to give way to the work and ministry of the Holy Spirit.

The entire work of witnessing to Christ, and leading the Church into all truth, has been committed to the Holy Spirit. Therefore all intervention of "angels," or audible voices from the spiritual realm, purporting to be from God, may be taken as counterfeits of Satan, whose supreme object is to substitute the working of his own wicked spirits in the place of God. In any case, it is best and safest in these days of peril to keep in the path of faith and reliance upon the Holy Spirit of God, working through the word of God.

HOW TO DETECT THE SOURCE OF A VOICE

In order to detect which is the "voice of God," and which is the "voice of the devil," we need to understand that the Holy Spirit alone is charged to communicate the will of God to the believer, and that He works from within the spirit of the man enlightening the understanding (Eph. 1: 17-18), so as to bring him into intelligent co-working with the mind of God.

The purpose of the Holy Spirit is, briefly, the entire renewal of the redeemed one, in spirit, soul and body, He therefore directs all His working to the liberation of every faculty, and never in any way seeks to direct a man as a passive machine, even into good. He works in him to enable him to choose the good, and strengthens him to act, but never--even for "good"--dulls him, or renders him incapable of free action, otherwise He would nullify the very purpose of Christ's redemption on Calvary, and the purpose of His own coming.

When believers understand these principles, the "voice of the devil" is recognisable, i.e., (1) when it comes from outside the man, or within the sphere of his circumference, and not from the central depth of his spirit, where the Holy Spirit abides; (2) when it is imperative and persistent, urging sudden action without time to reason, or intelligently weigh the issues; (3) when it is confusing and clamorous, so that the man is hindered from thinking; for the Holy Spirit desires the believer to be intelligent, as a responsible being with a choice, and will not confuse him so as to make him incapable of coming to a decision.

The speaking of evil spirits can also be a counterfeit of the apparent inner speaking of the man himself, as if he were himself "thinking," and yet with no concentrated action of the mind; e.g., a persistent and ceaseless "commentary" going on somewhere within, apart from volition or mind action, commenting on the man's own actions or the actions of others, such as "you are wrong," "you are never right ..... God has cast you off ..... you must not do that," etc., etc.

HOW TO DETECT THE SOURCE OF "TEXTS" SUPERNATURALLY SPOKEN

The "voice of the devil" as an angel of light is more difficult to detect, especially when it comes with wonderful strings of texts which makes it appear like the voice of the Holy Spirit. Voices from without, either as from God or angels, may be rejected, yet the believer may be deceived by "floods of texts" which he thinks are from God. In this case the detection needs more knowledge, i.e.,

(1) Does the believer rely upon these "texts" apart from the use of his mind or reason? This indicates passivity.

(2) Are these texts a prop to him? (a) undermining his reliance on God Himself; (b) weakening his power of decision, and (right) self- reliance.

(3) Do these texts influence him? and (a) make him elated and puffed up as "specially guided by God," or (b) crush and condemn him, and throw him into despair and condemnation, instead of leading him to sober dealing with God Himself, over the course of his life, with a keen and increasing knowledge of right and wrong obtained from the written Word by the light of the Holy Spirit?

If these, and other such like results, are the fruit of the "texts" given, they may be rejected as from the Deceiver, or at least an attitude of neutrality taken to them, until further proof of their source is given.

The voice of the devil as distinguishable from the voice of God may also be known by its purpose and outcome. Obviously if God speaks direct to a man, that man must be infallibly correct in regard to the specific matter in question. e.g ., A believer may say he is "led" to ask another to a meeting. The one asked must accept, or else give the lie to the other's "leading." If the one who believed he was "led" still holds to that position, he considers the one who declined as deceived, or else puts the matter aside without consideration, not realising that failure in guidance means that he has deceived himself, or else become deceived by deceiving spirits.

HOW EVIL SPIRITS ADAPT THEIR GUIDANCE TO THEIR VICTIM

Deceiving spirits carefully adapt their suggestions and leadings to the idiosyncrasies of the believer, so that they do not get found out; i.e., no "leading" will be suggested contrary to any strong truth of God firmly rooted in the mind, or contrary to any special bias of the mind. If the mind has a "practical" bent, no visibly foolish "leading" will be given; if the Scriptures are well-known, nothing contrary to Scripture will be said; if the believer feels strongly on any point, the "leadings" will be harmonised to suit that point; and, wherever possible, will be so adapted to previously true guidance from God, as to appear to be the continuance of that same guidance.

Here we see clearly the way of the enemy's working. The soul begins in God's will, but the purpose of the evil spirit is to draw it off into the carrying out of his will by counterfeiting the guidance of God. Satanic guidance alters the points of the life, and misdirects the energies of the man, and lessens his service value. To frustrate this artifice of the enemy, the believer should know that there are two distinct attitudes for guidance, which have serious results if their difference is not understood, i.e., (1) Trusting God to guide, and (2) trust that God is guiding.

The first means reliance upon God Himself, and the second is an assumption of being guided which can be taken advantage of by deceiving spirits. In the first, God does guide in response to definite trust in Him, and He guides through the spirit of the man who continues to co-operate with His Spirit; leaving every faculty free to act, and the will to choose intelligently the right step in the path before him.

In the second, when evil spirits take advantage of an assumption that God "is guiding," independently of momentarily watchful co-operation with the Holy Spirit, a slight compulsion may be noticed, slowly increasing in force, until presently the believer says "I was compelled" to do so-and-so, and "I was afraid to resist,"--the compulsion being taken as an evidence of the guiding of God, instead of recognised as contrary to God's principle of dealing with His children.

THE DECEIVED BELIEVER A SLAVE TO EVIL SPIRITS

If yielded to, and believed to be of God, the result is that the believer becomes a slave to a supernatural power which destroys all freedom of volition and judgment. He begins to be afraid to act himself, lest he should not fulfil, what he believes to be, a minute obedience to the "will of God." He asks "permission" to do the most obviously simple duties of life, and fears to take a step without "permission." As soon as the deceiving spirits have obtained perfect control, and the believer is so passively automatic that he is incapable of realising his condition, they do not need to work so much under cover. They insidiously commence to direct him to do the most absurd or foolish things, carefully working inside the range of his passive obedience to their will, so as to avoid the danger of awakening his reasoning powers. As a matter of "obedience," and not from any true conviction, or true principle, he is bidden to let his hair grow long, so as to be like Samson, a Nazarite; to go without his cap, to prove his willingness to obey in the smallest matters; he must wear faded clothes as a "test" of "no pride," or as a "crucifixion of self," or as a mark of "implicit obedience to God."

These things may seem trifles to others, who use their reasoning powers, but they have great issues in the purpose of the deceiving spirits, who, by these directions, aim at making the believer a passive, unthinking, or unreasoning medium, pliable to their will; in obedience to which--even in these trivial matters--their hold deepens upon him.

When these foolish and absurd actions are publicly visible, the lying spirits know that they have destroyed the testimony of the deceived man in the eyes of sober people; but there are vast numbers of devoted believers, known to the Church at large, who are not pushed to such "extremes" of exterior action; but who are equally misled, or in bondage to "supernatural" commands concerning matters of food, dress, manner, etc., which they think they have received from God. The spirit of judgment of others, and the secret self-esteem for their "consecration to God" which accompanies their "obedience," betrays the subtle workings of the enemy.

THE "PLANCHETTE" USE OF THE BELIEVER BY EVIL SPIRITS

As long as the believer thinks it is God who is directing him, so long the deceiving spirits are safe from exposure, and they can lead him on into more and more deception. When the man reaches a very high degree of Satanic deception, and possession, he finds himself unable to act unless the spirits in control allow him, so that he no longer even asks for "permission" to do this or that. In some cases they even establish communication with him from within his own bodily frame. If he desires to know whether he shall go here or there, he turns inward for guidance to the inner voice--supposed to be the "voice of God"--the answer "Yes," being by a movement of his head, caused by the spirit in possession, or "No" by no action at all; evil spirits making use of the body of the man in the same way as they reply to those who consult them through a "planchette" in other cases; showing their complete control over the nerves of the body and the whole being of the victim, who now believes that every supernatural movement in his body has signification since it may be originated by "God" in possession.

The possession by deceiving spirits at this stage is so great, that no arguments, reasonings, or outward considerations of any kind, influence the actions of the believer thus deceived; or turn him from obeying the "guidance," or "permission" of the inner voice, which he fully believes is of God. In truth should he endeavour to go against it in the smallest matter, the condemnation and suffering are so great, that he becomes terrified at any "disobedience," and would rather be condemned and misjudged by the whole world than go against it. His great horror is "disobeying the Holy Ghost," and the evil spirits deceiving him take every occasion to deepen this fear, so as to retain their hold upon him.

As the believer thus minutely obeys the spirit in control, he relies more and more upon supernatural help, for the moment he does something apart from it he is accused--apparently by the "Holy Spirit"--of "working apart from God."

It is at this stage that all the faculties fall into deepening passivity, as the man lets go entirely to the voice of guidance, and into a reliance upon the divine (?) speakings, which keep the brain in complete inaction.

Here also counterfeit manifestations in "miraculous gifts," prophecy, tongues, healings, visions, and supernatural experiences of every kind possible to the Satanic powers, may be given to the believer, with abundant "texts" and "proofs" to confirm their "Divine origin." He experiences a lightness of the body which makes it appear as if he were carried by invisible hands; he is lifted off his bed in what spiritists know as "levitation"; he can sing and speak, and do what he has never been capable of doing before. Constant contact with spirit forces gives the man a "mystical" look, but all lines of strength, which come from strenuous conflict and self-mastery, go out of the face, for the sense-life is being fed and indulged in a spiritual way as much as by fleshly habits, yet these, such as smoking, etc., have for a time no power.

THE COUNTERFEIT PERSONATION OF OTHERS

But counterfeits of God and Divine things are not the only "counterfeits" the angel of light has at his command. There are also counterfeits of the "human" and human things; such as the personation of others, and even of the believer himself. Others appear to be different from what they really are, jealous or angry, critical or unkind. "Self" is represented in another, in enlarged form, where there is really the very opposite manifestation of selflessness and love. Wrong motives appear to govern others where none exist; simple actions are coloured, and words made to mean and suggest what is not in the minds of the speakers; and sometimes seem to confirm the supposed wrong-doing of others.

Others of the opposite sex may also be personated to a believer in times of prayer or leisure, either in repulsive, or in beautiful form, with the object of arousing various dormant elements in the human frame, unknown to exist by the innocent believer; sometimes the reason for the personation is given "for prayer," or "fellowship" and "spirit-communion" in the things of God.

When their footing is in the body, the lying spirits' counterfeit representations of others, may be in the realm of the passions, and affections, seeking to rouse, or feed these in the possessed one; their faces, voices, "presence," being presented, as if they too were equally affected. This is accompanied with a counterfeit "love," or drawing to the other one, with a painful craving for their company, which almost masters the victim.

This subject of love, and its painful arousing, and communicating or counterfeiting by evil spirits, is one that touches multitudes of believers of all classes. Many are made to suffer poignant agonies of craving for love, with no specific person involved; others are wrought upon in their thoughts so as not to be able to hear the word love mentioned, without embarrassing manifestations of colour, wrought by evil spirits within the bodily frame; none of these manifestations being under the control of the will of the believer.

THE COUNTERFEIT OF THE MAN HIMSELF

In counterfeiting the believer himself, the evil spirit gives him exaggerated views, almost visions, of his own personality; he is "wonderfully gifted," and is therefore "puffed up"; he is "miserably incapable," and so is in despair; he is "amazingly clever," and thus undertakes what he cannot do; he is "helpless," "hopeless," "too forward," or "too backward"--in brief, a countless number of pictures of himself, or others, are presented to the mind of the man when once the lying spirit has gained a footing in the imagination.

So subtle is the identity of the deceiving spirit with a believer's individuality, that others see, what may be described as a "spurious personality," sometimes the person appears to be "full of self" when the inner man is deeply selfless; "full of pride" when the inner man is sincerely humble. In fact, the whole outer appearance of the man in manner, voice, actions, words, is often quite contrary to his true character, and he wonders why "others misunderstand," misjudge and criticise. Some believers, on the other hand, are quite unconscious of the manifestation of this spurious self, and go on happily satisfied with what they themselves know of their own inner motives, and heart life; oblivious of the very contrary manifestation which others behold, and pity or condemn. The spurious personality caused by evil spirits in possession, can also be in a beautiful form, in order to attract or mislead others in various ways, all unwittingly to the person, or to the victim. This is sometimes described as "unaccountable infatuation," but if it was recognised as the work of evil spirits, refused and resisted, the "infatuation" would pass away. It is so wholly apart from the action of the will in the persons concerned, that the work of evil spirits is clearly to be recognised, especially when the supposed "infatuation" follows supernatural experiences; and possession, through the accepting of counterfeits, has resulted.

COUNTERFEIT SIN

Evil spirits can also counterfeit sin, by causing some apparent manifestation of the evil nature in the life, and matured believers should know whether such a manifestation really is sin from the old nature, or a manifestation from evil spirits. The purpose in the latter case is to get the believer to take what comes from them, as from himself, for whatever is accepted from evil spirits gives them entry and power. When a believer knows the Cross and his position of death to sin, and in will and practice rejects unflinchingly all known sin, and a "manifestation" of "sin" takes place, he should at once take a position of neutrality to it, until he knows the source, for if he calls it sin from himself when it is not, he believes a lie as much as in any other way; and if he "confesses" as a sin what did not come from himself, he brings the power of the enemy upon him, to drive him into the sin which he has "confessed" as his own. Many believers are thus held down by supposed "besetting sins" which they believe are theirs, and which no "confessing to God" removes, but from which they would find liberty if they attributed them to their right cause. There is no danger of "minimising sin" in the recognition of these facts, because in either case, the believer desires to be rid of the sin or sins, or he would not trouble about them.

COUNTERFEIT SELF-CONDEMNATION

Again the believer is so acutely conscious of a "self" which he hates and loathes, that he is never free from the dark shadow of self-condemnation, self- accusation or self-despair, which no appropriation of identification with Christ in death, destroys; or else there is a self-confidence which continually draws the man forward into situations from which he has to retire abashed and disappointed. A spurious personality encompasses the true inner man, which few are aware of as possible, but which is a sadly real thing among multitudes of the children of God.

On the part of the soul beset with these constant presentations to his mind of his own personality, he only thinks he has a "vivid imagination," or still more that some of these things are visions of God, and that he is favoured of God, especially where the vision is of "great plans for God," or wide visions of what God is going to do! Always with the believer as the Centre, and special instrument of this service!

Many of the "plans" for "movements" which have gone even as far as print, in connection with Revival, have been of such a character; plans given by "revelation," and which have resulted in gaining but the few caught by them, and no others. Of such a character has been the aftermath of Revival, where men have left their regular calling, and followed a will-of-the-wisp revelation of "launching out on God," world-wide plans conceived, and dissipated in a few months. Such deceived believers become ultra-devotional, with an excess of zeal that blinds them to all things but the supernatural realm, and robs them of power to wisely meet the claims of other aspects of life. All this comes from an evil spirit's access to the mind, and imagination, through the deception of counterfeiting the presence of God.

COUNTERFEITS OF SATAN HIMSELF

Counterfeits of Satan himself also suit his purpose at times, when he desires to terrorise a man from actions, or prayer, adverse to his interests. There are occasions when Satan appears to fight against himself, only to cover deep schemes for obtaining fuller possession of a victim, or some greater advantage which he knows how to secure. Fear of the devil may always be regarded as from the devil, to enable him to carry out his plans of hindering the work of God. Of such a character may be the fearsome shrinking from hearing about him and his works, and the passive deadness of the mind in regard to all Scriptural truth concerning the forces of evil. Also the fear caused by reference to his name, given in order to frighten away believers from knowing the facts about him; whilst others who desire the truth may be given exaggerated impressions of his presence, and of "conflict.....clouds," "blocks," darkness, etc., until they lose the clearness of the light of God.

Especially is the work of the deceiver manifested in his efforts to make the children of God believe in his non-existence, and in the suggestion that it is only necessary to hear or know about God, as a protection from any form of the enemy's power. On the other hand, a deceived believer may be more deeply deceived, by seeing nothing but Satan's counterfeits everywhere.

Supernatural visions and manifestations are a fruitful source of revenue to deceiving spirits, and they have gained a strong footing somewhere in mind or body when these are given; especially when the believer relies upon, and quotes more from these experiences than the Word of God; for the aim of the wicked spirit is to displace the Word of God as the rock-ground of the life. It is true the Scriptures may be referred to and quoted, but often only as a warrant for the experiences, and to strengthen faith--not in God, but in His (apparent) manifestations. This secret drawing of faith from the bare Word of God to manifestations of God, as being more reliable, is a keenly subtle deception of the evil one, and it is easily recognised in a believer thus deceived.

COUNTERFEIT VISIONS

When evil spirits are able to give visions, it is an evidence that they have already gained ground in the man, be he a Christian or an unbeliever. The "ground" being, not of necessity known sin, but a condition of passivity, i.e., non-action of the mind, imagination, and other faculties. This essential condition of passive non-action as the means of obtaining supernatural manifestations is well understood by spiritist mediums, clairvoyants, crystal gazers, and others, who know that the least action of the mind immediately breaks the clairvoyant state.

Believers not knowing these main principles can unwittingly fulfil the conditions for evil spirits to work in the life, and ignorantly induce the passive state by wrong conceptions of the true things of God. e.g., They may (1) in seasons of prayer, sink into a passive mental condition which they think is waiting on God; (2) deliberately will the cessation of their mind action, in order to obtain some supernatural manifestation which they believe to be of God; (3) in daily life practise a passive attitude which they think is submission to the will of God; (4) endeavour to bring about a state of personal negation, in which they have no desires, needs, wishes, hopes, plans, which they think is full surrender to God, and their "will" lost in God.

BELIEVERS CAN IGNORANTLY DEVELOP MEDIUMISTIC CONDITIONS

In brief, believers may unknowingly develop mediumistic conditions, of which deceiving spirits are not slow to take advantage. They are careful not to frighten the believer by doing anything which will open his eyes, but they keep within the range of what he will receive without question. They will personate the Lord Jesus in the special way which will appeal to the person, e.g., to some as "Bridegroom" to others as seated on a throne, and coming in great glory. They will also personate the dead to those who grieve after their loved ones, and as they have watched them during life, and know all about them, they will give ample "proofs" to confirm the deceived ones in their deception.

Visions may come from one of three sources. The Divine, from God; the human, such as hallucinations and illusions because of disease, and the Satanic, which are false. "Visions" given by evil spirits, also describe anything supernatural presented to and seen by the mind or imagination, from outside; such as terrible pictures of the "future"; flashing of texts as if they were lit up; "visions" of widespread "movements," all counterfeiting either the true vision of the Holy Spirit given to the "eye of the understanding," or the normal and healthy action of the imagination. The Church is thus often made a whirlpool of division through believers relying upon "texts" for guiding their decisions, instead of the principle of right and wrong set forth in God's word.

THE DETECTION OF VISIONS FROM GOD OR SATAN

Apart from the "visions" which are the result of disease, the detection of Divine from Satanic visions depends a great deal upon knowledge of the Word of God, and the fundamental principles of His working in His children. These may be briefly stated thus:--

(1) That no supernatural "vision" in any form, can be taken as of God, which requires a condition of mental non-action, or comes whilst the believer is in such a condition.

(2) That all the Holy Spirit's enlightening and illuminating vision is given when the mind is in full use, and every faculty awake to understand; i.e., the very opposite condition to that required by the working of evil spirits.

(3) That all which is of God, is in harmony with the laws of God's working as set forth in the Scriptures, e.g., "World-wide movements" by which multitudes are to be gathered in, are not in accord with the laws of the growth of the Church of Christ as shown in (1) the grain of wheat (John 12: 24.); (2) the law of the Cross of Christ (Isa. 53: 10); (3) the experience of Christ; (4) the experience of Paul (1 Cor. 4: 9-13); (5) the "little flock" of Luke 12: 32 ; (6) the foreshadowed end of the dispensation given in 1 Tim. 4: 1-3; 6: 20.

Many a believer has left his path of "grain of wheat multiplication," caught by a vision of "world-wide" sweeping in of souls, given by Satan, whose malignant hatred, and ceaseless antagonism is directed against the true seed of Jesus Christ , which in union with Him, will bruise the serpent's head. To delay the birth, (John 3: 3,5), and growth of the Holy Seed (Isa. 6: 10), is the devil's aim. To this end he will foster any widespread surface work of the believer, knowing it will not really touch his kingdom, nor hasten the full birth into the Throne-life of the conquering seed of Christ.

The safe path for believers at the close of the age is one of tenacious faith in the written Word as the sword of the Spirit, to cut the way through all the interferences and tactics of the forces of darkness, to the end.

COUNTERFEIT DREAMS

All dreams also, as well as visions, can be classed, as to their source, under three heads: (1) Divine, (2) human, or (3) Satanic, each to be known, first by the condition of the person, and second by the principles distinguishing the working of God or Satan.

If the person is under any degree of possession, no dreams at night can be said with certainty to be either from natural causes or "Divine communication," but are simply night presentations of the same character as "visions" to the mind during the day, and are the counterfeits by evil spirits of these two causes.

Passivity of brain is an essential condition for the presentation to the mind of things by evil spirits. At night the brain is passive, and whilst activity of the mind in the daytime hinders, they have their occasion at night when the passivity is more pronounced in sleep.

Believers who are fighting possession, and the regaining the use of their mental faculties in normal action, can "refuse" these night presentations by evil spirits as definitely as they refuse their workings during the day, and in due time find their complete cessation.

Dreams arising from the natural condition of the person, and attributable to purely physical causes, may be recognised as natural (1) when there is no "possession," and (2) when such physical causes really exist, and are not used as a cover, by deceiving spirits, to hide their workings.

Apart from the condition of the person, the principle distinguishing Divine from Satanic in relation to dreams, is in the first instance, by their import and exceptional value (Gen. 37: 5-7; Matt. 1: 20, 2: 12), and in the latter, their "mystery," absurdity, emptiness, folly, etc. as well as by their effects on the person. In the first, the recipient is left normal, calm, quiet, reasonable, and with an open, clear mind. In the second, elated, or dazed, confused, and unreasonable.

The presentations of evil spirits at night is frequently the cause of morning "dullness" of mind, and heaviness of spirit. The sleep has not been refreshing because of their power, through the passivity of the mind during sleep, to influence the whole being. "Natural" sleep renews, and invigorates the faculties, and the whole system. Insomnia is, in a great degree, the work of evil spirits, adapting their workings to the over-wrought condition of the person, so as to hide their attacks under cover.

Believers who are open to the supernatural world should

specially guard their nights by prayer, and by definite rejection of the first insidious workings of evil spirits along these lines.

How many say "The Lord woke me," and place their reliance upon "revelations" given in a state of half-consciousness, when mind and will are only partially alert to discern the issues of the "guidance" or "revelations" given to them. Let such believers watch the results of their obedience to night-revelations, and they will find many traces of the deceitful workings of the enemy. They will find, too, how their faith is often based upon a beautiful experience given in the early hours of the morning; or, vice versa, shaken by accusations, suggestions, attacks and conflict manifestly of the evil one, instead of an intelligent reliance upon God Himself in His changeless character of faithfulness and love to His own.

All workings of the enemy at night can be made to cease by their recognition as of him, and definitely refused in the Name of the Lord, revoking all ground unknowingly given for such workings, in the past.

CHAPTER 7
Ground and Symptoms of Possession

In the summary given, the various ways in which ground is given for the deception and possession of evil spirits are briefly summarised.

Communication is possible with the believer without ground being given, but evil spirits can never interfere with the faculties of brain or body, unless sufficient ground for possession has been obtained by them.

Satan had power to communicate with Christ in the wilderness, for the Devil spoke to Him, and Christ replied, yet the Lord Himself said later on (John 14: 30) that although the prince of this world came to Him; he could find nothing in Him for his working. The devil also communicated with Eve in a state of innocence.

It is therefore no proof of ground, or sin in mind or life, that Satan is able to communicate with believers. But there is a certain class of "communication" which cannot be carried on without ground having been given. There is a difference, also, between "communication" and "communion"--communication is with the mind, as evil spirits suggest thoughts to it, but they have "communion" with the man through the senses, as these respond to "feelings" given by them to the senses.

Delicious, lulling, exquisite sensations in the body, arising from spiritual causes, may always be attributed to deceiving spirits, for they feed the sensuous, and nothing that comes from God in purity does this; nor does He in any degree by His manifestations, minister to a self-indulgent, self-satisfied, sensuous condition of the mind, or body of His redeemed ones; but on the contrary, the operations of God in man, are directed to the elimination of all that feeds the senses, and the invigoration of spirit, soul and body, for the keenest activities of life. The satiety of the senses, however, caused by evil spirits, sooner or later changes in manifestation, and the true character of the source stands revealed when irritable and disagreeable feelings take the place of the soothing influences hitherto given, to the horror of the one who had revelled in the exquisite "waves" of peace, thought to have come from God, and who is now convinced that he has lost God's presence and power. Where the disagreeable takes place now, may have been the place where an agreeable manifestation occurred in the past.

COLUMN 1: GROUND TO EVIL SPIRITS IN THE MIND

In the list of various ways by which ground is given to evil spirits, the first is by means of suggestions or thoughts admitted to the mind. Thoughts manifestly from Satan every believer rejects at once, when he becomes conscious of them; but thousands of "thoughts" come without any volition of the person, for few understand control of the mind, and how to "bring every thought into captivity to the obedience of Christ" (2 Cor. 10: 5).

One of the symptoms of demon possession is absolute inability, even after volition, to change the course of thinking, or subject of thought, for the mind appears stiff and laborious in action. The man cannot let a specific thought go from his mind, even after he wills to. The chief faculty open to the access of deceiving spirits is the mind, especially before the believer apprehends the need of a "renewed mind" (Eph. 4: 23), and realises that his mind can be open to, and used by evil spirits, notwithstanding the Divine operation of God in the innermost shrine of his being.

Also before he realises what he has admitted as ground for evil spirits in his past life, for all the "thoughts" inserted by the god of this world blinding the mind (2 Cor. 4: 4; Ephes. 2: 2), form material for his later working; such as "thoughts" lodged there unconsciously, perhaps years before; mental conceptions admitted without examination; floating ideas which have drifted into the ground of the mind, the believer knows not whence; a sentence in a paper, a word dropped in his hearing; the flotsam and jetsam of the mental world, leaving unthought of effect upon him, colouring Scripture, and placing the mind almost at the mercy of any suggestion of evil spirits, under certain conditions, later on.

HOW TO DETECT EVIL SPIRITS' INTERFERENCE WITH THE MIND

To detect the working of evil spirits upon the mind, let the believer note the way in which his "thoughts" come. If the mind is working easily, quietly, in normal action in the duty of the moment, and sudden "flashes," "suggestions," or apparent "thoughts" arise, not in sequence, or in orderly connection with the work he has in hand, then the enemy may be counterfeiting the operation of the person's own mind, and trying to insert his suggestions into it as if they were the outcome of the man's own thinking; for when he is in the process of thinking, the lying spirits seek to inject some thought, suggestion or feeling-- the first into the mind, and the last into the spirit.

The danger at this point is for the believer to be ensnared by the simultaneous working of his own mind, and the presentation to the mind of the evil spirit's "pictures" or visions, which he thinks come from his own "imagination"; or very subtly refined suggestions which have no appearance of being supernatural, or even distinct from the person at all.

Many think all that is "supernatural" is of necessity strikingly marvellous, and awesome, whereas the enemy's working is very ordinary--so ordinary that he is unrecognised, and the operations of the supernatural appear so "natural," that they are not looked upon as supernatural.

The Scripture statement of "the whole world lying in the evil one" is so true, that his speakings and workings are accepted and followed and yielded to, as the "ordinary" things of life, and as the ordinary operations of the mental faculties. The kingdom of darkness is near and "natural" to all the world under the rule of the prince of darkness.

SYMPTOMS OF INTERFERENCE WITH THE MIND

It is best to be suspicious of the abnormal in every shape and form. God does not interfere with the natural operations of the faculties. A sudden stoppage of thought, or sequence in the action of the mind, in thought or memory, as well as acute loss of the use of either, may indicate the interference of evil spirits.

The spirits of evil, in possession of some faculty of the mind, can either hold it, or suddenly release it for action--this holding or releasing power explaining much that is unaccountable in suddenness of action, or "change of mind" which, like much else, is left in obscurity as "unexplainable." "I can" one moment, then "I cannot" the next, generally being put down to an "erratic temperament," or other causes. The believer, however, may be unable to act, because of the interruption, or interference of the enemy, but he really has the ability for action, if the faculties were free.

Others whose lives are spent in the bondage of a "spirit of infirmity," are only conscious of a sense of inability, they are always "too tired," and have "no spirit," "no energy" for the ordinary demands of life, yet with no disease, or reasonable physical ground for their chronic inertness and feebleness.

A sudden inability to listen, described as "absent-mindedness" or "preoccupation," when the person is compelled to follow some "thought" suggested, or picture presented to the mind, or to follow the words of another, are all indications of the interference of evil spirits--the compulsions especially being a mark of their workings-- when the person is in a normal condition of health, and the brain is not diseased. For instance, in spiritual meetings, when people seem hardly able to listen to a vital truth, how many recognise the work of the prince of the power of the air taking away the Word (Matt. 13: 19), by the suggestion of other things, not appropriate to the moment, and by the mind being unable to follow the speaker's words, and to grasp and apprehend?

Streams of "texts," also, pouring through the mind, apart from concentration, and the volitional action of the mind, may overpower all that the speaker is saying, and "Carry away" the hearer into far away thoughts, and "daydreams," which appear so beautiful and "divine," yet after the "meeting" is over, have no solid result in practical life. Any admittance of these sudden suggestions, or passing thoughts, means ground given to the enemy.

TWO WAYS THAT THE ENEMY PUTS THOUGHTS INTO THE MIND

The Deceiver has two ways of putting thoughts into the mind: (1) By direct communication to the mind, and (2) indirect, by attacks on the spirit, causing undesirable feelings there, such as impatience through the attacks, which produce impatient thoughts in the mind, followed by impatient words.

The believer has a sense of being hindered persistently by some unseen obstacle, for the evil spirit beings suggest a certain action to him, and then when he attempts it, he is hindered, causing in him a sense of irritation for which he cannot account. Nothing he does seems to "go right," and his life seems made up of "pin-prick" troubles, too much for him to bear, causing a sense of moroseness and discontent which grows upon him in spite of himself. Feverish activity which accomplishes nothing is manifested occasionally, or else perpetual occupation which gives no moment of rest; difficulty with work in the day time; "dreams" at night, with no sense of rest or leisure at any time; suffering, confusion, difficulty of action, embarrassment, perplexity, all emanating directly, maliciously, and deliberately from evil spirits, unrecognised by the man.

Believers whose circumstances, and environment, should give them every cause for a glad and quiet mind, are harassed with terrible anxiety, and they are rarely free from troubled thoughts. The mind over-estimates everything, because the imagination and mental faculties are in bondage; anthills appear as mountains to them. Everything is exaggerated, so that they shrink from seeing others, as conversation is terribly difficult. They imagine they are only "thinking" in an ordinary sense, but it is not I "thinking" when a thing grips the mind, but when the mind grips the thing. Their "thinking" goes beyond the line of pure mental action.

CAUSES OF DEPRESSION APART FROM THE PHYSICAL CONDITION

Herein lies the real cause of depression as experienced by many believers, apart from purely physical conditions. The victim of depression and melancholia has admitted thoughts suggested by the deceiving spirits, until the mind is unable to shake them off, or else the enemy has obtained such a footing, that he holds the mental faculties in a grip of passivity, so that they cannot act. He feels as though they were in a vice, or weighted with some heavy pressure which obscures all light, and prevents him grasping the facts around him, or using his reason at all.

The malignant powers of darkness ofttimes succeed in keeping those who have given them opportunity to get them into their grip under the most harassing clouds and shadows. They rejoice over their own wicked deeds, and love to bind their victims, and keep them in bondage. This is truly the "oppression" of the enemy (Ps. 42: 9), and is the outcome of the earlier stages of the attacks of deceiving spirits upon the mind, which could have been quenched had they been dealt with at the beginning.

That the enemy takes advantage of any mental feebleness, or overstrain, or disease, is, of course, to be recognised; but in persons of normal health, with no disease of the mind, inherited or induced, much of the "depression" may be attributed to the inroads of the enemy, through ground given unconsciously at some previous time. The cause of "brain-fag" too, needs to be examined in this light, lest many attribute to natural causes what may have been supernaturally brought about.

COLUMN 2: GROUND TO EVIL SPIRITS THROUGH MISCONCEPTIONS

Wrong conceptions of spiritual things give ground to evil spirits, and these conceptions the adversary skilfully cultivates ready for use on later occasions.

Imaginations as to how God works in Revival power, and in "Pentecostal" measure, is specially a fruitful ground for evil spirits, i.e., a conception that God moves a meeting, and sways it as the wind sways the corn; and that God moves on the physical man, rather than from the centre of man's spirit only.

These imaginations prepare the believer for Satan's deceptions in these very forms. This entry of "thoughts" from any quarter comes from the deeper cause of a passivity of the mind which, as we have pointed out in Chapter 4, is the main object of the adversary to produce, ere he can succeed in his effort to obtain control of the believer's will.

The Lord's words in Matthew 13: 23, that the good ground hearer is "he that heareth the word and understandeth it," show that the mind is the vehicle through which the truth of God reaches men to win their affections, and bring back the will into intelligent and loyal co-operation with God.

In like manner the mind is the hindrance to Satan's carrying out his schemes to win back control of the believer.

For the success of his plans, the enemy knows that the mind must be lulled into inaction and disuse by some means or other, either by stratagem or attack. The arch-deceiver is well aware that any "teaching" of deceiving spirits accompanied by supernatural signs, may be received by the believer if his mind is lulled into passivity so that he does not question, or intelligently reason, what the teachings are, or what they involve in their ultimate issue.

PASSIVITY OF THE BODY AS RESULT OF PASSIVITY OF THE MIND

Passivity of body is the next stage in the development of passivity of the whole being, and is the ultimate consequence of passivity of the mind, for the mind dulled by passivity takes away alert action from the physical frame. The "dreamy," passive mind is seen in a dreamy walk and a lethargy of action in every department of the human frame. All this is deepening ground for deceiving spirits. The faculties are unused, there is lack of mental control, a lack of reasoning power, a ceasing to use the judgment, followed eventually by a disinclination to use the will.

The believer slowly loses power of decision, he becomes more and more tossed about by letting everything in his environment decide for him, and sometimes thinking and believing it is God choosing and deciding for him by "Providences"; he therefore does not choose or decide for himself, but passively drifts, and accepts the choice or decision made for him by "circumstances"; or else he is full of impulses, with no central poise of any kind. But God does not choose instead of the man, otherwise he would become a machine; neither does he decide in his stead. He chooses an eternal inheritance for him, but even this choice of God for the man cannot be fulfilled apart from the believer's intelligent co-operation.

PASSIVE YIELDING TO ENVIRONMENT

Therefore the passive yielding to environment and what the man sometimes calls "Providence," really means letting evil spirits decide for him, for they are the world rulers of this darkness, and readily seize the opportunity of playing upon his passive will, and thus he is deceived by them and thinks that he is yielding to the will of God.

In this way good men have become victims of others' sin, fearing to "resist evil" lest they disobey the commands of God, not intelligently understanding that they therefore fail to co-operate with God in fighting against sin (Heb. 12: 4; 1 Tim. 5: 20), and conquering the spirit of the age in their environment.

God has given man a will, and a deciding voice; and all the purpose of His working in man, is to restore that once enslaved will to its throne of intelligent volition, in the choosing of right instead of wrong, and God instead of Satan. But Satan's entire purpose is to drag back the will into captivity-- and thus the man himself--so that he becomes a passive, though unconscious slave to the world-rulers of the darkness around him, and hence subject to Satan, the god of this world, ruling through his hierarchy of evil powers.

The actions of the believer thus re-captured by Satan, through his emissaries of evil spirits, are the outcome of the subtle and unknown control of the adversary and the actions again give more ground to the enemy. Words are spoken, and deeds are done, almost blindly, either by impulse, or in the confusion of sudden revulsion of feeling; and often without the man intelligently apprehending the consequences of words or deeds. Old habits which ceased to be manifested, show themselves again, and sins which were once conquered, re-assert their power.

COLUMN 3: WHERE THE EVIL SPIRITS ENTER

Where evil spirits enter is the subject of the third column, and the list is very brief, since the widest ramifications of their workings in man can be covered by the words spirit, soul and body, for they bury themselves in the very structure of the human frame, some acting directly upon the organs or appetites of the body, others upon the mind or intellect, sensibilities, emotions and affections, and others more immediately upon the spirit. In the body they specially locate themselves in the spinal column, nervous system, and deepest nerve centres, through which they control the whole being; from the ganglionic nerve centre located in the bowels, the emotional sensibilities, and all organs affected by them, to the cerebral nerve centre in the head, the eyes, ears, neck, jaws, tongue, muscles of the face, and delicate nerve tissues of the brain.

They may obtain access gradually and insidiously, as already shown, but there are instances where they make a sudden assault, so as to rush the victim into involuntary surrender.

COLUMN 4: SYMPTOMS OF THE PRESENCE OF EVIL SPIRITS

When evil spirits have gained entry to the believer through the ground given to them, as already described, the symptoms of their presence are recognisable according to the degree of the possession and the place wherein they are located, whether deep in the innermost structure of the person, or in the mind and faculties which are more visibly affected by them.

Many of the symptoms have already been touched upon in previous chapters, especially in "Passivity as the chief basis of Possession" (4), and "Counterfeits of the Divine" (6) in spiritual experiences, and need not be recapitulated.

Here we need but sum up some of the characteristics of acute and fully developed possession in mind and body, when the passive surrender to deceiving spirits is very complete, and the whole of the outer man is open to their use in every part of his being. It must, however, be clearly understood, that (1) all the symptoms may be present in a very slight degree, so as to be almost indistinguishable from entirely natural causes; (2) they may be only manifested in the part of the human frame wherein the intruders are located; or (3) they may come into existence, and pass away through various causes, WITHOUT THE KNOWLEDGE of the victim.

CHARACTERISTICS OF ACUTE "POSSESSION" OF MIND AND BODY

When the possession is very pronounced, these intruders entirely dominate the outer man, using, or interfering with the vocal organs, the tongue, jaws, eyes, ears, smell, taste, muscles, the hands and feet, sometimes with uncontrollable and unconscious movements. They interfere with the head, and move it at their will, and with the five senses of the body, because they are the avenues of knowledge to the mind. They seek to dull and check the acute use of the senses, so that they may have more opportunity to control their victim, and when they do this, there is more or less difficulty in all the operations of the senses and faculties.

VOCAL ORGANS INTERFERED WITH

When evil spirits affect the vocal organs, they may interfere with all the vocal operations in audible reading, speaking, singing, or praying. In speaking, the enunciation may be heavy or blurred, slow or quick; the words may appear to run one into another, the pronunciation variable, and the accents, or emphasis, wrong, for emphasis in speech which is not the result of the mind controlling any emphasis, may be the effect of possession.

The supernatural power affecting the passive mind mixes up, so to speak, the words in the mind, and then in the speech; prevents the mind grasping thoughts, and causes the memory to fail in action. Words come to the mind, and do not remain long enough for speech; or, on the other hand, torrents of "thoughts" come, which "rush" the vocal organs into action beyond control. It is then easier to speak than to listen to another speaking. The tongue acts independently of the mind or will. Words are spoken unthought of by the mind, or intended by the will; sometimes the exact opposite to what was in the mind and intention, which astonish the speaker when he is afterwards reminded of what he has said.

GARRULITY OF CHRISTIANS

Much that has been called "garrulity," "talkativeness," and irresponsible use of the tongue among Christians, may be attributed to the cause here named; for many whose tongues are uncontrollable in gossip, slander and backbiting, are sincerely unconscious of what they do, or if they are conscious, are quite unable to control or check their grievous, irresponsible talking. Evil spirits may "possess" them only in the organs of speech, or practically have control of the tongue through the CHANNEL OF A PASSIVE MIND.

This may be the case in platform speakers, who have a voluminous flow of words which pour through the lips, or else a rapid rushing speech, or in staccato form, without any concentration or true action of the mind. Pulpit preaching is even possible in this way, evil spirits being unaffected by "preaching" which does not proclaim the atoning sacrifice of Christ, and is not in the power of the Holy Ghost.

VOICE AFFECTED BY EVIL SPIRITS

The voice of a man is more easily affected by supernatural power than many have thought. When evil spirits touch the man's spirit, it may be sometimes recognised by a harsh, metallic sound in the voice, or a hoarse and rough thickness; or these same effects may be noticed in an atmosphere which is very thickly charged by the powers of darkness; showing their effect upon the delicate vocal chords.

In the interference with, or use of the vocal organs and voice, may be placed the counterfeit "gift of tongues," or the exquisite singing which has been termed the "heavenly music," because of its manifest supernatural source, and its being beyond the singer's own natural power.

In pronounced demon possession, evil spirits may affect the voice in an apparently natural way, which is put down to natural causes. For instance, in singing, the man may be doing so with power, and with clear, and bell-like enunciation, but soon there comes weakness in the muscles of the throat, a dry cough, and tears in the eyes, and the singing ceases. The concentration of the eyes upon the music book grows weaker, a sense of heaviness comes on neck and spine; the playing goes on, but heedless, spiritless, dejected and heavy, the singer turns away, putting it all down to "difficulty of breathing," and physical impediment, when it has been entirely a manifestation of the evil spirits in possession.

INTERFERENCE WITH THE HEAD

In interference with the head, the jaws can be moved by the spirits of evil, and the nerves of the face manipulated in the production of smiles, which appear at unsuitable moments, manifestly apart from the cognisance of the person. Of such a nature is the mechanical smile, when the facial muscles seem made of elastic, or a stiffening of countenance which makes the face appear hard or cruel, dried up and withered, or painfully miserable.

Demon possession does affect the face, and cause expressions upon it which may be opposed to the true character of the person. Other effects upon the face produced by the controlling spirits may be repellent or beautiful, and appear natural and physical; such as a blushing red, impure look, or an angelic look of heavenly beauty, with exquisite smiles, and light as of glory, which may suddenly change into a stern unbending look, with lips set and brow furrowed, or into a dark cloud as of sudden storm and tempest.

In the drainage of vitality, caused by the grip of the spirits of evil, the temples may be sunken, and the hair become prematurely gray. In a sudden manifestation of the intruders, the nostrils may become tightened, the scent deadened, and the breathing gasping and short, with choking, suffocating feelings, and noises in the head.

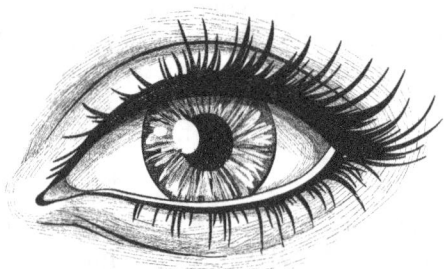

INTERFERENCE WITH THE EYES

No part of the nerves in the head are more affected than those of the eyes, for there can come about a passivity of the eyes, which permits them to be moved by evil spirits, and forced to see visible objects apart from the use of the volition. In reading, the eyes can be moved to see the printed words, and rapidly skim the pages of matter, without any of it entering the mind, and making any impression upon the memory. It is important, in connection with the use of the eyes, to notice whether mental action always governs their movements, or whether they look at objects independently of the intelligent volition; for evil spirit interference is most marked when the eyes roam about whilst the man is speaking to another person, or gaze upward or downward, or in any direction without any cause, ofttimes in a most unseemly or discourteous manner.

Particularly is the use of the eyes by evil spirits manifested in a set or fixed gaze upon various things, or upon the faces of others, the latter is especially dangerous, when the person is compelled by this fixity of gaze to take, unknowingly, a mediumistic attitude to another. Any persistent drawing of the eyes to another's face should be instantly resisted.

Especially in meetings where supernatural powers are manifestly present, a "fixed gaze" in listening to a speaker should be avoided, if it has the effect of causing non-action of the mind and a dazed condition, as it opens the listener to the workings of evil spirits through his passivity. In the same way, speakers in such gatherings should take care lest the spirits of evil find opportunity to use their eyes in fixity of concentration upon the people, to sway them by power and thus hinder the intelligent opening of their minds to the words that are being spoken.

IN ACUTE POSSESSION INTERFERENCE WITH THE EYES IS VERY MARKED

In acute demon possession, the eyes are affected very markedly. They are forced to see evil things, and bad things, so much so that they affect the person, and make him fidgety and complaining; the eyes cannot look straight in another's face, nor, indeed, look at anything without an "attack" of some kind, produced by the spirits of evil. These attacks may cause the person to look guilty in the eyes of others, when there is no ground for doing so.

There are two kinds of concentration: (1) Physical, through the eyes, and (2) mental, by the mental vision. The man himself is only acting in any action of the body, when concentration of mind and will is at the back of his every action. Visions may be physical, mental or spiritual. In the physical vision the eyes are needed; in the mental, the eyes of the mind; and in the spiritual the inward vision of the spiritual man.

When evil spirits control the physical eyes, visions of supernatural, and natural beings, and things, appear before them, and in ordinary matters of life things appear different from what they really are. The man receives impressions of things contrary to reality, such as the panel of a door appearing like a cross, lights in the sky in various figures, etc. The man declares he "sees" these things, but he does not know that evil spirits can present them to his vision.

The eyesight of necessity is affected by this manipulation of the eyes, and there are general feelings of weakness. Things look misty and blurred, and undefined. There may be short-sightedness, and inability to concentrate on any small object; concentration of the eyes is painful and difficult, the man complains of the light, tiredness of the eyes, and dark spots appear before them, either stable or moving, near or far; symptoms which might be looked upon as purely physical if it were not for the supernatural element accompanying them.

THE EARS AND HEARING AFFECTED

In interference with the ears, entire deafness may be caused by an evil spirit locating in the nerves of the ear, or there may be degrees of interference with the hearing, such as the loss of words, so that in listening there are moments when sentences, or words, are not heard at all; or there is a failure to grasp clearly what others say because the person hears partly what the speaker says, and partly what the evil spirit inserts, or suggests to the mind, hence "misunderstandings" of given instructions, or the clearly expressed language of others. This also causes an indisposition to listen to others speaking, and a restless impatience which cannot wait for them to complete their sentences, or communications, because the intruders are thrusting in their own suggestions to the mind, and claiming attention to their speaking. The believer has a sense of double listening, so to speak, which is an interior and exterior listening at one and the same time. That is, he may be trying to "listen" to feelings and movements within whilst listening to the voices of others outside. This causes difficulty in listening to music, speaking, and reading aloud. There is also a deadness to exterior sounds, because of a buzzing in the ears, and the sound in the ears is stronger than the sound outside, with the effect of an apparent absent-mindedness. The man needs to be released from listening to the supernatural speaking within himself, before he is free to listen to that which is external.

Evil spirits interfering with the sensory nerves of the ears, render exterior sounds acute in forced consciousness of them, producing confusion and irritation; the exaggerated sense of sound rendering concentration difficult. They also make strange sounds by interference with the sensory nerves, the man declaring that he heard voices, thunder, rustling as of a dress, etc., which no one around him hears.

THE "BUZZ" OF EVIL SPIRITS SPEAKING

This persistent "buzz" in the ears, makes the victim preoccupied, and almost unconsciously shake his head, as if shaking off something which is annoying him. It is so distracting that he is obliged to speak aloud to himself to make an impression on his own mind: he must read aloud in order to take in the sense of what he may be reading, or speak aloud to apprehend his own speech, because of the confusion caused in his mind by the inward "buzz" of the persecuting spirits. Because of this confusion, also, fresh ground is given to the powers of darkness, for deeper possession through the distraction caused by their interference.

The cause of this is, that, unknowingly, the believer has lent his ears to evil spirits, listening to their words and suggestions, often because he believed he was listening to God, or listening to himself. This comes particularly when there has grown a habit of listening for an inner voice; or an alert inside "listening" which in time enables the evil spirit to dull the outer ear, and acute attention to outer communications; or a "listening" inwardly to "feelings," sensations, movements,"drawings," whilst at the same time listening for voices, texts, and messages from without.

DESCRIPTION OF THE SPEAKING OF EVIL SPIRITS

The speaking of evil spirits may be described somewhat as follows:

(1) It is not like the vocal speaking of a human being, which must always be stronger than the speaking of spirits, because spirits have no force of breath; therefore if a man speaks aloud, he can always drown the speaking of evil spirits. On the same principle a man can also drown the voice of the Holy Spirit, because He is Spirit and His speaking is always in the spirit, or through conscience.

(2) It resembles more the "thinking" of a person, or the speaking in oneself, when the words are not uttered through the lips. When evil spirits are speaking to the inner ear, it seems like a ceaseless buzz of inner words, apparently belonging to the person himself yet not from his mind, nor the result of mental action, nor from his will, nor even expressing his own personal ideas or desires.

When this "buzz" of objectionable, or annoying, or irresponsible words are thus, in an indefinite way, claiming the inner attention of the man, and he has outer claims to deal with, he is liable to speak aloud with a strong voice, so as to overpower or dull the inner clamour, without being conscious that he is raising his voice, or why he is doing so.

UNCONSCIOUS USE OF LOUD VOICE

Unknowingly the man is making an impression on his own mind, through his own ear, by using a loud voice; otherwise his dulled mind would not be able to take in, or retain what he is saying; or get the impression into his mind.

The believer may not be conscious of the inner "buzz" of the evil spirits' words, and not conscious that his voice is raised to express his own thoughts in audible speech, or know why he finds himself obliged to speak to get clear in his own thinking. Unconsciousness is a symptom of the depth of the evil spirit's possession, and unconsciousness of facts concerning himself, is as detrimental to the person, as attempts of strangers to enter a house would be to a householder who is oblivious to all sounds.

Consciousness of all things connected with the inner life and environment is as keenly needed by the believer, and should be cultivated by him, as consciousness of all exterior matters connected with the duties of life. Unconsciousness by men of how they themselves act and speak, think or appear, in oblivion to all that is patent to others, or, on the other hand, an "unconscious" self-consciousness, or ultra- consciousness of the actions of self, may all be results of the work of deceiving spirits.

Some symptoms of thus having listened to supernatural voices,

may be described as:
  (1) *Difficulty in listening to others;*
  (2) *Face "screwed up" in difficulty, of grasping what is said;*
  (3) *A sense of dullness or heaviness in the ear or ears.*

The distinction between deafness through the interference of evil spirits with the ears, and what is the result of physical causes, depends upon whether the person has other symptoms of evil spirit possession, or whether he is in a normally "natural" condition.

VARIED SYMPTOMS

There are other varied symptoms showing disturbance of the entire system of the man when dominated by evil spirits in possession. In affecting the muscles, hands and fingers or feet, the nerves are held, and these act without control of the mind or will, sometimes in convulsive action, or in twitches, and prostration, or else in the paradox of being muscularly weak and strong consecutively, and in rapid succession. There are many accidents through possession, which are called "the visitation of God," "slips of the hand," unaccountable "failures of the mind," which are left unexplained, but these "happenings" are not really "accidents"-- they are the carrying out of the real designs of unseen spirit beings malignantly concerned in the world of men.

The insidious spirits have prepared for this manipulation, or interference with the person by their slow dulling of the mind; the weakening of the reasoning powers, which prevents him seeing the outcome of a certain step or action; the disuse of the judgment; the imperceptible loss of decision, and independent action of the will, so that it "snaps," so to speak, at a critical moment, with fatal results; for without this passivity of mind and will, the emissaries of Satan cannot have the full control of the body which they so keenly desire.

In affecting the body, the spirits of evil also interfere with all the functions at various times, and in various degrees, such as in eating and drinking, and the swallowing of food. The mastication of food, the saliva, the phlegm, the breath and breathing, physical weakness or strength, stiffness of limbs, heaviness, heat and cold, agreeable or disagreeable feelings, sleeplessness, dreams, restlessness at night, all can be irritated, produced or exaggerated by the presence and will of evil spirits.

MANIPULATION OF THE BODY

How evil spirits can manipulate the body through the nervous system, we find clearly defined in the Scriptures; but we never find a single instance of the Holy Spirit working in the same way. Not once in the Acts of the Apostles do we find "twitchings," "writhing," convulsions, or other effects of supernatural power on the human frame, recorded as results of being filled with the Holy Spirit. But we do read that evil spirits can convulse the body, tear it, bruise it (Luke 9: 39), cause it to pine away (Mark 9: 18), or give it strength (Mark 5: 4); they can make the man cry out suddenly with a loud cry (Luke 9: 39), or make him dumb, gnash his teeth, roll on the ground, cast him into the fire to burn him, or water to drown him (Matt. 17: 15).

In this acute form the symptoms of demon possession and insanity are almost indistinguishable. The difference lies in the fact that in pure demon possession the mind is not impaired, although it may be passive, or suspended in action, but in insanity the evil spirit takes advantage of a physical condition, "Insane" people are more "sane" than sane people think they are, and there is more truth in what they say than is believed. What they "see" is not always delusion, but the actual doings of evil spirits.

It is necessary, therefore, to distinguish between
1. Pure insanity,
2. Pure "possession,"
3. Insanity and possession.

Before declaring a person insane, from physical and natural causes, the physician should find out if there be any supernatural cause. Insanity may be caused by natural derangement, and by supernatural interferences of evil powers. True insanity can also be the result of possession, and be (humanly) irrecoverable.

In short, under the power of a lying spirit, the man loses control of his body, and is, for the time being, when the intruder manifests himself, irresponsible for his actions.

The spirits in possession of the body vary in character, and in manifestation, as much as when in possession of the mind, or spirit, in spiritual manifestations. Some are malignant, and some are milder in their actions, such as the "spirit of infirmity" or powerlessness described in Luke 13: 11, or the blind and dumb spirit in Matt. 12: 22. These Scriptures show there were cases of possession which looked like cases for healing, but the Lord's words and action proved that the woman who was bent for eighteen years, did not require healing, but deliverance. The bending of the back is one of the symptoms of demon possession, when the body is deeply affected.

PROPHETIC ECSTASY AND INSPIRATION

Another manifestation of evil spirits may be described as prophetic ecstasy, or "inspiration." Such was manifested in the girl with a "spirit of divination," which Paul cast out (Acts 16: 16-18). The danger of this kind of spirit is that the manifestations are more like those of the Holy Spirit, than when in the nervous system, or bodily frame. To distinguish between the two in the Corinthian Church was the object of the Apostle writing the 12th and 14th chapters of the first Corinthians: "Concerning the 'inspired'. . . I would not have you ignorant," he wrote, as he proceeded to show them how to detect the difference between the manifestations of deceiving spirits in demoniacal 'inspiration' or ecstasy, and the true inspiration of the Holy Spirit. The Spirit of God in one believer being in harmony with the manifestation of His power in others, and the demoniacal spirit producing "schism" or "mutiny" of the members of Christ's Body one against the other. The Holy Spirit causing interdependence, and honour of His workings in the one and in the other; the demoniacal spirit causing lawlessness, and confusion. "Harmony" and "confusion" being respectively the hallmark of the supernatural power being from God or Satan in the assembly of God's people.

COLUMN 5: EXCUSES USED BY EVIL SPIRITS TO HIDE THEIR PRESENCE

The excuses of the evil spirit to cover the ground held opens again a wide field of consideration. Once the ground is taken, and the mind is dulled from its power of critical discrimination, the lying spirit is apt in suggesting "excuses" to the believer to cover his location, and the ground he holds. The list of varied explanations is given in Column 4. If the mind labours in action, "it is natural" or "it is heredity," he suggests. Where the whole nervous system is involved, "it is disease" or "it is purely physical." "It is fatigue," or it is "spiritual." There may be, and there generally is, some basis for the "excuse," for the deceivers are keenly clever in working alongside natural conditions, either in circumstances, temperament or disturbance of the bodily functions, i.e., the attack may be in the natural and physical realm, but not from it as the source. They like to have, and watch for, some physical or mental ailment to serve as the cover, or "excuse" for their manifestation.

They attack a person because they are in possession, but make him think and believe it to be an indirect attack, i.e., through another person. The blame is placed on the man himself or someone else, or on anything but the true cause, so that the intruder may not be discovered and expelled. It is therefore important that all "excuses" should be examined, i.e., the "reasons" for such and such an unexplainable manifestation. The causes should always be gone into, for by believing a wrong interpretation of the manifestation, more ground is given to the lying spirits. The believer may be refusing ground on the one band, and giving new ground on the other, unless he examines all the suggestions which come to his mind concerning his condition.

The following tables show the stages of the advance in possession, and how wrong interpretation gives new ground:

1) Ground followed by
2) Possession, manifested by
3) For example "twitching of nerves" that the evil spirits give
4) Wrong interpret ion of the cause of the twitching, which if accepted by the believers admits new lies from them and gives more ground

Four sequences should be noted in this connection:

1) Ground because of a) ignorance resulting in b) deception
2) Followed by possession because of ground
3) Manifestation because of possession
4) Danger of wrong interpretation of manifestation

Deceiving spirits also persistently endeavour to keep the believer occupied with something else to fill up the mind, so that he may not discover his own need of deliverance. Workers are almost obsessed with the thought of "Revival," or the "need of others," whilst blind to their own condition. Devotion, singing, preaching, worship--all rightful things--may so possess the mind as to close it to all personal knowledge of the need of deliverance from the adversary's deception.

The effect on the believer of evil spirit possession, we have already dealt with, in the aspect of mental and bodily inertness. To this we add, general weakness of the whole man, spiritual, mental and physical. He becomes erratic in temperament, spasmodic in study, wavering in allegiance, and undecided in action; easily moved by (1) impulses, i.e., a sharp movement forward without volition; or (2) repulsion without reason, i.e., a sharp movement backward apart from volition.

THE LIFE FULL OF CONTRADICTION

The life becomes increasingly full of contradictions. The man seems strong and yet is weak, he is stoical and yet seeks love; he is spasmodic in his actions, erratic and dogmatic in his beliefs, and utterly illogical in his reasonings. All these symptoms may be visible or invisible, and manifested at different intervals, and in different degrees, concurrently or consecutively.

After a time the believer may become conscious of his condition, and then he has a painful shrinking lest these symptoms should be read by others, and thus cause attacks upon him. When they do become too manifest to be hidden or ignored, then he is often said to be suffering from a "nerve breakdown," for the symptoms coincide with all the characteristics of neurasthenia, and can only be distinguished from it by an examination into past spiritual experiences, and the discovery of the working of supernatural powers.

Should the apparent "neurasthenia" be really the possession of evil spirits, no prolonged rest or natural means will set the person free, although such means may give the body a renewing which will enable the victim to face the spiritual truth in due time.

This growing weakness of the circumference also weakens the spiritual life, by preventing its growth into vigorous manhood in Christ; for the inner spiritual man needs the outer man for expression, and development. But in possession through deception the mind is too passive to act, and express the inner life--the expression of the face is passive and dull, the eyes are dreamy and slow. In brief, the outer man becomes a "prison," so to speak, of the spirit life at the centre within.

Another very manifest effect is that as time goes on, the man lives more in the body than in the soul and spirit, the lawful appetites reassert control and the spirit-life is more unrecognised and less followed, whilst variations and inconsistencies in life, in state, in actions, all show increasingly the marks of "possession."

THE GENERAL EFFECT ON THE MAN OF SUPERNATURAL EXPERIENCES

A very little consideration of the characteristics of those drawn into abnormal supernatural experiences, will bear out this diagnosis. The invariable effect upon such believers is the weakening of the mental force, the reasoning and judging power; a weakening in moral force and will and ofttimes; a haunting sense of fear--fear of the future, fear of persons so that they cannot bear to hear them spoken of, or to speak to them; and a gradual general weakening of the physical frame. In time there comes an involuntary effect upon the nervous system, and there is impatience--manifestly "nervous" and not moral--and restlessness, and often an involuntary twitching action of the nerves.

In the moral realm comes an attitude of infallibility, positive assertion and unteachableness, with loss of the real power of choice, and personal control of mind, speech, manner, and actions--for persons thus "possessed" cannot choose or act, because they shall not; and they have acutely a sense that they "don't know what to do," on account of the evil spirit's hold of them.

COLUMN 6: EFFECTS OF POSSESSION ON THE BELIEVER

The effect of evil spirit possession as listed in Column 6 has already been more or less indicated in the preceding columns, and it is only necessary to compare Column 4 and 6 for their further summing up.

The subtilty of the deception has been that in multitudes of cases, all these "symptoms" are thought to be physically or morally the outcome of the individual personality, i.e., the "temperament" of the person, which must be borne with until released from the body of clay in the grave! "Self," they declare, is their trouble, which no acceptance of the Fulness of the Spirit, nor light upon identification with Christ, has altered. Wandering of mind in prayer, restlessness, talkativeness, or extreme reserve; and many other hindering troubles in the outer man remain, and are tolerated, or grieved over, without hope of change.

But how different the outlook, when much that troubles them is attributed to the true cause. "An enemy hath done this!" In many it is not "self" after all, but ground unwittingly given to deceiving spirits, who could be dislodged by the knowledge of the truth, and by refusal of ground.

CHAPTER 8
The Path to Freedom

It has been thought almost universally that the only way to deal with demon-possession is by the casting out of the evil spirit, by some Divinely equipped believer. But facts prove that this method is not always successful, for though the diagnosis of the intruder's presence may be correct, yet the ground that gave it occupation cannot be cast out; and unless the ground is dealt with, no full relief can be obtained, or change seen, in the majority of cases.

In others, when the evil spirit apparently departs, it must not be concluded that the person is entirely free, for it may be that what has occurred is only that a particular manifestation has ceased, and it is not unlikely that another manifestation may appear; possibly not a visible one, or one easily perceived or detected, but recognisable by any who have learned to discriminate between the workings of evil spirits, and those which are human or Divine.

It is possible also to suppress a certain manifestation for a time, and not entirely get rid of it; and the same manifestation may return again and again in different guise, unless the ground is dealt with.

In some instances, where the possession is so manifest that the true inner personality of the victim is almost entirely lost sight of, the relief may be immediate: but where the intruder hides himself so subtly in the mind, or body, as to be indistinguishable from the operations, or actions of the person--hidden in some state, or form, apparently natural or physical--the deliverance will not be obtained by "casting out" only, but by the truth being given to the mind, and the volition of the person actively refusing and disowning the ground.

The very first step to freedom is the knowledge of the truth as to the source and nature of experiences the believer may have had since his entrance into the spiritual life, which possibly may have been perplexing, or else thought with deepest assurance to be of God. There is NO DELIVERANCE FROM "DECEPTION" BUT BY THE ACKNOWLEDGMENT AND ACCEPTANCE OF TRUTH. And this facing of truth in regard to certain spiritual and "supernatural" experiences, means a keen edged knife to the man in his self-respect, and pride.

THE HUMILIATION OF THE UNDECEIVING PERIOD

It requires a very deep allegiance to the truth which God desires should reign in the inward parts of His children, for a believer to accept truth which cuts and humbles, as readily as he accepts that which is agreeable. The "undeceiving" is painful to the feelings, and the discovery that he has been deceived is one of the keenest blows to a man who once thought that he was so "advanced," so "spiritual," and so "infallible," in his certainty of obeying the Spirit of God.

"Was he not advanced?" Yes, to a degree above the "man of soul," but he had not reached the goal as he thought, for he had but begun the journey in the spiritual plane. The end of standard one is but the beginning of standard two. So after all, he believed a lie about himself and his experience.

He was not as "advanced" as he thought. Thus the truth breaks upon his mind, and its entrance is not agreeable. It is not easy to disbelieve absolutely, what he once believed so thoroughly. Then "Was he 'spiritual'?" He may have had spiritual experiences, but this does not make a man "spiritual." The spiritual man is a man who lives in, and is governed by, and understands his spirit, and co-operation with the Spirit of God. A great experience accompanying the ENTRANCE INTO THE PLANE OF THE SPIRIT does not make a believer "spiritual."

THE DISCOVERY OF THE TRUTH OF DECEPTION

The deceived believe, laid claim to positions to which he had no right, for with the entrance of truth he discovers he was neither so advanced, nor so spiritual, nor so infallible as he had thought. He built his faith about his own spiritual condition on assumption, and left no room for a doubt, that is, true doubt, such as doubting a statement that afterwards turns out to be a lie, but in due season doubt finds an entry to his mind, and brings his house of infallibility to the ground. He knows now that what he thought was an "advanced" experience, was only a beginning, and that he is only on the fringe of knowledge. This is the operation of truth. In the place of ignorance is given true knowledge; in the place of deception, truth.

Ignorance, falsehood and passivity; upon these three the enemy silently builds his castles, and unobtrusively guards and uses them. But truth pulls his strongholds to the ground. By the entry of truth, the man must be brought to the place where he acknowledges his condition frankly, as follows:-

(1) I believe that it is POSSIBLE for a Christian to be deceived and possessed by evil spirits.
(2) It is possible for ME to be deceived;
(3) I AM deceived by an evil spirit;
(4) WHY am l deceived?

Then comes the facing of the fact that (1) "ground does exist; and (2) the seeking for knowledge as to what the ground is.

In order to discover the ground, the believer must first, in a general sense, get a fair conception of what ground is; for he is liable to be deceived in (1) putting down to "possession" what belongs to something else, and (2) placing to something else what belongs to possession.

He may confuse ordinary conflict, i.e., the perpetual battle in spirit against the powers of darkness, with conflict which comes from possession. And when the deception and possession are of long standing, the spirits of evil may get the believer himself to defend their work in him, and through him fight tenaciously to guard the cause of his deception from being brought into light, and exposed as their work.

They thus get the believer himself, in effect, to take their side, and fight for them to keep their hold, even after he has found out his condition, and honestly desires deliverance; one of the greatest hindrances being the effect of an assumed position concerning spiritual experiences, which believers are loath to examine, and part with.

THE SPIRITUAL BASIS OF DELIVERANCE IN CALVARY'S VICTORY

The Scriptural ground for obtaining deliverance is the truth concerning Christ's full victory at Calvary, through which believer CAN BE DELIVERED FROM THE POWER OF BOTH SIN AND SATAN, but in actual fact the victory won at Calvary can only be applied as there is conformity to Divine laws.

As the deceptions of Satan are recognised, and the will of the person is set to reject them, he can, on the basis of the work of Christ at Calvary as set forth in Rom. 6: 6-13; Col. 2: 15; 1 John 3: 8, and other passages, claim his deliverance from these workings of the devil in deception and possession.

Just as there are various degrees of deception and possession, so there are degrees of deliverance according to the understanding of the believer, and his WILLINGNESS To FACE ALL THE TRUTH ABOUT HIMSELF, and all the ground given to the enemy.

In doing this the believer needs to have a steady grasp of his standing in Christ as identified with Him in His death on the Cross, and his union with Him in spirit in His place on the Throne (Ephes. 1: 19-23; 2: 6), and he must "hold fast" with steady faith-grip, the "Head" (Col. 2: 19) as the One who is, by His Spirit, giving him grace (Heb. 4: 16), and strength to recover the ground in mind and body which he has ignorantly yielded to the foe.

For the man himself must ACT to get rid of passivity; he must revoke his CONSENT given to evil spirits to enter, and by his own volition insist that they retire from the place (Ephes. 4: 27) they have obtained by deceit.

Since God will not act for him in regaining the normal condition of his outer man, nor exercise his choice for him, he must stand on the vantage ground of the Calvary victory of Christ, and claim his freedom.

Assuming, then, that the believer has discovered that he is a victim of the deceptions of deceiving spirits, what are the subjective steps in the path of freedom? Briefly, (1) acknowledgment of deception; (2) refusal of ground; (3) steadfast fight against all that possession means; (4) being on guard against excuses; (5) the detection of all the effects of possession; and (6) a discerning of the result of these actions. For the believer must learn to read the signs of dis-possession, as well as the symptoms of possession, lest he be deceived again by the Adversary.

COLUMN 1: DOUBT OF EXPERIENCE

Taking first for consideration the list.
1. Doubt of the experience, or "manifestation" being of God.

We cannot emphasise too strongly the need of not quenching, and not ignoring the first doubt, for the "doubt" is actually the initial penetration of truth to the mind, and hence the first step to deliverance.

Some have instantly quenched the first doubt, fearing to "doubt God," and in doing so, closed the mind to the first ray of light which would have led them into liberty. They have looked upon doubt as temptation, and resisted it, overlooking the distinction between true and evil, right and wrong, "doubt." This has its root in the mind of most Christians, in associating only evil with such words as "judging," "criticising," "doubting," and "enmity," "hatred," "unbelief," etc., all of which dispositions and actions they thought to be evil, and evil only, whereas they are evil or good according to their source in spirit or soul, and in relation to their object, e.g., "enmity" against Satan is God-given (Gen. 3: 15), "hatred" to sin is good, and "unbelief" of spirit manifestations is commanded until the believer is sure of their source. (1 John 4: 1).

To doubt God--which means not to trust Him--is sin; but a doubt concerning supernatural manifestations is simply a call to exercise the faculties, which all spiritual believers should use to discern "good and evil." The deep doubt concerning some supernatural experiences is therefore not a "temptation," but really the Holy Spirit moving the spiritual faculties to action according to 1 Cor. 2: 15, "He that is spiritual judgeth--i.e., examineth--all things," the "things of God" thus being "spiritually discerned" (A.V.).

NO "CONTRADICTION" IN WORKING OF SPIRIT OF GOD

A "doubt" generally first pierces the mind either (1) from truth pointed out by others, or (2) arises from some flaw in the experience which arrests the attention of the believer. In the case of some supernatural manifestation, for instance, which bore the appearance of being Divine, there was some slight contradiction which perplexed the soul. And as no contradictions can possibly occur in any of the workings of the Spirit of God, Who is the Spirit of Truth, one single contradiction is sufficient to reveal a lying spirit at work.

This axiom must not be ignored. For instance, a believer declares, under supernatural "power"--assumed to be Divine--concerning one who is ill, that God purposes the restoration of that one, yet the sick one dies. This is a "contradiction" which should be fully examined, and not put aside as among things "not to be understood;" for the supernatural element in the declaration could not be of the Spirit of God, Who cannot depart from truth in His revelation of the Will of God.

To "prove the spirits" (1 John 4: 1), so as to discern between the "Spirit of Truth" and the "spirit of error" is a clear command to the children of God, as well as to "prove all things," and hold fast that which is "good" (1 Thess. 5: 21); bring "to the proof . . . with all longsuffering" (2 Tim. 4: 2, R.V. m.). To question until all things have stood the test of full examination is the safest course, and is far removed from the doubting of God Himself, in His faithfulness and love, the only doubt which is sin.

2. ADMITTANCE OF POSSIBILITY OF DECEPTION

This is the second stage in the breaking of truth upon the mind, although it may sometimes precede the doubt. To admit the possibility of being deceived--or mistaken--in any aspect of new experience or action, or even view of truth, is really a possibility which should be acknowledged by every believer; and yet so subtle is the deception of the enemy, that almost invariably the attitude of each one is, that "others" may be open to deception, and he or she is the exception to the rule.

This certainty of personal exception is so deep seated with the most visibly deceived person, that the long battle is simply to obtain entrance to the mind for the one thought of possible deception, in any point at all. The believer seems armed with unshaken assurance that if others be misled, he certainly is not; he "beholdeth the mote" in his brother's eye, and is blind--blind to the "beam" in his own. But an open attitude to truth says, "Why not I as well as others? May not my assurance of safety be a deception of the enemy, as much as the deception I see in others?"

Why all believers should admit the possibility of deception by the deceiving spirits, may be considered just here.

THE BASIC FACT OF THE FALL

The primary fact to be recognised by every human being is the complete and utter ruin of the first creation at the Fall, when the First Adam admitted the poison of the serpent, which permeated and corrupted his whole being beyond repair. This fact of the utter corruption of the human race as a consequence of this is unmistakably declared in the New Testament:-"The old man, which waxeth corrupt after the lusts of deceit." (Eph. 4: 22 R.V.) "Being darkened in their understanding; alienated from the life of God." (Eph. 4: 18). "We all once lived in the lusts of the flesh, doing the desires of the flesh and of the thoughts, and were by nature the children of wrath, even as the rest." (Eph. 2: 3). Thus the Apostle described the whole race of man, Gentile and Jew, Pharisee and Publican--in all, he said, "the prince of the power of the air" wrought, as "the spirit that now worketh in the sons of disobedience."

These facts declared by the Word of God, and the reality of the blinded mind (2 Cor. 4: 4), and ruined condition of every human being, is the ONLY BASIS UPON WHICH THE TRUTHS WE ARE CONSIDERING IN THIS BOOK CAN BE UNDERSTOOD, AND PROVED TO BE TRUE, IN EXPERIENCE AND PRACTICE. ADMITTANCE OF POSSIBLE DECEPTION LOGICALLY REASONABLE

The second fundamental fact--and the logical outcome of the first--is that unless regeneration by the Holy Spirit, and the indwelling of the Spirit, means (1) sinlessness, and (2) the present possession of a resurrection body, every part of a believer not yet renewed, and freed by the redemption of Calvary from the effects of the Fall, MEANS GROUND FOR THE POSSIBLE ENTRY AND POSSESSION OF DECEIVING SPIRITS. Since absolute sinlessness, and the present possession of the resurrection body are not clearly taught in the Scriptures, as attainable whilst on earth, the admittance of possible deception, and entry of evil spirits to the outer man of mind or body, is logically and reasonably possible for all; even whilst the spirit and heart of the man is renewed by the Holy Spirit.

If we come to facts of experience, the proofs are so abundant as to be beyond our power to handle in the limited space of this book, not only in the unregenerate world, but in those who are undoubtedly children of God, and spiritual believers. If we knew ourselves, and our actual condition as sinners, simply as depicted in God's Word, we should be in greater safety from the enemy.

It is the ignorance of our true condition, apart from the new life from God implanted in us, and our blind confidence of safety, without an intelligent basis for our faith, which lays us open to being deceived by Satan through our very certainty of being free from his deception.

After admitting the possibility of deception in supernatural things, and a doubt has come in to the mind whether certain "experiences," either personal or otherwise, were of God after all, the next stage is,

(3) THE DISCOVERY OF THE DECEPTION

Light and truth alone can make free, and when once a doubt comes in, and the man opens his mind to the truth that he is as liable to be deceived as anyone else, then to the open mind and attitude, light is given (John 3: 21).

Sometimes the specific deception is seen at once, but more often the discovery is gradual, and patience is needed while the light slowly dawns. Certain facts in connection with various experiences of the past, which the believer has failed to note, may now emerge into the light, and the half truths of the Adversary which he had used to deceive, are clearly seen--the twisting of words, the wrenching of sentences out of their context in the Scriptures, all come into view as the light is given.

Then comes:-

(4) THE ACKNOWLEDGMENT OF THE DECEPTION

This is now imperative. The truth must not only be faced, but owned, so that things are called by their right names, and the father of lies defeated by the weapon of truth.

COLUMN 2: THE REFUSAL OF GROUND

This brings us to the crucial matter of Column 2 of the way in which the "ground" the evil spirit has held must be dealt with. Thoughts admitted to the mind, passivity of mind or body, faculties allowed to lie unused, lack of mental control, of the use of the will, of decisive power or judgment, etc. Now the believer must deliberately and steadily refusen all this ground to the enemy, especially and specifically the ground on the points wherein he has been deceived; for it is of primary importance that the one who is deceived should know the ground, and give it up

Since there is POSSESSION BECAUSE OF GROUND GIVEN, there must be DIS- POSSESSION BECAUSE OF GROUND REFUSED to the enemy. The deceived one must pray for light until the cause or causes of the deception are revealed, and honestly desire, and be willing for the light on every point (John 3: 21). He must be given light from God to detect symptoms and their causes, and in the recognition of these beware of introspection, i.e., a turning in upon himself, which is the contrary of a simple refusing of ground as it is brought into the light.

THE DANGER OF GIVING NEW GROUND

It may be said generally, that whatever the person shrinks from hearing about, or is troubled when reference is made to it, may reveal upon examination, ground given on that point. If the believer is afraid to examine something he shrinks from dealing with, then it is safe to examine that particular thing, for the enemy most probably has some footing there. What the believer cannot bear to hear about is probably the very thing that he is guilty of doing, or is in some way wrong in his relation to it. Then the ground--and the cause or causes of it--when revealed, must be taken back from the deceiving spirits, by the rejection, or refusal of these points upon which ground has been given, until the ground given has passed away; for ground which admits the evil spirit is the ground that keeps him in possession. There is also ground given which causes the believer, unknowingly, to take hold of evil spirits, and there are things, and ground given, which enable them to grip the believer, and his faculties. There is also the probability of giving new ground, by taking the lying spirits' interpretation of their manifestations, which on the believer's part is the accepting of lies from them in the present, as much as in the past, when ground was given to admit them.

THE FIGHTING THROUGH PERIOD

What it means by "fighting through" may be explained in a specific case. For instance, if the believer discovers that he has sunk into passivity, and that an evil spirit has fastened upon the passive faculties, and whilst they were lying passive, acted for, or in conjunction with him; when he gives up the ground, he finds it most difficult to act for himself again, and to regain the use of his faculties. If he has been drifting into passivity in the matter of decision, and, refusing this ground to the enemy, he decides now to "decide" for himself, and not to act under their control, he finds that, at first,

(1) He cannot act and decide for himself, and

(2) The evil spirits will not let him act, i.e., when their victim refuses them permission to control him, then they will not let their captive act without their permission.

The man has therefore to choose between "not acting" at all, or letting the evil spirit continue to act for him. This he will not do, and so for a while he is unable to use his own decisive power, and yet refuses to allow the enemy to use it. It becomes a fight for the use of his "free will," and for deliverance from passivity of the will, which destroyed his decisive power, and gave evil spirits control over him.

Why does not possession, and its effects, cease directly the man refuses all ground, as a whole, to the deceiving spirits? Because every detail of the ground must be detected; the man must be undeceived on every point; and the evil spirits must be dispossessed from every hold. Whatever caused possession, the opposite must be obtained for dispossession; instead of the lies of Satan, the truth of God; instead of passivity, activity; instead of ignorance, knowledge; instead of surrender to the enemy, resistance; instead of acceptance, refusal.

Actions are the result of thought and belief. The ground is always to be traced back to its radical cause, which is a THOUGHT AND BELIEF. Wrong thoughts and belief, which gave ground to evil spirits for possession, must be detected and given up. The basis of acceptance or refusal must be knowledge, not a passing thought, or impression. It is for this reason that understanding is such an important factor in deliverance, and the subsequent warfare.

In seeking for the ground of any trouble in the spiritual life, believers generally go back only as far as the first manifestation of conscious wrong, instead of seeking the radical cause of the manifestations.

Men in seeking for the root of a tree do not content themselves with the discovery of its manifestation above ground. They know that the cause of the growth they see lies deeper down. It is VERY IMPORTANT that believers diagnose the cause of their trouble as further back than the first conscious manifestation, i.e., some thought or belief which has given the enemy occasion for deception.

Example in matter of "unconsciousness."

RESULT: Ever since the believer admitted that "thought" and "belief," he became subject to the consequences of it, and all that evil spirits gained by it; for they came around and made true to the victim what he desired, i.e., "unconsciousness," which formed the ground of passivity for Satanic manifestations.

If the believer resists and refuses any specific ground for possession, and cannot get rid of it, he must seek light upon the cause, i.e., the ground in the past in thought and belief, when this is discovered and refused, the "possession" of necessity passes away.

THE REFUSAL OF ALL GROUND

This is why it is necessary to say that each point must be patiently "fought through," i.e., the refusal of all ground to evil spirits must be maintained, because refusing all ground, and getting rid of all ground, are two different things. All ground is not of necessity removed at the moment of refusal. The refusing must therefore be reasserted, and the believer refuse persistently, until each point of ground is detected and refused, and the faculties are gradually released to act freely under the will of the man. The faculties let go into passivity should regain their normal working condition, such as the operation of the mind kept to true and pure thinking, so that any subject being dealt with is mastered, and does not dominate beyond control. So with the memory, the will, the imagination, and the actions of the body, such as singing, praying, speaking, reading, etc. All must be brought back into normal working order, out of the passive, heavy state, into which they have fallen, under the subtle workings of the enemy.

THE REFUSAL OF THE WORKINGS OF EVIL SPIRITS

The refusal, also, of the workings of deceiving spirits in
possession, is necessary as well as the refusing of ground upon which they have obtained possession. The believer may say as his declaration of decision:

The "fighting through" period is a very painful time. There are bad moments of acute suffering, and intense struggle, arising out of the consciousness of the resistance of the powers of darkness in their contest for what the believer endeavours to reclaim. The moment he begins to advance from weakness into strength, he becomes aware of the strength of the evil spirits resisting him; consequently he feels worse when fighting through. This is a sign of "dispossession," although the believer may not think, or feel it to be so.

The order of dispossession is not the order in which possession took place. The last thing given to the spirits of evil is generally the first thing removed, because fight is given upon the experience of the moment, and deliverance from the bondage of the moment is the most urgent need. Sometimes it is the advanced stage of possession, with its terrible bondage, which reveals his condition to the man himself, and it is not until he starts, point by point, to fight back to his normal condition, that he discovers the depth of the pit he has fallen into, and the slow work of regaining the liberation of his whole being, from the power of the deceiving enemy.

> I refuse the "influence" of e.s.
> I refuse the "power" of e.s.
> I refuse to be "led" by e.s.
> I refuse to be "guided" by e.s.
> I refuse to "obey" e.s.
> I refuse to "pray" to e.s.
> I refuse to "ask" anything of e.s.
> I refuse to "surrender" to e.s

I refuse all "knowledge" from e.s.
I refuse to listen to e.s.
I refuse "visions" from e.s.
I refuse the "touch" of e.s.
I refuse "messages" from e.s.
I refuse all "help" from e.s.

The believer must revoke the consent he unknowingly gave to the workings of the deceivers. They have sought to work through him, therefore he now declares:

"I, myself, WILL to do my own work.

In the past I willed not to do my work. This I NOW REVOKE for ever."

IMMEDIATE EFFECTS OF DISPOSSESSION

The believer fighting back to freedom must not be deceived about the immediate effects of dispossession, for it may appear as he advances, that he is slipping back. For instance, when the man is in a passive state under the bondage of the enemy, he may be absolutely regardless of what he is, what he feels, and how he appears: and therefore he cannot feel and cannot be touched on these points; but as he fights back to the normal condition, these things become real to him again, and he thinks he has gone back; but the fact that he feels about these matters, proves a degree of dispossession, for his feelings, which had become numb, are once more regaining their normal condition.

The believer must not be off-guard when he knows much about dispossession, because there are new realms of deception, and he must take heed not to confuse ordinary wrestling in spirit with the powers of darkness, with manifestations of their workings through possession.

THE TACTICS OF THE ENEMY DURING THE FIGHTING THROUGH PERIOD

When the spirits of evil see their hold coming to an end, they never let go until the cause is fully removed, and they continue to attack if the thing they have attacked about still exists in any degree. When "fighting through," the enemy has various tactics to hinder the man's deliverance; and will dangle a thing before the mind which is not the true cause of the possession, so as to get the believer occupied with it, whilst he is gaining all the time, pouring in accusations upon his victim, until he is bewildered and confused. Charges, accusations, blame, guilt, direct from the enemy, or indirectly through others. Accusing spirits can say "You are wrong" when you are not wrong, and vice versa; and also say you are wrong, when you are wrong, and right when you are right, but it is very essential that the believer does not accept blame until he is absolutely sure that it is deserved, and then not from Satan's lying spirits, who have not been appointed by God to do the convicting work of the Holy Spirit.

When once the truth has dawned upon the victim of the powers of darkness, and they no longer hope to gain by deception, their one great attack all through, from the moment of undeceiving to final dispossession, is the perpetual charge, "You are wrong," so as to keep the man in ceaseless condemnation. The poor persecuted believer then goes to God, and tries to get victory over "sin," but in vain. The more he prays, the more he appears to sink into a hopeless bog. He seems to himself to be one mass of "sin," without hope of freedom. But it is victory over the powers of darkness he needs, and he will quickly prove this when he recognises the true cause of his trouble, and lays hold of the Calvary Victory over Satan.

THE WEAPON OF SCRIPTURE

In fighting back to freedom, the believer must wield Scripture as the Divinely provided weapon for victory over evil spirits. The ver ses used with immediate effect, and giving evidence of relief, indicate the specific nature of any attack; showing by the efficacy of the weapon used the immediate cause of the conflict, the believer reasoning back from the effectiveness of the weapon to the cause of the warfare. For instance, if the text wielded is that Satan is the "father of lies," and the believer declares that he refuses all his lies, brings liberty from the oppression of the enemy, it indicates that the enemy is attacking with some of his deceptive workings. Then the believer should not only refuse all his lies, but pray, "Lord, destroy all the devil's lies to me."

All this simply means that in the path to freedom, the deceived believer must act intelligently. He must know the truth, and by the truth being received and acted upon, he is set free. In going down into the deception the intelligence is unused, but in recovering freedom he must act with deliberate knowledge; i.e., he goes down "passively," but he must emerge to liberty actively that is, by the action of his whole being.

Force must be used against force. There are two aspects of the use of force in the fight against the powers of darkness; one of using spirit force against spirit force when the believer is free from possession, and the second of physical force brought into action against their power or grip of the body. Either of these the Deceiver may suggest as "self-effort," and deceive the man into taking up a passive attitude, and thus to cease his resistance against him.

When the believer is fighting free from possession, he must bring into action all the forces of his tripartite being, and must know the place of the spirit, the soul, and the body, in the conflict, e.g., if evil spirits have a hold on the muscles of the bodily frame there must be effort, and use of the muscles to dislodge them, and so in every other part of the being. The believer, therefore, must not be afraid to use force--pure force, which simply means ACTIVE USE OF SPIRIT, SOUL AND BODY in their various actions. Evil spirits, by possession, caused the forces of the tripartite man to be inactive and passive, and now these must be aroused to action against the force holding them. There must be liberation of the physical being from passivity, as well as mind and spirit.

THE DANGER OF A WRONG KIND OF "FIGHT"

But resistance, i.e., action of spirit, soul or body, must not take the place of refusal by the will. A man may "fight" without any result, if he does not first "refuse." There is an evil fight, i.e., a resistance in body or brain, which is due to possession. If it exists it must be refused. To be clear that this evil force is not in operation, the believer can say, "I refuse all evil fight now in spirit, soul or body." The believer may be resisting something in himself which is the fruit of his choice in the past, and which only his "refusal," or revoking of his past choice, can touch in the present. Fighting by force, or resistance, must therefore always have at the back of it the volitional attitude of refusal. For example (1) in the refusing stage of regaining the use of the memory, the man says "I will to remember," and so to speak, by the action of his will he lays hold of freedom; then follows (2) the actual fighting stage where he holds the liberty he has taken by refusal, and actively insists upon the enemy giving way, until the memory becomes really free from his possession.

A few brief suggestions for attitude and action may be added here in condensed form, for the guidance of any who are seeking freedom from the enemy's power:

Keep claiming the power of the blood (Rev. 12: 11).
Pray for light, and face the past.
Resist the devil persistently in your spirit.
Never give up hope that you will be set free
Avoid all self-introspection.
Live, and pray for others, and thus keep your spirit in full aggressive and resisting power.

Again it may be said:—
Stand daily on Rom. 6: 11; as the attitude to sin.
Resist the enemy (James 4: 7) daily on the ground of the blood of Christ (Rev. 12: 11)
Live daily for others; i.e., outward, and not inward.

THE FOOTING ON ROM. 6: 11, A WEAPON OF VICTORY

The standing on Romans 6: 11 means the attitude of the believer reckoning himself "dead unto sin . . in Christ Jesus." It is a declaration of death--a gulf of death--to evil spirits as well as sin; to evil spirits working in, through, for, instead of, or in conjunction with the man.

To resist the enemy on the ground of the blood of Christ, means wielding the weapon of the finished work of Christ, by faith; i.e., His death for sin, freeing the trusting believer from the guilt of sin; His death to sin on the Cross and the believer's death with Him, freeing the man from the power of sin, and His death victory on Calvary freeing the believer from the power of Satan.

A condensed form of the principles, and conditions for deliverance from the deception and possession of evil spirits in any degree, may be given as follows:—

Knowledge of the possibility of deception and possession;
Admission of actual deception and possession;
Attitude of neutrality toward all past experiences (spiritual) until truth concerning them is ascertained;
Refusal of all ground to evil spirits;
(In some cases) the casting out of evil spirits by the authority of the Name of Christ;
The believer taking position of death to sin (Rom. 6: 11);
The detection and refusal of all that belongs to possession;
The understanding of the criterion of the true normal condition so as to gauge signs of dispossession;
Active usage of the faculties so that they reach the normal condition.In another brief form a summary of the steps to deliverance may be given as follows:—

Recognise persistently the true cause of bondage; i.e., the work of an evil spirit or spirits.

Choose to have absolutely nothing to do with the powers of darkness. Frequently declare this.

Do not talk or trouble about their manifestations. Recognise, refuse and then ignore them.

Refuse and reject all their lies and excuses, as they are recognised.

Notice the thoughts, and the way in which they come, and when, and immediately declare the attitude of Rom. 6: 11 against all the interferences of the enemy.

Hindrances to deliverance from deception and possession may again be given here briefly, as:—

Not knowing it is possible to be deceived;

Thinking God will not allow a believer to be deceived;

Saying "I am safe under the Blood," without intelligent knowledge of conditions;

Saying "I have no sin," to open the door to an "evil spirit";

Saying "I am doing all that God wants, so all must be right"; without seeking to understand what the will of the Lord is. (Eph. 5: 10- 17).

Some hints on overcoming passivity of mind, are as follows:—

Act as far as you can, doing what you can.

Take the initiative, instead of passively depending on others.

Decide for yourself in everything you can. Do not lean on others.

Live in the moment, watch and pray step by step.

We your mind, and THINK--think over all you do, and say, and are.

THE SLOW WEAKENING OF POSSESSION AS THE BELIEVER MAINTAINS RESISTANCE

Col. 3: The possession by the enemy now slowly weakens as the ground which he held is steadily refused, and given up. The Deceiver fought long to obtain the ground, and the believer may have to fight a long time ere he is fully set free. The weakening of the possession, too, is according to the degree in which the ground is removed, and if the man does not meanwhile give more ground to the foe. This makes the deliverance gradual, it is true, but in most cases the snare may have been gradually woven about him for many years. Film after film may have slowly come upon the mind, preparing for the deception of after years.

Col. 4: Following the steady attitude of the refusal of the ground, light begins to break in, with the discovery of the "excuses" the enemy is making to hide the true location. For the persistent endeavour is to make the man believe that the manifestations are due to some other cause. The chief excuses over the manifestation of possession centre around the suggestions, "it is divine," "natural," "physical," or else temperament, circumstances, others' wrong doing, etc., in order to cover or hide the ground which is held. But as the excuses are recognised, the believer resists them, and calls the excuses by the right name of Satan's lies.

After getting rid of the counterfeits of the Divine workings, the difficult stage is the recognising and getting free from the counterfeits of the man himself. As the "excuses" or lies are recognised the believer becomes more acute in detection, and less ready to accept the "natural" and "physical" causes as true explanations, without examination and certainty, e.g., if he "cannot bear" to hear, or speak about a person, he asks Why? If an attack on a certain point does not cease, he asks Why?

The truth is, a believer cannot bear things because of attack through possession, and he cannot do things because of possession.

NAMING THE ATTACK A FACTOR IN VICTORY

Naming the "attack" is a great factor for victory. For example, an attack may be made to hinder, then the believer must be on guard against all hindrances, seen and unseen, which the Hinderer is placing in his way; it may be to make him impatient, then he must be on guard over all things liable to test his patience. The sooner the attack is recognised and named, the quicker the weapon can be called into use to destroy it.

It may be a flood of accusations of wrong doing, which need to be recognised, or tested as to their truth. When the Accuser charges the believer with some specific wrong over a certain thing, and he surrenders that thing to God, if the accusation does not then pass away, it shows that it is not the true ground for the accusation, but some other cause hidden from view. The believer should then seek light from God upon the hidden causes according to John 3: 21; and refuse the cause of the accusation without knowing what it is, saying, "I refuse the cause of this attack, whatever it is, and I trust the Lord to destroy it." But often, when the believer is charged with being wrong over a certain thing, and it is fought off again and again in this way, it does not pass away. Then the true cause of the attack is possession, and not a "thing" at all. The matter to be fought is possession as a whole.

The true location of the deceiving spirit will often be found in an opposite direction to the apparent one, for they know they are being exposed, and dislodged, and so they vigorously ply an attack upon some other place to divert attention.

THE SYMPTOMS SLOWLY PASSING AWAY

Col. 5: THE EFFECT OF THESE PRECEDING STEPS CAN NOW BE SEEN. The symptoms slowly pass away, and the believer, coming back to normal conditions, finds his faculties usable, and his thoughts once more under the control of his volition. It is a spiritual resurrection from a Satanic burial.

Now the one who is being freed must be on guard not to think it is final victory, or that the deceiving spirit has been fully dislodged because the manifestations have ceased; nor must he think that, when the intruder has been "cast out," in cases where casting out is possible and successful, that he is completely delivered, if there are no actual manifestations. It is necessary to watch and pray as never before. The evil spirit has been exposed, the soul has been undeceived; but the deeper the deception the longer is the time for the film of Satan upon the mind to be removed, and the passivity of the various faculties, of spirit, soul or body, to be destroyed. To be "undeceived," does not always mean to be fully delivered. The believer must therefore beware of the snare of ceasing the fight against possession when ease comes.

It is here that the believer needs to know himself, so as to be able to judge of the extent of his liberation; and this he does by having a clear criterion of his true normal condition, so as to detect whether he is above it, and therefore strained beyond his normal poise and measure, or below it, and therefore less capable in all the departments of his being.

THE IMPORTANCE OF KNOWING THE TRUE NORMAL

For these reasons it is essential and indispensable for full deliverance from the power of evil spirits, that a believer know the standard of his normal condition, and with this gauge before him, can judge of his degree of deliverance, physically, intellectually, and spiritually, so as to fight through with steady volition and faith, until every faculty is free, and he stands a liberated man in the liberty wherewith Christ has made him free.

As he judges himself by this criterion he may say, "Things are not the same as they were," and he then fights through by prayer to his normal condition. The deceiving spirits will suggest all kinds of excuses to stop the man's advance to freedom; e.g., if he is forty years of age, they will suggest that the "mind cannot be as vigorous as at twenty"; or "overwork" is the cause of his being below what he should be, but he must not accept reasons which appear to be "natural," IF HE HAS BEEN A SUBJECT OF POSSESSION. Let the believer know the highest measure of grace whereunto he has attained, for spirit, soul and body, and resist all attempts of the powers of darkness to keep him below it at any time. If he is vigilant he will know that the lying spirits will endeavour to deceive him about it, and he must resist their lies.

REGAINING THE NORMAL

Some practical ways of keeping the mind in its normal working condition, may be briefly suggested as follows:—

(a) ATTITUDE TO THE PAST. There should be no "regrets," or brooding over things done or undone. This is an ordinary operation of the mind in thinking over the past, entangled into an evil kind of thinking which is generally described as "brooding." The believer must earn to discern for himself when he is simply "thinking," or being drawn into a state of "regretting" or brooding. For victory in the life, there must be victory in regard to the past, with all its failures. The good of the past causes no trouble to the mind, but only the real or supposed evil. This should be dealt with by dealing with God, on the ground of 1 John 1: 7, and thus the believer be delivered from it.
In regaining the normal working of the mind, it needs first to be brought into action, and then into balanced action. This is very difficult, and at times impossible, whilst there is evil spirit possession. Possession must therefore pass away before balanced working is restored. This principle applies to every faculty.

(b) THE ATTITUDE TO THE FUTURE. The same may be said in the action of the mind in regard to the future. It is lawful to think of the past and think of the future, so long as the evil state of "brooding," brought about by sin, or Satan, is not yielded to.

(c) THE ATTITUDE TO EVIL SPIRITS. They must not be permitted to interfere, by the believer seeing to it that no new ground is given to them, either for possession, or interference.

(d) THE ATTITUDE TO THE PRESENT MOMENT. This should be a steady concentration of mind upon the duties of the moment, keeping it in active readiness for use as occasion requires. This does not mean ceaseless activity, for activity of the mind so that it is never at rest, can be a symptom of possession.

THE WEAPON OF THE WORD OF GOD

The believer must understand that the regaining of the facile use of the faculties, and the maintenance of the mind in healthy condition, after passive surrender to evil spirits, will mean a steady fight with the powers of darkness, which will require the use of the weapons of warfare given in the Word of God, as tried and proved by experience. Weapons, for instance, such as the truth in the text "Sufficient for the day is the evil thereof," for resisting brooding over the past, or torturing pictures of the future; "Resist the devil and he will flee from you," when the pressure of the enemy is severe; and other "fighting" texts, which will prove truly to be the "sword of the Spirit" to thrust at the enemy, in the evil day of his onslaught upon the escaping believer.

(e) THE STEADY ATTITUDE OR ACTION OF THE WILL. In keeping the mind in normal working condition, free from the interference of the enemy, the believer should maintain the attitude of the will steadily set; i.e., "I will that my mind shall not be passive;" "I will to have full control of, and to use my faculties;" "I will to recognise everything that comes from demon-possession;" all of which declares the CHOICE of the man, rather than his determination to do these things. The powers of darkness are not affected by mere determination--i.e., resolve--but they are rendered powerless by the act of volition definitely choosing, in the strength given of God, to stand against them.

THE RESULTS IN EXPERIENCE WHEN DELIVERED

Col. 6: The believer now finds the following results in experience. He has clear vision in the light of God, of the enemy's workings, without fear; a clear mind, intelligently in exercise in all its actions; a calm decision of the will, with a strong pure spirit in resisting, without hesitation, all he sees to be of the Adversary. Instead of acceptance of the enemy's workings, there is an established attitude of refusal; instead of a lie in the mind there is truth; instead of ignorance there is knowledge.

The delivered believer now has a deep longing for the deliverance of others he sees to be in the net of the fowler; acute insight into the devil's true character in his bitter enmity to Christ and His redeemed; past perplexities in spiritual experiences are now clearly understood, and the Adversary detected where it was little thought he had a place; the undeceived one now seeing with astonishment the "naturalness" of his supernatural workings. This man is never off guard now, but always alert, watching against the powers of darkness, whilst relying upon the strength of God, and there is a manifest development of resisting power against the wicked spirits attacking him in the heavenly places, instead of the weak and passive attitude of the past, which enabled them to hinder or mislead him.

The steps to deliverance which have been given, deal with the PRACTICAL ASPECT OF THE BELIEVER'S ACTIONS. On the Divine side, the victory has been won, and Satan and his deceiving spirits have been conquered, but the actual liberation of the believer demands his ACTIVE COOPERATION WITH THE HOLY SPIRIT, and the steady exercise of his volition, choosing freedom instead of bondage, and the normal use of every faculty of his being, set at liberty from the bondage of the enemy.

"He that doeth the truth cometh to the light" (John 3: 21) said the Lord. Evil spirits hate scrutiny, and so work under cover with deception and lies. The believer must come to the light of God for His light upon all spiritual experiences, as well as all other departments of the life, if he is to "cast off the works of darkness" (Rom. 13: 12) and put on the armour of God- -the armour of light.

THE SCRIPTURE ASPECT OF DELIVERANCE

The Blood of Jesus Christ, God's Son, cleanseth us from all sin, if we walk in the light; but the light must shine in for the soul to walk in it. The evil spirits can be cast out in the Name of the Lord Jesus, but the GROUND THEY HAVE GAINED CAN ONLY BE REMOVED BY THE INTELLIGENT CHOICE OF THE WILL REFUSING the ground given to them, and appropriating the deliverance by death with Christ on Calvary.

CHAPTER 9
The Volition and Spirit of Man

It is now necessary to see from the Scriptures the true way in which God works in the believer, in contradistinction to the way of Satan and his wicked spirits; for the principle of co-operation with God, and not passive control by Him, must be fully understood, not only as the basis of deliverance from deception and possession, but also as the basis for the warfare which will be dealt with in our next chapter.

Briefly, it may be said that the Holy Spirit dwelling in the regenerate human spirit, energises and works through the faculties of the soul and the members of the body, only in and with, the active cooperation of the WILL Of the believer, i.e., God in the spirit of man, does not use the man's hand apart from the "I will use my hand" of the man himself.

CO-OPERATION WITH GOD DOES NOT MEAN AUTOMATIC WORKING

When Paul said, "His working, which worketh in me mightily" (Col. 1: 29), he first said, "I labour according to" His working. The "I labour" did not mean that hands and feet and mind worked automatically in response to a Divine energising, as the engine works in response to the steam, but at the back of the "I labour" was the full action of Paul's will, saying "I choose to labour," and "as I labour, God's power and energy energises me in the acting," so that it is "I who live and move and work," and "yet not I, but Christ--the 'Spirit of Christ' in me." (See Gal. 2: 20; Phil. 1: 19).

It was so in the Greater than Paul, Who said, "I came not to do Mine own will, but the will of Him that sent Me," "The Son can do nothing of Himself," and yet He said also, "My Father worketh hitherto and I work." "The works that I do shall ye do also!" He had a separate will, but He came not to do His own will, but the will of the Father, and He was doing the Father's will when He said to the one who sought His healing power, "I WILL, be thou clean!" Thus it should be in the life of the believer.

Granted the essential union of his will with the will of God, and the energising power of the Holy Spirit, by his own deliberate choice of harmony with that Holy Will, the believer is actively to use his will in ruling himself in spirit, soul and body. God dwelling in his spirit co-working with him through his exercised volition.

GOD GOVERNS THE RENEWED MAN BY HIS CO-ACTING WILL

For deliverance from the power of sin and protection from deceiving spirits in their workings, it is important to have a clear apprehension of God's purpose in redemption. God created man, with dominion over himself. This dominion was exercised by his act of will, even as it was by his Creator. But man fell, and, in his fall, yielded his will to the rule of Satan, who from that time by the agency of his evil spirits has ruled the world, through the enslaved will of fallen man. Christ the Second Adam came, and taking the place of man, chose obedience to the Father's will, and never for one moment diverged from His perfect co-operation with that will. In the wilderness He refused to exercise the Divine power at the will of Satan, and in Gethsemane in suffering His will never wavered in the choice of the Father's will. As Man He willed the will of God right through, becoming obedient even unto death, thus regaining for regenerated man, not only reconciliation with God, but liberty from Satan's thraldom, and the restoration of man's renewed and sanctified will to its place of free action, deliberately and intelligently exercised in harmony with the will of God.

Christ wrought out for man upon Calvary's Cross salvation of spirit, soul, and body, from the dominion of sin and Satan; but that full salvation is wrought out in the believer through the central action of the will, as he deliberately chooses the will of God for each department of his tripartite nature.

The will of the man united to the will of God--and thus having the energising power of God working with his volition--is to rule his (1) "own spirit" (see Prov. 25: 28; 1 Cor. 14: 32); (2) thoughts or mind (Col. 3: 2) inclusive of all the soul-powers; and (3) body (1 Cor. 9: 27), and when, by the appropriation of God's freeing power from slavery to sin and Satan, the believer regains free action of his will so that he gladly and spontaneously wills the will of God, and as a renewed man re-takes dominion over spirit, soul and body, he reigns in life "through . . Jesus Christ" (Rom. 5: 17).

But the natural man does not reach this stage of renewal and liberation of his will, without first knowing the regeneration of his own human spirit. God is not in fallen man until the moment of his new birth (Ephes. 2: 12; 3: 16; John 3: 5-8). He must be "begotten of God;" the very fact of such a begetting being necessary, declares the non-existence of Divine life in him previously. After such a begetting, it is also necessary to understand that the regenerated man does not, as a rule, immediately become a spiritual man, i.e., a man wholly dominated by, and walking after the spirit.

THE "NATURAL" VERSUS THE "SPIRITUAL" MAN

At first the regenerated man is but a "babe in Christ, manifesting many of the characteristics of the natural man in jealousy, strife, etc., until he apprehends the need of a fuller reception of the Holy Spirit to dwell in the regenerated spirit as His sanctuary.

The unregenerate man is wholly dominated by soul and body. The regenerate man has his spirit (I) quickened, and (2) indwelt by the Holy Spirit, yet may he governed by soul and body because his spirit is compressed and bound. The spiritual man has his spirit liberated from bondage to the soul (Heb. 4: 12) to be the organ of the Holy Spirit in mind and body. It is then that, by the Holy Spirit's power, his volition is brought into harmony with God in all His laws and purposes, and the whole outer man into self-control.

Thus it is written "The fruit of the Spirit . . . is self-control" (Gal. 5: 23, m). It is not only love, joy, peace, longsuffering, and gentleness, manifested through the channel of the soul--the personality--but in a true dominion over the world of himself, (1) every thought brought into captivity, in the same obedience to the will of the Father as was manifested in Christ (2 Cor. 10: 5); (2) his spirit "ruled" also from the chamber of the will, so that he is of a "cool spirit" and can "'keep back" or utter at his will what is in his spirit as well as what is in his mind (Prov. 17: 27, m.), and (3) his body so obedient to the helm of the will, that it is a disciplined and alert instrument for God to energise and empower; that body an instrument to be handled intelligently as a vehicle for service, and not any longer master of the man, or the mere tool of Satan and unruly desires.

THE CALL TO DECISIVE ACTION OF THE WILL

All this is fully made clear in the New Testament Epistles. "Our old man was crucified with Him" is said of the work of Christ at Calvary, but on the part of the one who desires this potential fact made true in his life, he is called upon to declare his attitude of choice with decisive action, both in the negative and positive positions.

The Apostle appeals again and again to the redeemed believer to act decisively with his will, as the following few passages show:- Negative "Cast off the works of darkness." Rom. 13: 12. "Put away the old man." Eph. 4: 22. "Put off the old man with his doings." Col. 3: 9. "Put to death your members." "Put off the body of the flesh." Col. 3: 5. Col. 2: 11. Positive "Put on the armour of light." Rom. 13: 12. "Put on the new man." "Put on the new man." Eph. 4: 24. Col. 3: 10. "Present your members unto God." Rom. 6: 13. "Put on the Lord Jesus Christ, and make no provision for the flesh." Rom. 13: 14. See also Ephes. 6: 13, 16 "Take up the whole amour. . . . "Put on a heart of compassion." Col. 3:12 "Put on the whole armour of God." Eph. 6: 11

All these passages describe a decisive act of the will, not toward exterior things, but toward things in an unseen, immaterial sphere, incidentally showing the effect in the spiritual sphere of a man's volitional action. They also emphasise the effect of the decisive use of the will of man, when it acts in harmony with the liberating power of Christ.

Christ has done the work on Calvary's Cross, but that work is applied in fact through the action of the believer's own will, acting as if he himself had power to "cast off" the invisible works of darkness, and finding with this action of his will, the co- working of the Spirit of God making the casting off effectual. In saving the man, God calls him into co-action with Himself, to "work out his own salvation," for it is God Who works with and in him, to enable him to will and to do His pleasure.

GOD CALLS A MAN INTO CO-ACTION FOR HIS OWN SALVATION

In the hour of his regeneration God gives to man the decisive liberty of will to rule over himself, as he walks in fellowship with God. And by this restoration of a will free to act in choosing for God, SATAN LOSES HIS POWER.

Satan is the god of this world, and he rules the world through the will of men enslaved by him, enslaved not only directly, but indirectly, by his inciting men to enslave one another, and to covet the power of "influence," whereas they should work with God to restore to every man the freedom of his own personal volition, and the power of choice to do right because it is right, obtained for them at Calvary. In this direction we can see the working of the world-rulers of darkness in the realm which they govern, directly in atmospheric influence, and indirectly through men, in (1) hypnotic suggestion, (2) thought reading, (3) will controlling, and other forms of invisible force, sometimes employed for the supposed good of others.

The danger of all forms of healing by "suggestion," and all kindred methods of seeking to benefit men in physical or mental ways, lies in their bringing about a passivity of the will, and mental powers, which lays them open to Satanic influences later on.

THE BELIEVER'S RIGHT OF DECISION OF WILL

The liberation of the will from its passive condition, and control by the prince of this world, takes place when the believer sees his right of choice, and begins to deliberately place his will on God's side, and thus choose the will of God. Until the will is fully liberated for action, it is helpful for the believer to assert his decision frequently by saying, "I choose the will of God, and I refuse the will of Satan."

The soul may not even be able to distinguish which is which, but the declaration is having effect in the unseen world, i.e., God works by His Spirit in the man as he chooses His will, energising him through his volition to continually refuse the claims of sin and Satan; and Satan is thereby rendered more and more powerless, whilst the man is stepping out into the salvation obtained potentially for him at Calvary, and God is gaining once more a loyal subject in a rebellious world.

On the part of the believer the action of the will is governed by the understanding of the mind, i.e., the mind sees what to do, the will chooses to do it, and then from the spirit comes the power to fulfil the choice of the will, and the knowledge of the mind.

For example, the man (1) sees that he should speak, (2) he chooses or wills to speak, (3) he draws upon the power in his spirit to carry out his decisions. This means knowledge of how to use the spirit, and the necessity of knowing the laws of the spirit, so as to fully co-operate with the Holy Ghost.

THE SPIRIT ENERGISED BY THE HOLY SPIRIT AT THE BACK OF THE WILL

But the believer thus co-operating with God in the use of his volition, must understand that the choice of the will is not sufficient alone, as we see by Paul's words in Rom. 7: 18. "To will is present with me, but to do . . .is not." Through the spirit, and by the strengthening of the Holy Spirit in the "inward man" (the regenerate human spirit--Eph. 3: 16), is the liberated will desirous and determined to do God's will, empowered to carry out its choice. "It is God which worketh in you . . to will," i.e., to enable the believer to decide or choose. Then it is "God which worketh in you . . to do His pleasure" (Phil. 2: 13), i.e., energises the believer with power to carry out the choice. That is, God gives the power to do, from the spirit where He dwells, and by the believer understanding the using of his spirit, as clearly as he understands the use (1) of his will, (2) of is mind, or (3) of his body. He must know how to discern the sense of his spirit, so as to understand the will of God, before he can do it.

THE DISTINCT ORGANISM OF THE SPIRIT

That the human spirit is a distinct organism, as separate from the soul and body, is very clearly recognised in the Scriptures, as these few verses show. "The spirit of man." 1 Cor. 2: 11. "The Spirit Himself beareth witness with our spirit." Rom. 8: 16. "My spirit prayeth." 1 Cor. 14: 14. ". . .my spirit. . ." 1 Cor. 5:4. "Relief in my spirit." 2 Cor. 2: 13.

There is also a separation of "soul and spirit" required and carried out by the Word of God--the sword of the Spirit--made known in Heb. 4: 12, because through the Fall, the spirit in union with God which once ruled and dominated soul and body, fell from the predominant position into the vessel of the soul and could no longer rule. In the "new birth" which the Lord told Nicodemus was necessary for every man, the regeneration of the fallen spirit takes place. "That which is born of the Spirit is spirit" (John 3: 6), "a new spirit will I put within you" (Ezek. 36: 26), and through the apprehension of the death of the old creation with Christ as set forth in Rom. 6: 6, is the new spirit liberated, divided from the soul, and joined to the Risen Lord. "Dead to the law . . . joined to Another . . having died . . . that we might serve in newness of the spirit" (Rom. 7: 4-6).

The believer's life is therefore to be a walk "after the spirit" minding "the things of the spirit" (Rom. 8: 4-5). In the R.V. the word "spirit" is not written with a capital "S" denoting the Spirit of God, but with a small "s" as referring to the spirit of man. But the believer can only thus walk "after the spirit," if the Spirit of God dwells in him (Rom. 8: 9), the Holy Spirit lifting his spirit to the place of rule over soul and body--"flesh," both ethically and physically--by joining it to the Risen Lord, and making it "one spirit" with Him (1 Cor. 6: 17).

That the believer retains volitional control over his own spirit is the important point to note, and through ignorance he can withdraw his spirit from co-operation with the Holy Spirit, and thus, so to speak, "walk" after the soul, or after the flesh unwittingly. A surrendered will to do the will of God, is therefore no guarantee that he is doing that will--he must understand what the will of the Lord is (Eph. 5: 17) and for the doing of that will seek to be filled in spirit to the utmost of his capacity.

The knowledge that the Spirit of God has come to indwell the shrine of the spirit, is not enough to guarantee that the believer will continue to walk in the spirit, and not fulfil the lusts of the flesh (Gal. 5: 16). If he "lives" by the Spirit he must learn how to walk by the Spirit, and for this understand how to "combine" and "compare" spiritual things with spiritual (1 Cor. 2: 13, R.V. margin), so as to interpret truly the things of the Spirit of God, exercising the spirit faculty by which he is able to examine all things, and discern the mind of the Lord.

Such a believer should know how to walk after the spirit, so that he does not quench its action, movements or monitions as it is moved or exercised by the Spirit of God, cultivating its strength by use, so that he becomes "strong in spirit" (Luke 1: 80), and a truly spiritual man of "full age" in the Church of God (1 Cor. 2: 6; Heb. 6: 1).

HOW BELIEVERS IGNORE THE HUMAN SPIRIT

Many believers are not intelligently conscious that they have a "spirit" or else they imagine that every experience which takes place in the realm of their senses is spirit or "spiritual." If they seek a Baptism of the Holy Spirit, and become conscious of His indwelling, believers sometimes think that then He alone acts in them, and they are infallibly, or specially guided by Him, with the result that everything which takes place in their inner life is necessarily His working.

In these three cases the man's own spirit is left out of account. In the first instance, the believer's religious life is, if we may say so "spiritually mental," that is the mind is illuminated and enjoys spiritual truth, but what "spirit" means he does not clearly know; in the second the believer is really "soul-ish" although he thinks he is spiritual; and in the case where the believer thinks that the Holy Spirit's indwelling means every movement to be of Him, he becomes specially open to the deception of evil spirits counterfeiting the Holy Spirit, because without discrimination he attributes all inner "movements" or experiences to Him.

In this case the man's spirit comes into action, and into his cognisance through the reception of the Holy Spirit, but believers need then to understand that the Holy Spirit does not act through them as a passive channel, but requires them to know how to co-work with Him in spirit, otherwise their "own spirit"--the human spirit--can act apart from Him whilst they may think He alone is the source of action.

THE HUMAN SPIRIT CO-WORKING WITH THE HOLY SPIRIT

Walking "after the spirit," and "minding the spirit," does not only mean mind and body subservient to the spirit, but the man's own spirit co-working with the Holy Spirit in the daily life, and all the occasions of life. To do this, the believer needs to know the laws of the spirit, not only the conditions necessary for the Holy Spirit's working, but the laws governing his own spirit, so that it may be kept open to the Spirit of God.

When the Holy Spirit takes the spirit of man as His sanctuary, evil spirits attack the spirit to get it out of co-working with God. They first get access to mind or body, their object being to close the outlet of the Spirit of God dwelling at the centre; or when the man is "spiritual," and the mind and body are subservient to the spirit, the spiritual forces of Satan can come into DIRECT CONTACT with the spirit, and then follows the "wrestling" referred to by Paul (Eph. 6:12).

If the man becomes "spiritual" through the Baptism of the Spirit, and yet is ignorant of the laws of the spirit, especially the tactics of Satan, he is liable to yield to an onslaught of deceiving spirits by which they (1) force his spirit into strained ecstasy, or elation, or (2) press it down, as it were into a vice. In the former he is given "visions" and revelations which appear to be divine, but afterwards are proved to have been of the enemy, by their passing away with no results; in the latter the man sinks into darkness and deadness as if he had lost all knowledge of God.

THE BELIEVER'S CONTROL OVER HIS SPIRIT

When the believer understands these direct onslaughts of wicked spirits, he becomes able to discern the condition of his spirit, and to retain control over it, refusing all forced elation and strain, and resisting all weights and pressure to drive it below the normal poise, in which it is capable of co- operation with the Spirit of God.

The danger of the human spirit acting out of co-operation with the Holy Spirit, and becoming driven or influenced by deceiving spirits is a very serious one, and can be increasingly detected by those who walk softly and humbly with God, e.g., a man is liable to think his own masterful spirit is an evidence of the power of God, because in other directions he sees the Holy Spirit using him in winning souls; another may have a flood of indignation inserted into his spirit, which he pours out thinking it is all of God, whilst others shrink and are conscious of a harsh note which is clearly not of God.

This influence on the human spirit by evil spirits counterfeiting the Divine workings, or even the workings of the man himself, because he is out of co- working with the Holy Spirit, needs to be understood and detected by the believer who seeks to walk with God. He needs to know that because he is spiritual his "spirit" is open to two forces of the spirit realm, and if he thinks that only the

Holy Spirit can influence him in the spiritual sphere, he is sure to be misled. If it were so, he would become infallible, but he needs to watch and pray, and seek to have the eyes of his understanding enlightened to know the true workings of God.

SOME LAWS GOVERNING THE TRUE SPIRIT LIFE

Some of the laws governing the spirit life may be summarised briefly as follows--(1) The believer must know what is spirit, and how to give heed to the demands of the spirit, and not quench it, e.g., a weight comes on his spirit, but he goes on with his work, putting up with the

pressure; he finds the work hard, but he has no time to investigate the cause, until at last the weight becomes unendurable, and he is forced to stop and see what is the matter, whereas he should have given heed to the claims of the spirit at the first, and in a brief prayer taken the "weight" to God, refusing all pressure from the foe.

(2) He should be able to read his spirit, and know at once when it is out of co-operation with the Holy Spirit, quickly refusing all attacks which are drawing his spirit out of the poise of fellowship with God.

(3) He should know when his spirit is touched by the poison of the spirits of evil; by the injection, for instance, of sadness, soreness, complaint, grumbling, fault-finding, touchiness, bitterness, feeling hurt, jealousy, etc.-- all direct from the enemy to the spirit. He should resist all sadness, gloom, and grumbling injected into his spirit, for the victory life of a freed spirit means joyfulness (Gal. 5: 22). Believers think that sadness has to do with their disposition, and yield to it without a thought of resistance or reasoning out the cause. If they are asked if a man with a strong disposition to steal should yield to it, they would at once answer "no," yet they yield to other "dispositions" less manifestly wrong, without question.

In the stress of conflict, when the believer finds that the enemy succeeds in reaching his spirit with any of these "fiery darts," he should know how to pray immediately against the attack asking God to destroy the causes of it. It should be noted that this touching of the spirit by the various things just named is not the manifestation of the "works of the flesh," when the believer is one who knows the life after the spirit; although they will quickly reach the sphere of the flesh if not recognised, and dealt with in sharp refusal and resistance.

(4) He should know when his spirit is in the right position of dominance over soul and body, and yet not driven beyond due measure by the exigencies of conflict or environment. There are three conditions of the spirit which the believer should be able to discern and deal with, i.e.:—

(1) The spirit depressed, i.e., crushed or "down."

(2) The spirit in its right position, in poise and calm control.
(3) The spirit drawn out beyond "poise," when it is in strain, or driven, or in "flight."

When the man walks after the spirit, and discerns it to be in either of these conditions, he knows how to "lift" it when it is depressed; and how to check the over-action by a quiet act of his volition, when it is drawn out of poise by over-eagerness, or drive of spiritual foes.

SOME LIGHT ON TRUE GUIDANCE AFTER THE SPIRIT

In "guidance," the believer should understand that when there is no action in his spirit, he should use his mind. If in everything there must be the "Amen" in the spirit, there is no use for the brain at all, but the SPIRIT DOES NOT ALWAYS SPEAK. There are times when it should be left in abeyance. In all guidance the mind decides the course of action, not only from the feeling in the spirit, but by the light in the mind.

In coming to a decision, the deciding is an act of mind and will, based upon, either mental process of reasoning, or sense of the spirit, or both, i.e.:--

(1) Decision by mental process, reasoning, or
(2) Decision by sense of the spirit: i.e., movement, impelling; drawing or restraint; spirit as if "dead"--no response. Contraction of spirit; openness of spirit; fulness of spirit; compression of spirit; burden on spirit; wrestling in spirit; resisting in spirit.

God has three ways of communicating His will to men. By (1) vision to the mind, which is very rare, and can be given only to very matured spiritual men, such as Moses; (2) understanding by the mind; and (3) consciousness to the spirit, that is, by light to the mind, and consciousness in spirit. In true guidance, spirit and mind are of one accord, and the intelligence is not in rebellion against the leading in the spirit, as it is so often in counterfeit guidance by evil spirits, when the man is COMPELLED TO ACT, in obedience to what he thinks is of God, supernaturally given, and fears to disobey.

This all refers to guidance from the subjective standpoint, but it must be emphasised in addition, that ALL TRUE GUIDANCE FROM GOD IS IN HARMONY WITH THE SCRIPTURES. The "understanding" of the will of God by the mind, depends upon the mind being saturated with the knowledge of the written Word. and true "consciousness in the spirit" depends upon its union with Christ through the indwelling Spirit of God.

The mind should never be dropped into abeyance. The human spirit can be influenced by the mind, therefore, the believer should keep his mind in purity, and unbiased; as well as an unbiased volition. Passivity can be produced by seeking for a "leading" in the spirit all day, when there may be no action in the spirit to go by. When there is no movement, or "draw," or "leading" in the spirit, then the mind should be used in reliance upon the promise of God, "the meek will He guide in judgment." (Ps. 25: 9). An example of this use of the mind, when Paul had no consciousness in his spirit of any special guidance from God, is clearly given by him when he wrote to the Corinthians that in one matter he had commandment (1 Cor. 7: 10), but in another he said, "I have no commandment of the Lord, but I give my judgment" (1 Cor. 7:25); in the one case he had the guidance through his spirit; in the other he used his mind, and clearly said so--see verse 40--"after my judgment."

Through ignorance a large majority of believers walk "after the soul," i.e., their mind and emotions, and think they are "walking after the spirit." The Satanic forces know this right well, and use all their wiles to draw the believer to live in his soul or body, sometimes flashing visions to the mind or giving exquisite sensations of joy, buoyancy of life, etc., to the body, and the believer "walks after the soul," and "after the body" as he follows these things, believing that he is following the Spirit of God.

Depending upon supernatural things given from outside, or spiritual experiences in the sense realm, checks the inward spiritual life through the spirit. By the experiences of the senses, instead of living in the true sphere of the spirit, the believer is drawn out to live in the outer man of his body; and ceasing to act from his centre, he is caught by the outer workings of the supernatural in his circumference, and loses the inner co-operation with God. The devil's scheme is therefore to make the believer cease walking after the spirit, and to draw him out into the realm of soul or body. Then the spirit, which is the organ of the Holy Spirit in conflict against a spiritual foe, drops into abeyance and is ignored, because the believer is occupied with the sense- experience. It is then practically out of action, either for guidance, power in service, or conflict.

THE COUNTERFEIT OF THE HUMAN SPIRIT

Evil spirits then seek to create a counterfeit of the spirit, and they do this by getting a footing in the person so as to produce other feelings than those of the spirit, then when these get a hold they become strong enough to silence or overpower the true spirit-action, or spiritual feelings. If the believer is ignorant of the tactics of the enemy in this way, he lets go the true spirit-action--or allows it to sink into disuse--and follows the counterfeit spiritual feelings, thinking he is walking after the spirit all the time.

When the true spirit-action ceases, the evil spirits suggest that God now guides through the "renewed mind," which is an attempt to hide their workings, and the man's disuse of his spirit. On the cessation of the spirit co-operation with the Holy Spirit, and counterfeit "spirit" feelings taking place in the body, counterfeit light to the mind, reasoning, judging, etc., follows, the man thus walking after mind and body, and not after the spirit, with the true illumination of the mind which comes from full operation of the Holy Spirit.

To further interfere with the true spirit life, the deceiving spirits seek to counterfeit the action of the spirit in burden and anguish. This they do by first giving a fictitious "Divine love" to the person, the faculty receiving it being the affections. When these affections are grasped fully by the deceivers, the sense of love passes away, and the man thinks he has lost God and all communion with God. Then follow feelings of constraint and restraint, which will develop into acute suffering, which the believer thinks is in the spirit, and of God. Now he goes by these feelings, calling them "anguish in the spirit," "groaning in the spirit," etc., whilst the deceiving spirits, through the sufferings given by them in the affections, compel the man to do their will.

All physical consciousness of supernatural things, and even undue consciousness of natural things, should be refused, as this diverts the mind from walking after the spirit, and sets it upon the bodily sensations. Physical consciousness is also an obstacle to the continuous concentration of the mind, and in a spiritual believer an "attack" of physical "consciousness" made use of by the enemy, may break concentration of the mind, and bring a cloud upon the spirit. The body should be kept calm, and under full control; excessive laughter should be avoided, and all "rushing" which rouses the physical life to the extent of dominating mind and spirit. Believers who desire to be "spiritual" and of "full age" in the life in God, should avoid excess, extravagance, and extremes in all things (See 1 Cor. 9: 25-27).

Because of the domination of the physical part of the man, and the emphasis placed upon supernatural experiences in the body, the body is made to do the work of the spirit, and is forced into a prominence, which hides the true spirit life. It feels the pressure, feels the conflict, and THUS BECOMES THE SENSE INSTEAD OF THE SPIRIT. Believers do not perceive where they feel. If they are questioned as to where they "feel," they cannot answer. They should learn to discriminate, and know how to discern the feelings of the spirit, which are neither emotional (soulish), or physical. (See for example Mark 8: 12; John 13: 21; Acts 18: 5 A.V.).

SOME DESCRIPTIONS OF THE SPIRIT

The spirit may be likened to the electric light. If the man's spirit is in contact with the Spirit of God it is full of light, apart from Him it is darkness. Indwelt by Him "the spirit of man is the candle of the Lord" (Prov. 20: 27). The spirit may also be likened to elastic; when it is bound, or pressed, or weighted, it ceases to act, or to be the source of power and "spring" so to speak, in the life. If a man feels weighted, he should find out what the weight is. If he is asked, "Is it your body?" he would probably say "No," but that he "feels bound inside." Then what is it that is "bound" or "weighted?" Is it not the spirit? The spirit can be compressed or expanded, up or down, in or out of place, bound or free. The possibilities and potentialities of the human spirit are only known when the spirit is joined to Christ, and united to Him is made strong to stand against the powers of darkness.

The great need of the Church is to know and understand the laws of the spirit, so as to co-work with the Spirit of God in fulfilling the purpose of God through His people. But the lack of knowledge of the spirit life has given the deceiving spirits of Satan the opportunity for the deceptions, of which we have spoken in the previous pages of this book.

Note—That the children of God may more readily discern the true workings of God from the counterfeits of Satan. A summary of some of these is given in concise form in "Supplementary Notes."

CHAPTER 10
Victory in Conflict

In a previous chapter we have seen the way of deliverance from possession by evil spirits. The great question here is, how to be victorious over the powers of darkness as a whole. How to have authority, and victory over the wicked spirits in place of their mastery over the believer; who, having learnt the devices of the enemy, and the way of deliverance, is now deeply concerned that others should be set free, and brought into the place of victory "over all the power of the enemy." For this he must now understand that the degree of Christ's "authority" the Spirit of God will energise him to exercise over the spirits of evil, will be according to the degree of victory he has over them in the personal conflict, which he must now settle down to face in the sphere of the spiritual life into which he has emerged.

DEGREES OF DELIVERANCE AND VICTORY

The believer needs to have thorough knowledge and understanding of their ways and works, and of the laws of the spirit, and how to keep in mastery of spirit in all the vicissitudes of life. As there are (1) degrees of deception, and degrees of possession and deliverance from possession; so there are (2) degrees of victory over the devil; (3) degrees of temptation, and victory over temptation.

The power to co-operate with the Holy Spirit in the wielding of Christ's authority will also be in degrees, and gained according to the aggressive spiritual strength obtained by overcoming the devil in his various workings; just as victory over sin deepens in its strength as the man overcomes temptation to sin; and victory over the world (1 John 5: 4-5) is increasingly known by faith in the Son of God. These degrees of overcoming power with the consequent degree of reward, are to be clearly seen in the Lord's call to the churches recorded in the Apocalypse. Degrees also of the future authority in the reigning with Christ are indicated in His words in one parable, "Be thou ruler over ten cities . . over five . ." (Luke 19: 17-19).

The believer delivered from deception and possession by the spirits of evil, must now learn to walk in personal victory over the devil at every point, if he is to have the fullest victory over the powers of darkness. For this, just as he needs to know the Lord Christ in all the aspects of His Name and character, so as to draw upon His power in living union with Him, so the believer must learn to know the adversary in his various workings, as described in his names and character, that he may be able to discern his presence, and all his wicked spirits, wheresoever they may be, either in attacks upon himself, in others, or working as "world-rulers" of the darkness in the world.

VICTORY OVER SATAN AS TEMPTER

Victory over the Devil as a Tempter, and all his temptations personally, direct and indirect, must be learnt by the believer in experimental reality; remembering that all "temptations" are not recognisable as temptations, nor are they always visible, for half their power lies in their being hidden.

A believer thinks that he will be as conscious of the approach of temptation, as of a person coming into the room, hence the children of God are only fighting a small proportion of the devil's workings; that is, only what they are conscious of as supernatural workings of evil. Because their knowledge of the devil's character and methods of working is limited and circumscribed, many true children of God only recognise "temptation" when the nature of the thing presented is visibly evil, and according to their limited knowledge of evil, so they do not recognise the Tempter and his temptations when they come under the guise of natural or physical, or lawful and apparent "good."

When the prince of darkness and his emissaries come as angels of light, they clothe themselves in light, which, in their case, stands for evil. It is a "light" which is really darkness. They come in the guise of good. Darkness is opposed to light, ignorance is opposed to knowledge, falsehood is opposed to truth. Darkness is a term applied to evil morality and moral darkness.

The believer may need to discern evil spirits in the realm of the supposed good. That which comes to them as "light" may be darkness. The apparently "good" may be really evil; the apparent "help" which they cling to may be really a hindrance.

For instance, a difficulty in work may arise out of accepting a degree of weakness, which is really the result of demon possession; so while desiring strength the believer may fulfil conditions which make him weak. The devil then tempts him because he is weak, and he succumbs.

There needs to be a choice between good and evil perpetually by every man, and the priests of old were specially called to discern and teach the people the difference between "the holy and the common," the "unclean and the clean" (Ezek. 40: 23). Yet is the Church of Christ today able thus to discern what is good, and what is evil? Does she not continually fall into the snare of calling good evil, and evil good? Because the thoughts of God's people are governed by ignorance, and limited knowledge, they call the works of God, of the devil; and the works of the devil, of God, and they are not taught the need of learning to discern the difference between the "unclean and the clean", nor how to decide for themselves what is of God, or what is of the devil, although they are unknowingly compelled to make a choice every moment of the day. Neither do all believers know that they have a choice between good and good, i.e., between the lesser and the greater good; and the devil often entangles them here.

VARIOUS KINDS OF TEMPTATIONS

There are unseen temptations, and temptations in the unseen. Physical temptations, soulish temptations, spiritual temptations; direct and indirect temptations, as with Christ when He was directly tempted in the wilderness, or indirectly through Peter.

The believer must not only resist the devil when he tempts visibly, or attacks consciously, but BY CONSTANT PRAYER HE MUST BRING TO LIGHT HIS HIDDEN AND COVERED TEMPTATIONS, knowing that he is a "Tempter," and therefore is always planning temptation for the believer. Those who thus, by prayer, bring to light these hidden workings, are by experience, widening their horizon in knowledge of his work as a Tempter, and becoming better able to co-work with the Spirit of God in the deliverance of others from the power of the enemy; for in order to be victorious over the powers of darkness, it is essential to be able to recognise what they are doing.

Paul, on one occasion, did not say "circumstances," but "Satan hindered me" (1 Thess. 2: 18), because he was able to recognise when circumstances, or the Holy Spirit (Acts 16: 6), or Satan, hindered or restrained him in his life and service. There are degrees also in the results of temptation. After the wilderness temptation, which settled vast and eternal issues, the devil left Christ, but he returned to Him again and again with other degrees of temptation (John 12: 27; Matt. 22: 15) both direct and indirect.

DIFFERENCE BETWEEN "TEMPTATION" AND "ATTACKS."

There is also a difference between the "temptations" and "attacks" of the Tempter, as may again be seen in the life of Christ. "Temptation" is a scheme or a plot, or compulsion on the part of the Tempter to cause another to do evil, whether consciously or unconsciously; but an attack is an onslaught on the person, either in life, character, or circumstances, e.g., the devil made an onslaught on the Lord through the villagers, when they sought to hurl Him over the brow of the hill (Luke 4: 29); when His family brought a charge of insanity against Him (Mark 3: 21); and when He was charged with demon possession by His enemies (John 10: 20; Matt. 12: 24).

Temptation, moreover, means suffering, as we see again in the life of Christ, for it is written, "He suffered being tempted" (Heb. 2: 18), and believers must not think they will reach a period when they will not feel the suffering of temptation, as this is a wrong conception, which gives ground to the enemy for tormenting and attacking them without cause.

PRAYER BRINGING HIDDEN TEMPTATIONS TO LIGHT

For perpetual victory, therefore, the believer must unceasingly be on guard against the Tempter, praying for his hidden temptations to be revealed. The degree of understanding his working will be determined by the degree of victory experienced, for "In vain is the net spread in the sight of any bird."

We have given in preceding chapters much knowledge needed by the believer, if he is to gain victory over every aspect of the Tempter's workings, but especially does he require power of discrimination between what is temptation from the Tempter working upon the uncrucified "old man"; tempting through the things of the world (1 John 2: 15, 16; 5: 4, 5); and temptation direct from the spirits of evil.

In temptation the crucial point is for the tempted one to know whether the temptation is the work of an evil spirit having gained access to him, or from the evil nature. This alone can be discerned by the experimental knowledge of Romans 6 as the basis of the life. Temptation from the fallen nature should be dealt with on the foundation of "Reckon ye also yourselves to be dead unto sin, but alive unto God in Christ Jesus" (Rom. 6: 11), and practical obedience to the resulting command "Let not sin reign in your mortal body."

In the hour of temptation to sin--to visible, known sin--the believer should take his stand on Romans 6: 6, as his deliberate position of faith, and in obedience to Romans 6: 11, declare his undeviating choice and attitude as death to sin, in death union with Christ. If this choice is the expression of his real will, and the temptation to sin does not cease, he should then deal with the spirits of evil, who may be seeking to awaken sinful desires (Jas. 1: 14), or to counterfeit them. For they can counterfeit the old nature in evil desire, evil thoughts, evil words, evil presentations, and many honest believers think they are battling with the workings of the old nature, when these things are given by evil spirits. But if the believer is not standing actively on Romans 6, the "counterfeits" are not necessary, for the old fallen creation is always open to be wrought upon by the powers of darkness.

VICTORY OVER SATAN AS ACCUSER VICTORY OVER THE DEVIL AS AN ACCUSER:

The difference between the accusation of the enemy and his temptations, is that the latter is an effort on his part to compel, or draw the man into sin; and the former is a charge of transgression. Temptation is an effort to cause the man to transgress the law, accusation is an effort to place the believer in the guilty position of having transgressed the law. Evil spirits want the man to be wrong, that they may accuse and punish him for being wrong.

"Accusation" can be a counterfeit of conviction--the true conviction of the Spirit of God. It is important that the believer should know when the charge of transgression is made, whether it is a Divine conviction, or a Satanic accusation. (1) The devil may accuse when the man is truly guilty; (2) he may accuse when the man is not guilty, and cause him to think, and believe that he is guilty; (3) he may endeavour to pass on his accusations as a conviction, and cause the man to think that it comes from the evil nature, when he is not guilty at all.

Evil spirits are able to infuse a sense of guilt. Sin itself comes from the evil nature within, but it is not forced into the personality from without, apart from the person. How can the believer tell if evil spirits are at the back of involuntary sin? If the man is right with God, standing on Romans 6, with no deliberate yielding to known sin, then any manifestation of sin coming back again unaccountably, may be dealt with as from evil spirits.

The believer must therefore never accept an accusation--or a charge, supernaturally made, of having transgressed--unless he is fully convinced by intelligent knowledge and clear decision that he has done so; for if he accepts the charge when innocent, he will suffer as much as if he had really transgressed. He must also be on guard to refuse any compulsory drive to "confession" of sin to others, which may be the forcing of the enemy to pass on his lying accusations.

BELIEVER SHOULD MAINTAIN NEUTRALITY TO ACCUSATIONS UNTIL SOURCE PROVED

The believer should maintain neutrality to accusations, until he is sure of their real source, and if the man knows he is guilty, he should at once go to God on the ground of 1 John 1: 9, and refuse to be lashed by the devil, as he is not the judge of God's children, nor is he deputed as God's messenger to make the charge of wrong. The Holy Spirit alone is commissioned by God to convict of sin. The steps in the working of evil spirits in their accusations and false charges, are these, when the believer accepts their accusations:-(1) The believer thinks and believes he is guilty; (2) Evil spirits cause him to feel guilty; (3) They cause him, then, to appear guilty; (4) They cause him then to be actually guilty through believing their lies, it matters not whether he is guilty or not in the first instance.

Malicious spirits try to make the man feel guilty by their nagging accusations, so as to make him act, or appear guilty before others; at the same moment flashing, or suggesting to others the very things about which they are accusing him, without any cause.

All such "feelings" should be investigated by the believer. Feeling wrong is not enough for a man to say he is wrong, or the Accuser to accuse him of being wrong. The man says he "feels" wrong. He should ask "Is the feeling right?" He may feel wrong, and be right; and "feel" right, and be wrong. Therefore he should investigate, and examine the question honestly, "Am I wrong?"

"FEELINGS" INJECTED BY EVIL SPIRITS

There are physical, soulish, and spiritual "feelings." Evil spirits can inject feelings into either of these departments. Their aim is to move the man by "feelings" to substitute these for the action of his mind, so that the believer is governed by the deceiving spirits through his feelings. Also to substitute feelings for the conscience in its recognition of right and wrong. If believers "feel" they can do a thing, they do it, without asking whether it be right or wrong, if it is not visibly sinful.

For victory over the deceitful enemy, it is essential that the children of God cease to be guided by "feelings" in their actions. Again: If believers in any course of action "feel relief," they think that sense of relief is a sign that they have been doing God's will. But a man gets rest when his work is done, not only in the spiritual, but in ordinary life.

A "sense of relief" in any line of action, is no criterion that it is in the will of God. The action must be judged by itself, and not merely by its effects upon the doer of it. For instance, a believer says he "felt happy" after doing such and such a thing, and that it was "a proof that he was doing the will of God"; but peace and rest and relief are no proof at all of being in God's will. Believers also think that if they do some action that the devil wants them to do, they will "feel condemned" at once, but they overlook the fact that Satan can give pleasant feelings.

There are innumerable variations of feelings caused by evil spirits, from countless attacks, and countless false suggestions, which call forth all the spiritual discernment of the believer, and his understanding of spiritual things, to recognise them.

NEED OF DISCERNING ACCUSATION FROM TRUE CONVICTION

The devil as a Tempter very quickly becomes the Accuser, even if he does not succeed in getting the man to yield to his temptations. As we have seen, deceiving spirits can cause apparent "sin" to be manifested to the consciousness of a believer, and then lash and accuse the man for their own workings.

They counterfeit some sin, which may be called with sadness, "my besetting sin," in the believer's life; and as long as it is believed to be sin from the evil nature, no "confessing" or seeking victory over it, will cause it to pass away.

They can also hide behind real sin. A sense of guiltlessness does not necessarily lead to absolute happiness, for even with the peace of conscious innocence there may be suffering, and the suffering have its source in some sin which is not known.

Walking by known light, and measuring his guiltlessness by his knowledge of known sin, is very dangerous to him who desires a fathomless peace, for it leads only to superficial rest, which may be disturbed at any moment by the attacks of the Accuser, who directs his darts to a joint in the armour of peace, hidden from the believer's view.

For obtaining victory over the Deceiver's accusing spirits, spiritual believers should, therefore, understand clearly whether any consciousness of sin, is the result of real transgression, or is caused by evil spirits. If the believer accepts the consciousness of sin, as from himself, when it is not, he at once leaves his position of death to sin, and reckons himself alive to it.

This explains why many who have truly known victory over sin by the "reckon" of Romans 6: 11, surrender their basis, and lose the position of victory; because the Accuser has counterfeited some manifestation of "self" or "sin," and then accused the man of it, with the taunt that " Romans 6 does not work," and by this device made him surrender his basis of victory, causing him to fall into confusion, and condemnation, as into a pit of miry clay and darkness.

NEED OF UNFLINCHING WARFARE AGAINST SIN

On the other hand, if the believer in the slightest degree is tempted to treat sin lightly, or attribute it to evil spirits when it is from himself, he is equally on false ground, and lays himself open to the old fallen nature regaining mastery over him with redoubled force. The warfare against Satan must be accompanied with a vigorous, unflinching warfare against sin. Any known sin must not be tolerated for a moment. Whether it be from the fallen nature, or from evil spirits forcing it into the man, it MUST BE CAST OFF AND PUT AWAY; on the basis of Rom. 6: 6 and 12.

Two misconceptions which give great advantage to the watching enemy are the thoughts in many believers' minds, that if a Christian commits sin he will at once (1) know it himself, or (2) that God will tell him. They, therefore, expect God to tell them when they are right or wrong, instead of seeking light and knowledge according to John 3: 21.

Believers seeking victory over all the deceptions of the enemy, must take an active part in dealing with sin. Based upon a wrong conception of "death" they may have thought that God would remove sin out of their lives for them, with the result that they have failed to actively co-work with Him in dealing with evil, within and in their environment, in others and in the world.

For a life of perpetual victory over Satan as Accuser, it is very important that the believer should understand, and detect any inconsistency between the attitude of the will and the actions in his life. He should read himself from his actions as well as from his will and motives. For instance, a person is charged with doing a certain thing, which he at once denies, because the action does not agree with his will-attitude, and therefore, he says, it is impossible that he should have acted or spoken in the way stated. The believer judges himself by his own inner standpoint of will and motives, and not by his actions as well as his will. (1 Cor. 11: 31).

On the Godward side the cleansing power of the Blood of Christ is needed (1 John 1:7) continuously for those who seek to walk in the light, cleansing themselves from all defilement of flesh and spirit, perfecting holiness in the fear of God. (2 Cor. 7: 1).

The devil as an Accuser also works indirectly through others, inciting them to make accusations which he wants the man to accept as true, and thus open the door to him to make them true; or he accuses the believer to others by "visions" or "revelations" about him, which causes them to misjudge him. In any case, whatever may come to the believer from man or devil, LET HIM MAKE USE OF IT FOR PRAYER, and by prayer turn all accusations into steps to victory.

VICTORY OVER SATAN AS A LIAR

VICTORY OVER THE DEVIL AS A LIAR (John 8: 44): "He was a murderer from the beginning, and stood not in the truth, because there is no truth in him. When he speaketh a lie, he speaketh of his own; for he is a liar, and the father thereof." This does not mean that the enemy never tells the truth, but his truth has the objective of getting the believer involved in evil; e.g., when the spirit of divination spoke the truth, that Paul and Silas were the servants of God, it was to suggest the lie that Paul and Silas derived their power from the same source as the girl under the evil spirit's power. The devil and his wicked spirits will speak, or use, ninety-nine parts of truth to float one lie, but Paul was not deceived by the witness of a soothsaying prophetess acknowledging their divine authority. He discerned the wicked spirit and its purpose, exposed it, and cast it out.

Even so must the believer be able to triumph over Satan as a liar, and be able to recognise his lies, and those of lying spirits, in whatever form they are presented to him. This he does by knowing the truth, and using the weapon of truth.

VICTORY OVER FALSEHOOD BY TRUTH

There is no way of victory over falsehood but by truth. To have victory over the devil as a liar, and over his lies, the believer must be determined always to know the truth, and speak the truth about everything, in himself, in others, and around him.

Satan the liar, through his lying spirits, persistently pours lies on the believer all day long; lies into his thoughts about himself, his feelings, his condition, his environment; lies misinterpreting everything in himself, and around him; about others with whom he is in contact; lies about the past and the future; lies about God; and lies about himself, magnifying his power and his authority. To have victory over this persistent stream of lies from the father of lies, the believer must fight (1) with the weapon of God's truth in the written Word, and (2) truth about facts in himself, others and circumstances. How persistently to "refuse" all lies from the Liar, and his emissaries, is explained in other parts of this book. As the believer increasingly triumphs over the devil as a liar, he grows better able to discern his lies, and equipped to strip away the covering for others.

VICTORY OVER SATAN AS A COUNTERFEITER

VICTORY OVER THE DEVIL AS A COUNTERFEITER, OR FALSE "ANGEL OF LIGHT": "Even Satan himself fashioneth himself into an angel of light," and his "ministers" ("false apostles, deceitful workers," 2 Cor. 11: 13) also fashion themselves as "ministers of righteousness" (2 Cor. 11: 14-15). This aspect of victory over Satan runs on the same lines as the preceding ones; i.e., by the knowledge of truth, enabling the believer to recognise the lies of Satan, when he presents himself under the guise of light.

Light is the very nature of God Himself. To recognise darkness when clothed in light-supernatural light--needs deep knowledge of the true light, and a power to discern the innermost sources of things that in appearance look God-like and beautiful. How the Adversary counterfeits the very light of God, so as to appear as God, has been already set forth in Chapter 6. The main attitude for this aspect of victory over the Adversary, is a settled position of neutrality to all supernatural workings, until the believer knows what is of God. If any experience is accepted without question, how can its Divine origin be guaranteed? The basis of acceptance or rejection must be knowledge. The believer must know, and he cannot know without examination, nor will he "examine" unless he maintains the attitude of "Believe not every spirit" until he has "tested" and proved what is of God.

VICTORY OVER SATAN AS A HINDERER

VICTORY OVER THE DEVIL As HINDERER: "We would fain have come unto you . . . but Satan hindered us" (1 Thess. 2: 18), wrote Paul, who was able to discern between the hindering of Satan, and the restraining of the Holy Spirit of God (Acts 16: 6). This again means knowledge, and power to discern Satan's workings and Schemings, and the obstacles he places in the paths of the children of God; obstacles which look so "natural," and so like "Providence," that numbers meekly bow their heads and allow the Hinderer to prevail.

Power to discern comes (1) by knowledge that Satan can hinder; (2) by observing the objective of the hindrances, and (3) close observation of his methods along this line; e.g., is it God or Satan withholding money from missioners preaching the Gospel of Calvary, and giving abundance to those who preach error, and teachings which are the outcome of the spirit of anti- Christ?

Is it God or Satan hindering a believer by "circumstances," or, "sickness," from vital service important to the Church of God? Is it God or Satan urging a family to remove their residence, without reasonable grounds, to another neighbourhood, when it involves the removal of another member from a strategic vantage ground of service to God, with no other worker to take his place? Is it God or Satan leading Christians to put first their (1) health, (2) comfort, (3) social position, in their decisions, rather than the needs and the exigencies of the kingdom of God? Is it God or Satan who "hinders" service for God through members of a family making objections; or troubles in business which give no time for such service; or through property losses, etc.? Knowledge of the Hinderer, means victory by prayer over his schemes, and workings. The believer should therefore know his wiles.

VICTORY OVER SATAN AS MURDERER

VICTORY OVER THE DEVIL AS A MURDERER (John 8: 44): Satan as the prince of death watches every occasion to take the life of the servants of God, if in any wise he can get them to fulfil conditions which enable him to do so. (1) By their willful insistence on going into danger without being sent of God; (2) by trapping them into danger through visions, or supernatural guidance, drawing them into actions which enable him to work behind the laws of nature for destroying their lives. This is what Satan tried to do with Christ in the wilderness temptation: "Throw Thyself down," he said; then quoting Scripture to show that the Lord had Scriptural warrant for believing that angel hands would bear Him up (Luke 4: 11), and not allow Him to fall. But the Son of God recognised the Tempter and the Murderer. He knew that His life would end as a Man, were He to give occasion to the malignant hate of Satan, by one step out of God's will; and that the Deceiver would not propose anything, however apparently innocent, or seemingly for God's glory, unless some great scheme for his own ends was deeply hidden in his proposition.

Christ now holds the "keys of death and of Hades" (Rev. 1: 18), and "him that hath the power of death, that is, the devil" (Heb. 2: 14, R.V., m.), cannot exercise his power WITHOUT PERMISSION, but when the children of God, knowingly or unknowingly, fulfil the conditions which give Satan ground to attack their physical lives, the Lord with "the keys of death" works according to law, and does not save them, UNLESS BY THE WEAPON OF PRAYER they enable God to interpose, and give them victory over the law of death, as well as the law of sin, through "the law of the Spirit of life in Christ Jesus" (Rom. 8: 2).

"The last enemy that shall be destroyed is death." Death is therefore an enemy; to be recognised as an enemy; and to be resisted as an enemy. The believer may lawfully "desire to depart and be with Christ" (Phil. 1: 23), but never to desire death merely as an end of "trouble," or to allow the lawful desire to be "with Christ," make him YIELD TO DEATH WHEN HE IS NEEDED FOR THE SERVICE OF THE CHURCH OF GOD. "To abide in the flesh is needful for you," wrote the Apostle to the Philippians, therefore "I know that I shall abide" (Phil. 1: 24-25).

BELIEVERS SHOULD RESIST DEATH AS AN ENEMY

The will of the believer "will"-ing physical death, gives the Adversary power of death over that one, and no believer should yield to a "desire to die" until he knows beyond question that God has released him from further service to His people. That a believer is "ready to die" is a very small matter; he must be ready to live, until he is sure that his life work is finished. God does not harvest His corn until it is ripe, and His redeemed children should be "garnered as a shock of corn in its season."

It is ofttimes the prince of death as a Murderer, working through the ignorance of God's children, (1) as to his power, (2) the conditions by which they give him power, and (3) the victory of prayer by which they resist his power, who cuts off God's soldiers from the battlefield. It is Satan as a Murderer, who gives "visions of glory," "longings to die," to workers of value to the Church of God, so that they yield to death, even in days of active service, and slowly fade away.

Believers who would have victory over Satan at every point, must resist his attack on the body, as well as on the spirit and mind. They must seek knowledge of God's laws for the body, so as to obey those laws, and give no occasion to Satan to slay them. They should know the place of the body in the spiritual life; (1) its prominence, and yet (2) its obscurity. Paul said, "I keep under my body." They must understand that the more knowledge they have of the devices and power of the Adversary, and of the fullness of the Calvary victory within their reach for complete victory over him, the more he will plan to injure them. The whole of his schemes against God's children may be summed up under three heads: (1) To cause them to sin, as he tempted Christ in the wilderness; (2) To slander them, as Christ was slandered by family and foes; (3) To slay them, as Christ was slain at Calvary, when, by the direct permission of God, the hour and power of darkness gathered around Him, and He by the hands of wicked men was crucified and slain (Acts 2: 23).

As the believer gains victories over Satan, and his deceiving and lying spirits, by thus recognising, resisting and triumphing over them in their varied workings, his strength of spirit to conquer them grows stronger; and he will become more and more equipped to give the truth of the finished work of Calvary as sufficient for victory over sin and Satan; in the power and authority of Christ by the Holy Spirit; which will set others free from their power.

CONFLICT AND ATTACK

It will, of course, be clearly recognised that victory over Satan in these aspects will not be without great onslaughts from him and sharp conflict, which may well be called "the evil day" (Eph. 6: 13). In these attacks and conflicts there are some points which need to be understood. First, that it is always essential to know whether the attack and conflict are because of ground in oneself or others. For one reason why believers get attacks, and do not get through the conflict into victory, is because the cause of the attack and conflict lies in themselves.

POSSIBLE FRESH GROUND

The believer must understand that although he has been delivered from the deception and possession he fell into, yet in the succeeding life of aggressive warfare against the powers of darkness, he may again give fresh ground to the enemy through lack of knowledge, by accepting some lie from lying spirits, or by taking their misinterpretations of experiences, conditions, etc. For it must never be forgotten that wrong interpretation of any experience gives new ground to them, GROUND BEING ANYTHING IN A PERS0N WHEREBY EVIL SPIRITS GAIN. The believer may attribute the attack and conflict to a wrong cause, i.e., (1) to an outside cause, or (2) to the maliciousness of the devil, or (3) to "local" conflict; meaning the enemy's workings around him in his environment, or through others.

When attacks and conflict come, lest he should give fresh ground to the enemy, the believer must know why they come, and in prayer ask God for light. In attacks, two or more may be in action simultaneously, therefore he should at once set himself to understand, and watch and observe all the workings of the enemy in the new conflict, or anything that will throw light on the situation, and show him what to refuse, and how to pray.

POSSIBLE WRONG WEAPONS

When there is ground, or the cause of the conflict or attack is in the believer himself, if he takes the attack pure conflict, i.e., as part of warfare for the Church, he will fight with the wrong weapons, and not get through to victory until the true cause is discovered, and the ground given up, and refused. For what is thought to be an "attack" from outside, may be a symptom, or manifestation of an evil spirit inside, who has regained a footing unknown to the believer, or has remained in some hidden location, when thought to have wholly gone. When the believer, therefore, finds himself in conflict, he should at once question "Is there ground?" in the following three aspects of the evil spirit's workings:--

(1) In attacks. Is there ground, or is it purely an attack?
(2) In conflict. Is there ground, or is it pure conflict?
(3) In communication, (i.e., suggestions, thoughts, whisperings of the enemy). "Is there ground?" or is it purely from outside, as Satan communicated with Eve ?

The believer should then declare his attitude in the three cases, as follows: "I refuse all ground, and the cause or causes of it!"

The last word spoken, alters, ratifies, or nullifies previous ones; for instance, the believer may "refuse" in the present moment, what may be the product through evil spirits' workings of something he asked for in the past. He may say, "Although I asked for, believed in, and accepted such and such a thing in the past, I now refuse it." His present refusal nullifies his previous acceptance.

THE VALUE AND PURPOSE OF "REFUSING."

THE PRINCIPLE EMBODIED IN REFUSING: It is essential that believers should understand the value of the act of refusal, and the expression of it. Briefly: REFUSAL IS THE OPPOSITE OF ACCEPTANCE. Evil spirits have gained by the believer giving them (1) ground, (2) right of way, (3) use of their faculties, etc., and they lose when this is all withdrawn from them. What was given to the enemy by misconception and ignorance, and given with the consent of the will, stands as ground for them to work on and through; until, by the same action of the will, the "giving" is revoked, specifically and generally. The will in the past was unknowingly put for evil, and it must now be put unceasingly against it.

Once understood, the principle is very simple. The choice of the will gives: the choice of the will withdraws or nullifies the previous giving. The value and purpose of refusing stands the same toward God and toward Satan. The man gives to God, or refuses to give. He takes from God, or refuses to take. He gives to evil spirits--unknowingly or not--and he refuses to give. He finds he has given to them unwittingly, and he nullifies it by an act of withdrawal and refusal.

THE RELATION OF FRESH GROUND GIVEN, TO THE VICTORY IN CONFLICT

The relation to the aggressive warfare of freshly discovered "ground" given to deceiving spirits, is, that every new ground, discovered as given to them, and refused, means a renewed liberation of the spirit, with an access of deepened enmity to the foe as his subtle deceptions are increasingly exposed, and consequently more war upon Satan and his minions. It means more deliverance from their power, and less footing for their possession, or ground in the believer as he realises that "symptoms," "effects," and "manifestations" are not abstract "things," but revelations of active personal agencies against whom he must war persistently.

Moreover all growth in experimental knowledge means increased protection against the deceiving enemy. As new ground is revealed, and fresh truth about the powers of darkness, and the way of victory over them, is understood, the truth delivers from their deceptions, and hence protects the believer up to the extent of his knowledge, from further deception; and he finds in experience that directly the truth ceases to operate by the believer's active use of it, he is open to attack from the watching foe, who ceaselessly plans against him. For example, let the believer who has been undeceived and dispossessed cease to use the truth, of (1) the existence of evil spirits; (2) their persistent watching to deceive him again; (3) the need of perpetual resistance and fight against them; (4) the keeping of his spirit in purity and strength in co-operation with the Spirit of God; and other truths parallel with these--the knowledge of which he has gained through so much suffering--he will sink down again into passivity, and possibly deeper depths of deception. For the Holy Spirit NEEDS THE BELIEVER'S USE OF TRUTH to work with in energising and strengthening him for conflict and victory, and does not guard him from the enemy apart from his co-operation in watching and prayer.

PERSISTENT REFUSAL OF GROUND TO EVIL SPIRITS

The way to refuse, and what to refuse, is of primary importance in the hour of conflict. As we have seen, the believer needs to maintain an active attitude, and, when necessary, expression of refusal continually and persistently, this pre-supposing the man standing in faith upon the foundation of his identification in death with Christ at Calvary.

In the hour of conflict, lest there should have been new ground given to evil spirits unknowingly, by accepting something from them, or believing some lie they have d to the mind, the believer should refuse all the things whereby they may have gained a new footing; the conflict, or attack, immediately passing away or ceasing, directly the means by which the enemy has regained ground is dealt with.

The believer himself will know, from his past experience, most of the ways by which the deceiving spirits have hitherto gained advantage over him; and he will instinctively turn to the points of refusal which have been of the most service to him in his fight to freedom. The refusing in this way takes ground from them in many directions. The widest scope covered by the act and attitude of refusal, the more thoroughly is the believer separating himself, BY HIS CHOICE, from the deceiving spirits, who can only hold their ground by the consent of his will. By refusing all he once accepted from them he can become comparatively clear of ground to them, so far as his choice and attitude is concerned.

REFUSAL AN AGGRESSIVE WEAPON IN CONFLICT

In the hour of conflict, when the forces of darkness are pressing upon the believer, the expression of his active refusal becomes an aggressive warfare upon them, as well as a defensive weapon. It is then as though the will at the centre of " Mansoul, " instead of sinking down in fear and despair when the enemy assaults the city, issues forth in aggressive resistance against the foe, by declaring its attitude against him. The battle turns upon the choice of the will in the citadel being maintained, in unshaken refusal to yield to, or admit any one of the attacking spirits of evil. The whole power of God, by the Holy Spirit, will be at the back of the active resistance of the man in his attitude of refusal to the enemy.

It is important to understand the effectiveness of this refusal of the will, on the part of the undeceived believer, as a barrier against the foe, because the outer man, in "feelings, " and nervous system, bears the scars long after his deliverance from the pit of deception into which he has been beguiled. When once the wall of the outer man has been broken into by supernatural forces of evil, it is not quickly rebuilt so that they cease to have any effect upon it in times of severe conflict. Believers who are emerging from deception and possession, should therefore know the power of an aggressive turning upon the enemy in the moment of his attacking them, with an active expression of their choice and will in regard to him. In such a way the aggressive becomes a defensive action. The believer in conflict may say with effect:

"I refuse all the authority of evil spirits over me: their right to me: their claims upon me: their power in me: their influence in or upon me .. ."

The same weapon of refusing works in many phases of the conflict; for example, in speaking or writing, if the believer is conscious of difficulties, obstacles, or interference in what be is doing, he should at once refuse all ideas, thoughts, suggestions, visions (i.e., pictures to the mind words, impressions, the spirits of evil may be seeking to insert, or press upon him, so that he may be able to co-operate with the Holy Spirit, and have a clarified mind for the carrying out of His will.

That is, the believer by his refusal, and resistance of all supernatural attempts to interfere with his outer man; is actively to resist the powers of darkness, whilst he seeks to co-work with the Holy Spirit within his spirit. At first this means much conflict, but as he maintains active resistance, and increasingly closes his whole being to the spirits of evil, and is on the alert to recognise, and refuse their workings, his union with the Risen Lord deepens, his spirit grows strong, his vision pure, his mental faculties clear to realise a perpetual victory over the foes who once had him in their power.

Especially is he on guard against, what may be described as, the "double counterfeits" of the deceiving spirits. That is, the counterfeits by the enemy in connection with attacks upon himself. For example, the devil attacks him manifestly and visibly, so that he clearly knows it to be an onslaught of the spirit beings of evil. He prays, resists, gets through to victory in his will and spirit. Then comes a great "feeling" of peace, and rest, which may be as much an "attack" as the onslaught, but more subtle and liable to mislead the believer if he is not on guard. The enemy suddenly retreating and ceasing the furious attack, hopes to gain the advantage by the second which he failed to obtain in the first.

FIGHTING FROM PRINCIPLE

It is essential to understand how to "fight," so to speak, "in cold blood"; i.e., wholly apart from feelings of any kind; for the believer may "feel" it is "victory" when it is defeat, and vice versa. All dependence upon feeling, and acting from "impulse" must be put aside in this warfare. Before the man received the Baptism of the Spirit, he acted from principle in the natural realm, and he must now come back to that same position as a spiritual man. Some can only recognise "conflict" when they are conscious of it, so to speak; they fight spasmodically, or by accident, when forced to it by necessity; but now the "fight" must be permanent and part of the very life. There is a ceaseless recognition of the forces of darkness in "cold blood," because of knowledge of what they are, and a consequent "fight" from principle. A fight against the unseen foes when there is nothing to be seen of their presence, or workings, remembering that they do not always attack when they can, i.e., if they were to attack on some occasions, they would lose by it, because it would reveal the character of the thing and the source.

The believer knows that the devil, as a Tempter, is always tempting, and therefore, he resists from principle. In brief, he who desires perpetual victory, must understand that it is a question of principle versus feeling, and consciousness. It can only be intermittent victory if the warfare is governed by the latter rather than the former. For instance, when the enemy attacks the believer, he will find a strong, primary weapon of victory in declaring deliberately, his basic position toward sin and Satan, as standing on the Calvary ground of Rom. 6: 6-11. The man reckoning himself in the present moment "dead indeed unto sin, and alive unto God," refuses to yield to sin and Satan, in any, or all of the points, or cause, or causes, of the attack or conflict.

As the believer thus declares his position in the hour of conflict and onslaught from the foe, he will often find himself obliged to wrestle in real combat with the invisible enemy. Standing on the finished work of Christ in death to sin, the spirit of the man becomes liberated for action, and energised to stand against the hierarchic hosts of Satan, the principalities and powers, the world-rulers of the darkness and the hosts of wicked spirits in the heavenly (or spiritual) sphere.

WRESTLING AND WHAT IT MEANS

It is only possible to wrestle against the powers of darkness, by the spirit. It is a spiritual warfare, and can only be understood by the spiritual man, that is, a man who lives by and is governed by his spirit. Evil spirits attack, wrestle with, and resist the believer. Therefore he must fight them, wrestle with them, and resist them. This wrestling is not with soul or body, but with the spirit; for the lesser cannot wrestle with the higher. Body wrestles with body in the physical realm; in the intellectual, soul with soul; and in the spiritual, spirit with spirit. But the powers of darkness attack the three- fold nature of man, and through body or soul seek to reach the spirit of man. If the fight is a mental one, the will should be used in decisive action, quietly and steadily. If it is a spirit fight, all the forces of the spirit should be brought to join the mind. If the spirit is pressed down and unable to resist, then there should be a steady mental fight when the mind, as it were, stretches out its hand to lift up the spirit.

The objective of evil spirits is to get the spirit down, and thus render the believer powerless to take the aggressive against them; or else they seek to push the spirit beyond its due poise and measure, into an effervescence which carries the believer beyond the control of his volition and mind, and hence off guard against the subtle foe; or incapable of exercising due balance of speech, action, thought, discrimination, so that under cover they may regain ground, or some advantage for themselves. A GREAT VICTORY MEANS GREAT DANGER, because when the believer is occupied with it, the devil is scheming how to rob him of it. The hour of victory therefore calls for soberness of mind, and watching unto prayer, for a little over-elation may mean its loss and a long sore fight back to full victory.

When the spirit triumphs in the wrestling and gains the victory, there breaks out, as it were, a stream from the spirit, of triumph and resistance against the invisible, but very real foe; but sometimes in the conflict the enemy succeeds in blocking the spirit through his attack on body or soul.

The spirit needs soul and body for expression, hence the enemy's attacks to close the spirit up, so as to render the man unable to act in resistance against him. When this takes place the believer thinks that he is "reserved," because he feels "shut up"; or he has "no voice to refuse"; in audible prayer the "words seem empty," he "feels no effect," it seems a "mockery," but in truth it is that the spirit is closing up through the wrestling enemy gripping, holding and binding it. The believer must now insist on EXPRESSING HIMSELF IN VOICE, until the spirit breaks through into liberty. This is "the word of testimony" which is said, in Rev. 12: 11, to be part of the overcoming power over the dragon. The wrestling believer stands on the (1) ground of the Blood of the Lamb, which includes all that the finished work of Calvary means in victory over sin and Satan; he (2) gives the word of his testimony in affirming his attitude to sin and Satan, and the sure, certain victory through Christ; and (3) he lives in the Calvary spirit, with his life surrendered to do the will of God, even unto death.

PRAYER AND PERSONAL CONFLICT

Closely bound up with the wrestling of the spirit is the necessity of prayer. Not so much the prayer of petition to a Father, as the prayer of one joined in Spirit with the Son of God, with the will fused with His, declaring to the enemy the authority of Christ over all their power (Ephes. 1: 20-23).

Sometimes the believer has to "wrestle" in order to pray; at other times to pray in order to wrestle. If he cannot "fight" he must pray, and if he cannot pray he must "fight. " For example, if the believer is conscious of a weight on his spirit, he must get rid of the weight by refusing all the "causes" of the weight; for it is necessary to keep the spirit unburdened to fight, and to retain power of detection. The delicate spirit-sense becomes dull under "weights," or pressure upon it, hence the enemy's ceaseless tactics to get "burdens" or pressure on the spirit, unrecognised as from the foe, or else recognised and allowed to remain.

The man may feel "bound up" and the cause be in others, i.e. (1) no open spirit or open mind in another to receive from the spirit and mind of the one who feels bound up; (2) no capacity in the other to receive any message of truth; (3) some thought in the mind of the other, checking the flow from the spirit.

If in the morning the believer finds a "weight" or heaviness on his spirit, and it is undealt with, he is sure to lose the position of victory through the day. In dealing with weight on the spirit, the moment it is recognised, the believer must at once act in spirit, and (1) stand (Eph. 6: 14); (2) withstand (Eph. 6: 13); and resist (Jas. 4:7) the powers of darkness. Each of these positions means spirit-action, for these words do not describe a "state," or an "attitude" (which is mainly an attitude of the will), or an act by soul or body.

To "stand" is a spirit-action repelling an aggressive move of the enemy; to "withstand" is to make an aggressive move against them; and to "resist" is actively to fight with the spirit, as a man "resists" with his body another who is physically attacking him.

THE WILES OF THE DEVIL

The word "wiles" in the original means "methods," and bears in its varied forms, the thought of "craft," or artifice; to "work by method," to over-reach, to outwit, to go in pursuit; also the thought of system, or a way, or a method of doing things.

Satan's war on the saints can be summed up in the one word "Wiles of the devil." He does not work in the open but always behind cover. The methods of the deceiving spirits are adapted to each one, with a skill and cunning gained by years of experience. Generally the wiles are primarily directed against the mind, or "thoughts," and apart from yielding to known sin, most of the workings of Satan in a believer's life may be traced back to a wrong thought or belief, admitted into the mind, and not recognised to be from deceiving spirits, e.g., if a believer only thinks and believes that all that Satan does is manifestly bad, Satan has only to clothe himself with "good" to gain full credence with that man. The war, therefore, is a war of deceit and counterfeit, and only those can stand against all the wiles of the deceiver, who seek the fullest truth from God, about God, Satan and themselves.

KNOWING THE WILES OF THE DEVIL

The Apostle said that the believer was to be able to stand against the wiles of the devil, and that he was to put on the whole armour for doing this. How can a man stand against a wile, if he does not know what the wile is? There is a difference between temptation and wiles; between the principles, and working of Satan and his emissaries, and their wiles; i.e., they themselves are tempters. Temptation is not a wile. A wile is the way they scheme to tempt. Paul did not say that the believer must stand against "temptations" or lies, or mention any other specific characteristic of evil spirits; but he must be "able to stand" against their wiles. The spiritual man is to be on guard lest he is caught by their wiles. If they can be detected, then their objective can be frustrated and destroyed. The spiritual man needs the fullest concentration, and sagacity of mind for reading quickly his spirit sense, and detecting the active operations of the foe; he also requires alertness in using the message his spirit conveys to him. A spiritual believer ought to be able to read the sense of his spirit, with the same instinctive adroitness, as a person recognises the physical sense of cold, when he feels a draught, and immediately uses his mental intelligence for actively protecting himself from it. So the spiritual man needs to use his spirit sense in locating and dislodging the foe by prayer.

Again, an "objective" and a "wile" are quite distinct. The wile is a means used by the foe to gain an objective. The evil spirits must use "wiles" to carry out their objective. Their objective is possession, but their "wiles" will be counterfeits. They are liars, but how can they succeed in getting their lies into the mind of a man? They do not need wiles to make themselves liars, but they need the wile to get the lie accepted by the believer.

The wiles of the devil and his emissaries are countless, and fitted to the believer. If he is to be moved by suffering from any course of action detrimental to their interests, they will play upon his sympathies by the suffering they cause to one near and dear to him; or if he shrinks from suffering in himself, they will work upon this to make him change his course. To those who are naturally sympathetic, they will use the counterfeit of love; those who can be attracted by intellectual things will be drawn from the spiritual sphere by being driven to over study, or be given mental attractions of many kinds. Whilst others, who are over sensitive and conscientious, may be constantly charged with blame for apparently continuous failure. The lying spirits lash the person for what they themselves do, but if the believer understands how to refuse all blame from them, he can use their very doings as a weapon against them.

THE ARMOUR FOR THE CONFLICT

For this conflict with the powers of darkness the believer must learn experimentally how to take and use the armour for the battle, described by the apostle in Ephes. 6. The objective in Ephesians 6 is clearly not victory over sin--this is assumed--but VICTORY OVER SATAN. The call is not to the world, but to the Church. A call to stand in armour; to stand in the evil day; to stand against the powers of darkness; to stand after accomplishing the work of overthrowing them--"having overcome all," verse 13, A.V. m.--by the strength given of God.

The armour in detail, as set forth in Ephes. 6 is provided that the child of God should be "ABLE to stand" against the wiles of the devil; clearly showing that a believer can be made able to conquer all the principalities and powers of hell, if he fulfils the necessary conditions, and uses the armour provided for him.

It must be a REAL ARMOUR if it is provided for meeting a REAL FOE, and it must demand a REAL KNOWLEDGE of it on the part of the believer; to whom the FACT of the provision, the FACT of the foe, and the FACT of the fight, must be as REAL FACTS as any other facts declared in the Scriptures. The armoured and non- armoured believer may be briefly contrasted as follows:The believer who takes up the whole armour of God as a covering and protection against the foe, must himself walk in victory over the enemy. He must have (1) his spirit indwelt by the Holy Spirit, so that he is strengthened with the might of God to stand unshaken; and be given continuously a "supply of the Spirit of Jesus" to keep his spirit sweet and pure; (2) his mind renewed (Rom. 12: 2) so that he has his understanding filled with the light of truth (Eph. 1: 18) displacing Satan's lies, and destroying the veil with which Satan once held it; the mind clarified so that he intelligently understands what the will of the Lord is; (3) his body subservient to the Spirit (1 Cor. 9: 25), and obedient to the will of God in life and service.

The armoured Christian.

Armoured with truth.

Righteousness of life.

Making and keeping peace.

Self-preservation and control.

Faith as a shield.

Scriptures in the hand.

Prayer without ceasing.

The non-armoured Christian

Open to lies, through ignorance.

Unrighteousness through ignorance.

Divisions and quarrels.

Reckless unwatchfulness.

Doubt and unbelief.

Relying on reason instead God's Word.

Relying on work without prayer.

CHAPTER 11
War upon the Powers of Darkness

In the path to freedom from deception and possession, the believer discovers the need of MAKING WAR AGAINST THE POWERS OF DARKNESS, for the undeceiving and the dispossession which follows, reveals to him the depths of the wickedness of Satan and his hosts of wicked spirits. The believer sees that he must (1) make war against their possession of him; (2) against all their works; and (3) against their deception and possession of others, as well as the need of a perpetual daily fighting against all their onslaughts, which come upon him apart from his giving them ground.

The believer who is dispossessed is born into the war, and compelled to fight to maintain his freedom. Just as a child is born into the natural world, and must breathe to maintain life, so there is a birth into the warfare through the sufferings and pains of being undeceived, and delivered from the thraldom of Satan.

Through his aggressive warfare against the foe, the believer understands the systematic workings of the forces of Satan. Through the knowledge gained by reading the symptoms of deception and possession in his own case, he is now able to read them in others, and see their need of deliverance, and finds himself compelled to pray for them, and work toward that goal.

AGGRESSIVE AND DEFENSIVE WARFARE

In war, whether natural or supernatural, there are two principles governing the warfare, viz.: aggressive and defensive, i.e., the attacking force must be able to defend itself as well as to take the aggressive against the enemy. Between the period of undeceiving and dispossessing, the believer learns to know his weak points, and vulnerable parts; and becomes able to recognise the methodical, planned and systematic attacks of the forces of the enemy upon those points.

By these attacks, the knowledge of the active operations of the lying spirits, and of the need of unceasing warfare against them, is deepened in him. He knows that he must stand against them daily, or again be entrapped by their wiles, and fall a victim to their wicked devices; for he discovers that even the lesser attacks, which, before the time of his deception and possession, would be unfelt, quickly overwhelm him, and cause him to lose his equilibrium, or spiritual balance, immediately. He knows, therefore, by the lessons of his fight to freedom, that he must ever after be on his guard, and watch against the attacks of the subtle foe, whether they come through things around him, or directly--or indirectly--through others, the indirect onslaughts being often the most violent.

During the period of his undeceiving, the eyes of the believer also become open to the supernatural operations of the forces of evil; for just as God is seen by His workings (John 14: 10, 11), so the powers of darkness are to be recognised by their activities.

Both the Divine and Satanic workings are invisible to the physical eye, but the effects are perceptible to him who has the power to read the signs. The one who has been dispossessed, can see how much that others attribute to God's sovereignty is nothing else but the results of the Satanic world-rulers' work. He sees that the primary cause of the apathy and deadness of the Church is Satanic, and that much which has been put down to sin, or the evil nature, is nothing but the work of evil spirits.

Hence he must war against the false teaching, which settles down to accept Satanic workings in the world as the "operations of God." Through his own undeceiving his old thoughts about things connected with God, and with Satan, fall to the ground as untested theories, and he receives two blessings through his undeceiving; i.e. (1) a purified "theology," (2) and a true demonology.

SOME OF THE RESULTS OF THE UNDECEIVING

The undeceived and dis-possessed believer also becomes intensely practical. He finds that God is "practical." The devil is practical, and man must be practical to join with the One against the other.

The believer sees that one of the ways in which the Son of God destroys the work of the devil, is through the instrumentality of prayer, and that he must now live a prayer-life, since prayer is the mightiest weapon against the foe. Through his undeceiving, the undeceived believer has been made conscious of the actual force which the powers of darkness bring to bear upon and against his tripartite being, and thus learns that all the strength of his redeemed, renewed, and liberated powers--mental, spiritual and physical--must be set against them in order that he may keep at liberty.

In the experience he has gone through, he has become more and more conscious of his own spirit, and the need of using it in strength, purity, and power against them. He has also discovered that in the perpetual war which the deceiving spirits wage against him, neither time, place, nor season, are exempt from their attacks.

Therefore, wherever he is, whatever he does, whatever state he is in, he must wage equally persistent war upon them. If he finds himself in keen suffering and anguish, he knows that it is "the hour and power of darkness"; and learns by the suffering they cause that they are unmerciful, as well as evil; intensely evil; nothing but evil;

aiming at nothing but evil, and with all the power they are able to wield, endeavouring to draw him into evil, doggedly, silently, persistently, wickedly, always at work; actuated by undying hatred and malice against the human race. Enemies they are, and will be. What they are they were, and what they were, they are still--evil, and evil only.

Thus he learns and knows that he must resist them and, that the fight to keep his spirit strong, pure and buoyant for victory over them needs all the force of his being, in the power of God, to enable him to be victorious.

THE BELIEVER FINDS HE IS AT WAR WITH ALL HELL

In the discovery of the wickedness and hatred of the supernatural powers of evil against him, the believer learns he is not fighting against the intelligence of one supernatural being, but against principalities and powers, with vast resources at their command, and that IF HE STANDS VICTORIOUS AGAINST THEIR WILES, HE HAS CONQUERED, NOT ONLY ONE EVIL SPIRIT, BUT ALL HELL.

He finds that the powers of darkness will not allow one single believer to be victor over them, until they as a whole (Ephes. 6: 12) have failed to conquer him. Hence their onslaught on him who elects to be victorious over them all, in vital union with the Victor Lord, Who put them to open shame through His death on the Cross of Calvary.

The believer is called to triumph over all the powers of darkness, but to reach the goal he must put on the whole armour of God, and lay hold of Divine strength, truth, righteousness, peace, faith, the mighty sword of the Scriptures, watchfulness and prayer. This armour, and the weapons belonging to it, will enable him to "stand against all" the wiles of Satan.

If he stands, all heaven sees it; if he is defeated, all hell knows it. If he triumphs, the hosts of darkness are not only conquered, but discouraged, and rendered less effective in their schemes.

The believer who would overcome such a disciplined and pertinacious foe, will never dare put his armour by, or give himself to careless work, for he finds that the foe is as tenacious and desirous to conquer as he himself is. But he who fully knows the foe and the warfare, and its eternal issues, finds his joy in the joy of war against an enemy devastating the earth, and the joy of victory, as a foretaste of the future triumph with the Lord Christ over all His foes. (Heb. 10: 13; 1 Cor. 15: 25, 26).

It is essential to study the powers of darkness from the point of view of their depraved nature. To be conquered, or to lose a point, is torment to them, for the fallen nature, both of men and angels, rebels against confessing itself vanquished. In the days of Christ, to be driven out of their hiding places, commanded to go, and thus be deprived of rest, was to demons "torment" before their time (see Matt. 8:29). They are being thus tormented by any truth made known about them today. The truth concerning them and their workings, with its consequent liberation of men from their power, is disturbing their rest at the present time, and what happened when Christ was on earth, will happen again when the casting out of evil spirits will become a recognised part of all Christian and ministerial activity. The Gospels record how Satan and his minions objected to Christ's presence on earth, for He moved about as the Victor, and they were shown to be the vanquished ones.

THE USE OF CHRIST'S AUTHORITY OVER THE POWER OF THE ENEMY

The believer who has thus learnt, through fire, the real schemes and workings of the Satanic forces, and realises that he must make war upon them for his own defense, as well as for the liberation of others, now discovers that Christ has given authority over "all the power of the enemy" (Luke 10: 19) to all who will lay hold of it, as part of the finished redemption of Calvary. That in union with Him He gives the believer power to wield His Name, and in His name to have authority to cast out demons.

This was one effect of the enduement of power upon the believers of the early Church. Christ said, on the eve of His Cross, "Hitherto ye have asked nothing in My name. " But after Pentecost they wielded the Name, and found the Spirit of God witness to its authority. "Such as I have, I give unto thee. In the Name . . rise . ." said Peter. "I command thee in the Name of Jesus . . come out . . " said Paul to the evil spirit (Acts 16: 18). "In My Name shall they cast out demons . ." said Christ of His followers. "The spirits are subject to you . . " (Luke 10: 20) must be true of all who are in actual experience "one spirit" (1 Cor. 6: 17) with the Lord.

The authority of Christ is, therefore, open to the faith of all His children who are united to Him in spirit, even though they may not be wholly free, through ignorance, from the power of deceiving spirits in their outer man.

THE AUTHORITY OF CHRIST IS NOT INHERENT IN THE BELIEVER

This is reasonably so, because the authority of Christ as Conqueror over the evil hosts of Satan, is not inherent in the believer, but is laid hold of by him through the power of the Holy Spirit, and is borne witness to by Him only in response to faith. Should, however, a believer by faith thus command evil spirits to depart they will make the most of any occasion he may give them, after he has dared to assert the authority of their Victor's Name.

This is to be explained by the facts dealt with in earlier pages of this book, that it is possible for the believer who is fully joined to Christ in spirit, and in whose spirit the Holy Spirit dwells, to have foreign spirits located, unknowingly, in mind and body, who have obtained a footing by deception.

The Holy Spirit does not give up His Place in a child of God who has received Him, because an intruder, against the man's real desire, and by guile, has gained admission. The entrance of a demon to a man, in any part of him, does not make him a demon, any more than the entrance of the Holy Spirit makes a man God. It is when the believer knows the truth, and will not take an attitude of refusal to the ground giving place to the enemy, and thereby clings to known sin and gives known ground to evil spirits, that his innermost life becomes seriously affected, just as known sin which the man will not part with, brings a cloud between him and God. God uses a man, so long as he is honestly true to known light, whilst glaring inconsistencies--unknown to himself-may stumble others.

DEGREES IN THE RESULTS OF USING THE AUTHORITY OF THE NAME

There are degrees in the manifestation of Christ's authority through the believer, over the spirits of evil, according to the degree of his personal victory described in our last chapter. Two believers may have faith to wield the authority of Christ, and have different results because of the difference in their knowledge of the workings of the powers of darkness, and hence a difference in their discernment, and consequent diagnosis of the case before them; that is, if one believer apprehends that he can cast out evil spirits by "commanding" only, and he does not know how the GROUND should be dealt with, he will not find the same results as the one who knows that the ground must be dealt with, before the evil spirits are really cast out.

Knowledge and discernment enables the believer to see where the Spirit of God would have him lay hold of the authority of Christ, and when to do so. For instance, authority over evil spirits to cast them out, is of no use in meeting their lies. Truth is the weapon of authority then. The truth of God, spoken with the authority of knowledge that it is the truth, will set the soul free.

KNOWLEDGE A FACTOR IN AUTHORITY

The degree of authority over evil spirits, then, depends not only upon personal victory, but also upon knowledge, and the believer who desires to know how to lay hold of the fullest authority over evil spirits for the sake of the deliverance of others, must set himself to understand their workings, as well as to be

VICTORIOUS IN ALL, AND OVER ALL HE PASSES THROUGH. Let him note how much is said in the Scriptures about knowledge and understanding. The Apostle wrote to the Colossians about their being filled with "the knowledge of God's will in all spiritual understanding" (Col. 1: 9), and the Lord said "This is life eternal, to know Thee. . . " (John 17: 3); "If we walk in the light ... fellowship."

To walk in the light is to know God, and knowing God, we in relative degree know the powers of darkness; for light makes manifest the works of darkness (see Eph. 5: 11-13). Those of full age in the spiritual life, have by reason o use, their "senses exercised to discern both good and evil" (Heb. 5: 14, A.V.). The believer must be willing for the price of the knowledge necessary for discernment, for he cannot take an attitude of resistance to a thing he believes is of God, or is good, or towards which he is neutral.

He must KNOW whether a thing is of God or no, therefore the degree of knowledge he has about the workings of the spirits of evil determines the degree of his (1) discernment, (2) resistance, and (3) authority over them in wielding the Name of Christ, whether exercised in "casting out," commanding to leave a person, or dispersing them by the light of truth. The believer must know their wiles, schemes, methods and accusations, weights on the spirit and their causes, and when hindrances and obstacles are brought about by the enemy, so as to be able to discern all these things, and resist them.

EVIL SPIRITS SUBJECT TO THE BELIEVER JOINED TO THE LIVING CHRIST

Knowledge also affects faith. The believer must KNOW that it is God's will that evil spirits should be, not only potentially, but actually subject to him as one joined in vital union to the Holy One of God, Who was Victor over them all when He walked on earth, and gave His messengers authority over them through using His Name (Cf. Luke 10: 17 to 24).

Some of the expressions used in Scripture describing the attitude of the Church, and of individual members of Christ toward the powers of darkness, clearly show God's will and purpose for His people. Paul said that God would "bruise" Satan under the feet of His children (Rom. 16: 20); the principalities and powers were to be "wrestled against" (Ephes. 6: 12) --surely not with a view to their triumph over the Christian; to be "resisted" by a steadfast attitude of faith (1 Peter 5: 8-9)-surely not by ignoring their presence and workings; "withstood" (Ephes. 6: 13), in their onslaughts-- surely not by ignorance of such attacks; "devices" recognised to be guarded against (2 Cor. 2: 1011); and "cast out" with the word of command by the authority of the Name of Jesus (Mark 16: 17), as those who were compelled to go, when a believer identifies himself with their Conqueror, and acts in reliance upon the authority of His Name.

Knowledge again affects the use of the will, in resistance to the enemy. How can the believer take an attitude of resistance to evil spirits in a meeting, unless he has knowledge whether the power in that meeting is Divine or Satanic? The senses also, when acute, are factors in knowledge. If they are dulled by possession, the knowledge necessary actually to read and discern the workings of the powers of darkness is hindered.

KNOWLEDGE GOVERNS PRAYER.

Abraham was seeking knowledge as to the conditions upon which God could spare Sodom, when he reverently questioned the Lord about the doomed city. He wanted to know God's conditions, before he was able to pray for Sodom.

KNOWLEDGE NEEDED FOR EFFECTIVE PRAYER

It is essential that the believer understand the workings of the powers of darkness for effective prayer against them. Without knowledge they may be actively at work all around him, and he be unable to stop them by prayer BECAUSE HE IS UNCONSCIOUS OF THEIR PRESENCE, OR WHAT THEY ARE DOING. That this is true can be seen by the way the devil is working among God's people notwithstanding much prayer. They are not able to defeat him by prayer against his works, because they are unable to recognise them.

In the war upon the powers of darkness, prayer is the primary and mightiest weapon, both in (1) aggressive war upon them and their works; (2) in the deliverance of men from their power, and (3) against them as an hierarchy of powers opposed to Christ and His Church; for the believer should pray against them, not only for himself, but for the whole Church (Ephes. 6: 18), and for the whole world, which in due time will be absolutely freed from their presence and power.

There is a systematic warfare of prayer possible against the kingdom of darkness, which would mean co-operation with the Spirit of God in the liberation of the Church, and hasten the ultimate binding of the great serpent, and casting him down to the pit. (Rev. 20: 1-3). A material "chain" could not bind a supernatural being, and it may be that "the great strong angel" typifies the mystical "Christ"; consisting of the Head and members--the "Man-Child" caught up to the Throne--when the members will have been liberated from the power of the enemy, and then commissioned to lay hold of the Deceiver to cast him into the abyss, and shut him up for the thousand years.

THE ANGELS' MINISTRATION OF WAR FOR THE SAINTS

How much prayer has to do with the setting in motion the hosts of light against the hosts of evil we do not fully know. There are many passages in the Scriptures which show that the unfallen angels have a ministration of war for the saints on earth, which the latter have but faintly realised. In the Old Testament the heavenly company is shown round about Elisha as in battle array; and in the New Testament, in Revelation 12, Michael and his angels are seen warring against the Dragon and his angels, the Church on earth sharing in this war. The united forces of the angelic hosts, and the Church on earth, are manifestly joined against the Satanic hosts: the latter "fighting" by the "word of testimony" and faith in the precious Blood, not only as single individuals, but as an united company--"They overcame him . ."- -recognising their union against a common foe.

The angels' ministration of war against the powers of darkness on behalf of the saints on earth, is strikingly revealed in Daniel 10, where Michael, the archangel, resists the interference of the Satanic "prince of Persia" and "prince of Grecia" with God's messenger, charged with an interview with Daniel. In the same way they fight against Satan and his angels as shown in Rev. 12. The Lord referred also to the "legion of angels" which He could call to His aid, to protect and deliver Him in the hour and the power of darkness (Matt. 26: 53), but He elected to fight the battle through alone, accepting no heavenly succour but that of the angel sent to strengthen Him in Gethsemane.

TRAINING IN THE WAR OF PRAYER

If a systematic warfare of prayer against the forces of darkness is possible to the believer, whereby God could hasten the deliverance of the Church of Christ, in preparation for the Lord's appearing, and its future destiny; such a warfare by prayer needs to be learnt as much as any other subject of knowledge in the world of men.

If we liken the war by prayer, systematically carried out against the forces of darkness, to a war in the natural sphere, those who would lead must be willing to be trained, and to take the same learner's attitude as a recruit in the natural sphere. Such believers need not only to understand the intelligent use of the weapon of prayer, but to obtain knowledge of the organised hosts of darkness, and how to exercise their spiritual vision so that "by reason of use" it becomes acute in discerning the operations of the enemy in the spiritual sphere. The believer must learn to observe, and learn by observation their methods in the war against the people of God.

The Church of God now needs "leaders" trained in the

knowledge of the world- campaigns of the enemy; believers able to foresee his "wiles," and to guide the rank and file of the Church into the aggressive war against him. Leaders skilled in the knowledge of the armour, and the weapons of warfare provided in the Word of God, so as to detect any weak places in their use, especially in prayer as an intelligent, systematic, aggressive COUNTER-CAMPAIGN AGAINST THE STRATEGIC METHODS OF THE HIERARCHY OF SATAN, against the Church.

The believer who makes war upon Satan, must learn both the defensive and the aggressive sides of the warfare; for to take the aggressive against such a wily foe, without fully understanding how to maintain the defensive position, means that the enemy soon ends the aggressive prayer warfare, by such attacks upon the undefended places in his life or environment, as will quickly compel him to draw back in defense of his own position. For instance, the believer makes war upon the foe and presses out into the open with a bold testimony to the way the weapon of prayer drew some stronghold to the ground, but it is not long before the testimony is challenged by some onslaught upon his inner circle, or upon himself, and the eager warrior finds he has failed to guard by prayer his own domain.

THE DEFENSIVE WARFARE OF EPHES. 6.

The importance of the defensive aspect of the warfare against the powers of darkness, and of the standing power of the believer being made immoveable, is shown in Ephes 6, where seven verses are given to describe the armour and the defensive position, with one verse only embodying the aggressive war by prayer.

The prayer-warrior fully armed must be alert in the defensive position, ready to stand against all the wiles of the devil, or the hosts of wicked spirits, whether they come as "powers," or with darkness, or in a rush of numbers upon him. He must know how to withstand in the "evil day" (5: 13) of the Satanic onslaughts, and "having overcome all" (A.V., m.), how to stand in the hour of victory, by discerning all their new attacks upon him in a change of tactics suited to the moment of triumph.

To maintain his defensive position the believer needs to know what evil spirits can cause to be done to him, and about him, and be especially on guard lest he yields to their workings, thinking he is submitting to God. He must know that lying spirits can "burden" other Christians about him; give visions to them, and misinterpret things about him; cause these "burdened" ones to write about him to others, and suggest thoughts to others to his detriment; in brief, use every possible device to move him from his position of victory over them in his own personal life and environment. The greater his position of triumph--"having overcome them all" (Ephes. 6: 13, m.)--the keener the new schemes of the wily foe to dislodge the victorious one from his armour-encased position. If by any of these means they can get him to turn from the aggressive warfare upon them, or be disturbed by the apparent misjudgments of others, or beguiled into looking upon these things as a "cross" he must bear, he will have failed to discern the tactics of the wily foe.

But when the believer knows what evil spirits can do to him, and about him, he can distinguish their workings through others, and, standing steadily in his defensed position, he protects himself by aggressive warfare upon them as they work in these special ways, and does not settle down to accept all these things as "the will of God," but sets himself to extinguish them by a systematic and persistent counter-campaign of prayer.

PRAYER AGAINST THE WORKS OF THE DEVIL

In the war upon the powers of darkness, prayer can be persistently and specifically directed against the works of the devil, as the believer moves about in his ordinary avocations, and sees their doings. It can be brief and ejaculatory, but it is effectual. It need only be "Lord, destroy that work of the devil!" or "May God open the eyes of that man to the deceptions of Satan around him!"

There is also prayer for others, directed specifically against evil spirits in them; but this first needs knowledge to discern the symptoms of their presence, and ability to distinguish between the man himself and the evil spirit or spirits. Any uncertainty here will weaken the force of prayer. If the prayer- warrior has a doubt about the source of certain characteristics in another, which cause the man to act as if he were two persons, one contradictory to the other, and one manifestly not his true character, he can pray that any evil spirit present may be exposed, so that the man himself will recognise it, or that the prayer-warrior may be sure of the source of certain things, that he may direct prayer upon the right cause.

One special mark of an evil spirit's presence in, or with, or operating upon, or through another, in every degree of possession, however slight, is antagonism to all truth in connection with the powers of darkness, especially that about evil spirits; the antagonism being unreasonable and unreasoning. For a man who is untouched by them, can calmly open his mind to knowledge about them, as easily as about the things of God. There is also resistance in such believers, in mind or spirit, to other aspects of truth; whether it be Scriptural truth as applied to themselves personally; or truth concerning facts in their spiritual experience, or about themselves or their actions, which the lying spirits do not wish them to know. Just as a special mark of the Presence of the Holy Spirit operating upon, or through another is an OPENNESS TO TRUTH; a desire and even a keen hunger for truth, irrespective of consequences, or feelings of pain. Believers of all degrees of spiritual life place themselves on the side of the God of Truth when they specifically declare, "I open myself to all truth," and by so doing they enable the Spirit of Truth to do His work.

It is important that the prayer-warrior should discriminate the working of evil spirits in possession of others, as IN, but not OF the person; so as not to be diverted from direct dealing with the enemy by blaming the one in whom they have obtained a footing for their manifestations.

HOW EVIL SPIRITS CAUSE BELIEVERS TO RESIST THE TRUTH THEY NEED

The believer seeking to help another under the possession of evil spirits, must be prepared for the deceiving spirits misusing to the captive one the very truth he himself desires, and needs for his deliverance, as well as misrepresenting to him the one seeking to help him to freedom. Sometimes the truth which is meant to, and does deliver the deceived one in spite of all that appears to the contrary, is used as a whip to beat him, by the lying spirits in possession. The poor captive has the actual sense of being lashed with rods as real as if the stripes fell on his body, and it appears as if the words of the other giving him the light he needs, and which he himself desires to have spoken to him, are as rods beating him. But if the deceived believer refuses to be moved by the pain of the lashing, lays hold of the truth told him, and at once TURNS IT

INTO PRAYER and fight against the enemy, he grasps the weapon of victory. For example, if a man is told "the enemy is now deceiving you," and he at once replies "It is against my will. May God reveal all deceptions from Satan to me, and to the whole Church!" he at once lays hold of a weapon for victory.

All truth imparted to a deceived believer should inspire antagonism to the lying spirits of Satan, instead of causing despair or resistance to the truth, or attempted laboured explanations to prove other causes for such and such a manifestation. The believer who desires freedom should thankfully receive all light that will expose the enemy, saying, "How can I get the benefit of this as a weapon against the foe?"

But in the stress, and ofttimes confusion, of the dispossessing period, the deceived and possessed person unwittingly fights against his deliverance by covering and siding with the evil spirits who have deceived him. The will may be set, and declared to be for deliverance, yet when the truth is given, evil spirits manifest their presence in the circumference of the man, or wherever they may be located, by arousing feelings of rebellion against the very truth, or messenger of truth, which the man in his will has chosen to receive. In brief, they bring into play all the resources they have at their disposal. They pour a flood of confusing thoughts into the mind, with suggestions utterly foreign to the desires of the person, and sometimes raging feelings in the body, as if it were being wrenched with pain, the spine and nerves

appear to be racked with irritation, and the head as if it would burst with pressure--none of this arising from any physical cause. For the time being the messenger with truth for the deliverance of this captive believer, appears to have done far more harm than good to the victim of Satan; but if the truth has been given, and the prayer warrior stands unmoved by the outward storm, quietly resisting by prayer the evil spirits arousing it, sooner or later the captive emerges into freedom, and a greater degree of deliverance, if not full victory.

THE CASTING OUT OF EVIL SPIRITS

Prayer against evil spirits in others may have to be accompanied by the inaudible commanding of them to leave the person, or else in casting out the demon, or demons, directly and audibly. There are several conditions for doing this, which need careful and prayerful consideration, ere such a course is taken. The possessed person may first need (1) truth upon his condition, and the ground wherein the evil spirit has found lodgment. This requires knowledge and discernment on the part of the worker, and sometimes very exhaustive dealing with the possessed one; (2) the ground which has been discovered must be given up definitely and specifically by the victim, or the "casting out" may fail; (3) definite prayer to God for His will to be revealed concerning the whole matter, and how the Spirit of God would have it dealt with, is primarily necessary; (4.) the authority of Christ needs to be specifically taken by the one called upon to deal with the man, and (5) wrestling prayer which reaches "fasting" may be needed if the case is a very difficult one.

The fasting which is of spiritual effect in such a case, means, that the one who is dealing with the possessed person, is brought into such a hand to hand conflict of spirit with the evil spirit, or spirits, in possession, that the sense of any bodily need ceases until the victory is won.

THE TRUE FASTING FROM FOOD IN CONFLICT

The Lord's wilderness conflict throws light upon this, for it appears that it was not until after Satan had left Him, and the tension of the conflict was over, that His physical needs asserted themselves, and "He hungered" (Matt. 4: 2). True "fasting," therefore, appears to be not so much the result of a believer's choice and determination to fast from food, as the result of some spirit-burden, or conflict, which constrains him to fast because of the dominance of the spirit over his body, and no sense of physical need at all. But when the conflict is over and the spirit disengaged, the requirements of the body make themselves felt once more.

There is also a permanent attitude toward the body, which may be described under the word "fasting," which is a necessary condition for continuous victory over evil spirits. Especially for the casting out of evil spirits, it is imperative that the believer has complete mastery over his body, able to discriminate between its legitimate demands, and the spirits of evil seeking to gain a footing behind its lawful needs, and to detect all the wiles seeking to rob him of victory over them.

THE VOICE IN CASTING OUT

In the casting out of evil spirits, the voice may be strong or weak, as it is governed by the circumstances of the occasion. If it is weak, the weakness may be caused by fear, ignorance, an immaturely developed spirit, or it may be the result of the strength of the opposing spirit. The Holy Spirit who energises the man for the act of "casting out," is of necessity hindered in His operations by these factors in the believer. Especially is an undeveloped spirit a limitation, for this shows the non-use of the spirit in general conflict. The spirit grows strong in maintained resistance and conflict with the powers of darkness, and by obtaining complete mastery over soul and body, as did John the Baptist in the wilderness (Matt. 3: 4); for "every man that striveth for the mastery" (1 Cor. 9: 25) over himself, gains a capacity of spirit for the Holy

Spirit's energising, which can be obtained in no other way.

The special influx of the Holy Spirit which equips believers for co-operating with Him in wielding the authority of Christ over evil spirits, is dealt with in another chapter (Acts 13: 8, 9, 10). The Holy Spirit in the spirit of the believer, is the power at the back of the act of casting out, and the servant of God should watch keenly not to move to any aggressive step apart from Him. Paul endured for many days the attack of the evil spirit upon him through the woman possessed with a spirit of divination, but there was a moment when, "sore troubled," the Apostle turned upon it (Acts 16: 18), and, speaking direct to the spirit and not to the girl, commanded it to come out of her. The believer who can discern the sense of the spirit knows that moment, and co-working with the Spirit of God moving in his spirit, finds the power of the Name of Jesus over the demons of Satan, as effective to-day as in the time of the Apostles and the Early Fathers of the Church.

The chief factor in the casting out, or commanding evil spirits to come out of a man, is FAITH IN THE POWER OF THE NAME OF JESUS. This faith is based on knowledge that evil spirits must obey the authority of Christ, exercised by Him through those who are united to Him. Any doubt on this point will render the commanding fruitless.

The casting out is always done by speaking directly to the spirit in possession, and in the Name of Christ, the believer saying:

"I charge thee in the Name of Jesus Christ to come out. . . ." Acts 16: 18.

CAN EVIL SPIRITS BE TRANSMITTED

There is no danger of the evil spirit when cast out, entering into, or being transmitted to the one who has dealt with them, unless there is ground for their doing so, or consent is obtained for their entry by trick of the enemy. Believers called upon to deal with evil spirits in others should deliberately declare their stand upon the Calvary basis of Romans 6: 6-11, ere they do so, as the only safe way of dealing with the basic ground of the old creation, which may give place to the enemy.

The casting out of an evil spirit from another may also be an occasion for the manifestation of one hidden unknowingly in the believer who is dealing with the other possessed person. If this is so, when he finds an immediate manifestation of the enemy's workings in himself he is liable to attribute it to a transmission to himself, or an attack upon himself, of the expelled spirit.

Through this wrong interpretation he now seeks deliverance from the supposed "transmission," and thereby gives new ground to the deceiving spirit, because he does not seek for the cause of the manifestation in his past life; that is, he deals with it as an "attack," instead of a symptom, and hence the cause, or ground, is left undealt with, and undiscovered.

Neither does the laying on of hands by a person unknowingly possessed, transmit evil spirits. If it appears so, it is but an occasion for an evil spirit already hidden in the person, to manifest itself, and then to suggest a wrong cause for the manifestation, so as to throw him off the track in the discovery of ground. In brief, if there are already deceiving spirits in possession, the conditions are favourable for their manifestation, for ALL MANIFESTATION OF EVIL SPIRITS IN A PERSON MEANS GROUND for their occupation, which should be dealt with at once. If a symptomatic manifestation is called an "attack" from outside, no deliverance will be known until the true cause is recognised.

It may be said at this point that whatever signification there may be in the "laying on of hands," the result should be spiritual, and in the spirit, not in physical sensations, or any conscious feelings in the Senses.

THE GIFT OF DISCERNING OF SPIRITS

Much of the knowledge needed for the "discerning of spirits" can be obtained by careful perusal of preceding chapters, but there is a gift of "discerning of spirits" referred to in 1 Corinthians 12, as a manifestation of the Holy Spirit in the members of the Body of Christ. Like all the Gifts of the Spirit, it needs the full co-operation of the believer for use, and becomes clearer and stronger as it is used. For this reason, it may appear so ordinary in its exercise, and so much like the using of a spirit sense faculty belonging to the man, that it escapes the attention of others. That is, it may not appear supernatural, nor operate in a miraculous way. Also like all the other gifts, it is not for show but for profit (5: 7), and it is only recognisable when it is in operation, and even then, may need a spiritual man to discern its presence and manifestation.

The power of discerning of spirits proceeds from the spirit of the believer, as the place from whence the Holy Spirit manifests His Presence and power, and develops in manifestation through the mind, as the man grows in knowledge and experience of spiritual things, and learns to watch and observe the ways of God, and the workings of the evil supernatural powers. Discernment is a "gift of the Spirit," but it is manifested as a fruit of watchfulness, and watchfulness is the fruit of keen alertness on the part of the believer. It needs great patience, great skill and great perseverance to become proficient in discrimination and discernment.

The faith necessary for laying hold of, and exercising the authority of Christ over the spirits of evil cannot be MADE; and if there is any effort in its exercise the believer should know that there is something at fault which needs examination; and seek to understand the hindrances to the working of true faith. When a prayer-warrior finds it difficult to "believe," he should find out the cause; whether it is from the (1) opposition of the powers of darkness; or (2) the non-working of the Holy Spirit with him in respect to the matter in hand. (Cf. Mark 16: 20).

There is what may be described as an "evil" faith, that is, a compulsion to "believe," which comes from evil spirits. The fact that the devil fights against the exercise of faith, is no proof of that "faith" being a true faith, or vice versa. It is true that the devil tries to quench true faith, and the believer may fight to keep it alive; but he must examine and know the nature of the faith that is in him. Is it of God in the spirit, or is it from the mind, or will, and based on a personal desire? In brief, is its origin from the man himself, or from God?

OTHER ASPECTS OF THE PRAYER WARFARE

There are many aspects of the war by prayer against the powers of darkness, which space precludes dealing with fully, such as lessons from the act of Moses, lifting up his hands on the hill-top, which was an outward expression of a spiritual DEED. The result of his action was seen in the plain, when the forces of Israel triumphed. The cause of the victory was invisible. Something in the spiritual realm was accomplished by the outward, visible attitude of the man upon the hill, which was manifest to him and the men with him, when he let down his weary hands.

The powers of evil attacking Israel through Amalek are the same forces against the Church of Christ to-day. Moses could not have kept the assertion of faith in Jehovah as Victor, audibly expressed without intermission throughout the prolonged fight; and that no intermission in the act of faith was vital is to be seen in that the moment his hands went down, the enemy triumphed, and as they went up, Israel prevailed.

There are times in a prolonged fight with the hosts of Satan, when it is clear to the spiritual vision, that the enemy gains ground as the "word of testimony" flags, and that the forces of God conquer as the Lord's praying ones maintain the cry of victory. In hours such as these, some physical act expressing the maintenance of the attitude of victory, to relieve mind and body from overstrained tension, may be admissible, and uplifted hands, or stretched out hands, may instinctively come about in the "hill-top" conflict for the Church of Christ.

There are hours, too, when the battalion of wicked spirits stand back, and the prince of darkness himself stands against the believer, as in Zech. 3: 2. Then the words, "The Lord rebuke thee, 0 Satan," never fails.

When prayer, also, needs focussing upon some stronghold of the enemy, in patient, persistent prayer for a prolonged period; or a wrestling in spirit in a great crisis
    battle against the forces of darkness, holding some position they

have taken; there are many weapons available to the armour-clad believer as he stands in Christ, withstanding the hosts of wicked spirits in high places. Not only the lifted hands of Moses, and the rebuking words of Michael, but the holding the curse of God upon the Prince of darkness, and all his hosts--that curse upon the great spirit-being, clothed in the guise of a serpent, which the Lord God pronounced upon him in the Eden tragedy of the Fall. That curse, which has never been revoked, and which Satan knows lies before him in its final climax in the lake of fire. The reminder of this curse is often an effective weapon against the foe.

PRAYER AND ACTION

The believer who has been patiently and persistently labouring in prayer, and conflict with the enemy, for others, must hold himself ready for action, for God may use the one who has prayed to be the instrument of the deliverance of the one prayed for. It is essential to have action as well as prayer. Many think it is quite enough to pray, because God is omnipotent; but God needs men to pray who are ready also to act. Cornelius prayed, and then acted in sending for Peter (Acts 10: 7-8). Ananias had prayed about Paul, and then was sent to speak to him (Acts 9: 11). Moses prayed for the deliverance of Israel, but he himself was called to be a great factor in the answer to his prayers (Ex. 3: 10).

There is also a time for answered prayer (Luke 2: 26), and there are hinderers to answered prayer (Dan. 10: 13). Those who pray for the deliverance of others, must have patience to plod in prayer for many days. There is sometimes a wrong thought in expecting a "flow" of prayer, if it is truly in the spirit. Because believers find no easy flow they cease to persevere in prayer, whereas prayer, when OPPOSED TO THE ENEMY, often means a hewing out words in a real fight against the hinderers to prayer. Believers must not expect those who are deeply deceived, to be delivered in a few weeks; for it may take months and even years of prayer. Contact with those who are being prayed for may hasten their deliverance, for the reason that God can work more quickly when He can use others to help immature Christians, when they do not understand. Indirectly, we answer our own prayers when we go to the ones we are praying for, and give them the light they need.

Patience and perseverance are needed, because, as we have seen, believers needing deliverance hinder through ignorance, when they side with evil spirits in believing their suggestions, and excuses; even whilst they sincerely desire to be liberated from their power.

PRAYER AND PREACHING

The one who prays may be called upon to act by transmission of truth by preaching. If so, he will need to understand the place of prayer in his preaching. That he needs the prayers of others for effective utterance (Ephes. 6: 19); and that he must carry out the warfare himself experimentally when he is transmitting truth which affects the kingdom of Satan. If by prayer he deals with the powers of darkness before preaching, the flow through his spirit may be unhindered; but if evil spirits are hindering his message he may have to fight his words out with difficulty, because his spirit is at the same time resisting the obstacles in the spiritual realm. This may cause his voice to sound harsh because of the resistance in the atmosphere, the voice breaking through into clear tones when the resistance gives way. Whenever the spirit is thus engaged in conflict the outer man is affected and less calm in action or speech. Whilst the believer is actually preaching, deceiving spirits can endeavour to interfere with his delivery by a stream of "comments," so to speak, charging him with their own workings, i.e., they will be whispering to him every cause but the true one for the condition of the meeting,pouring accusations into his mind whilst he is speaking, challenging the words coming out of his mouth. If he is speaking of the holiness of life necessary for the children of God, he is told how far he comes short of what he is preaching to others; the challenge being so persistent that the speaker may suddenly insert into his message depreciative words about himself, and through these words, suggested by evil spirits, and thought by the speaker to be his own, they pour a stream into the atmosphere of the meeting, which brings a dark cloud upon the people.

PRAYER AS A DESTROYING WEAPON

Prayer fulfils some law which enables God to work, and makes it possible for Him to accomplish His purposes. If such a law does not exist, and God has no need of the prayers of His children, then asking is a waste of time, but in fact, prayer is the greatest conceivable weapon of destruction at the disposal of the believer, destroying obstacles to God's working, either from sin or the works of the devil.

Prayer is DESTRUCTIVE as well as constructive, but to this end it must be radical, piercing to the very source of things, destroying the cause, or causes of hindrances to the operations of God. Prayer needs to be specific and radical, first in the sphere of the personal, then out through the local to the universal. Activity in prayer should be in the order of (1) Personal prayer, covering personal needs; (2) Family prayer, covering family needs; (3) Local prayer, covering environment needs; (4) Universal prayer, covering the needs of the whole Church of Christ, and the whole world (1 Tim. 2: 1; Ephes. 6: 18).

UNIVERSAL PRAYER

If the prayer-warrior prays for the universal, without first having dealt with personal and local needs, the enemy will touch these smaller spheres, and thus by the force of personal and local attack, draw the believer down from the universal outlook. The order of prayer is therefore, first exhaustive prayer for all personal and local spheres, praying through these out to the wider range of the universal. Prayer not only exhaustive, but persistent. The believer needs for all this (1) strength to pray, (2) vision to pray, (3) knowledge of what to pray; for there is a sequence in prayer which needs to be understood intelligently, and a work of prayer, demanding as much training and equipment as is needed for preaching.

The trained prayer-warrior knows something of all the various aspects of prayer, such as: The prayer of asking (John 14: 13); the prayer of interceding (Rom. 8:26);

"saying" (Matt. 21: 21; Mark 11: 23-25) and burden prayer, which may be a burden in the spirit or on the mind (Col. 2: 1; 4: 12). He knows that burdens of prayer may be conscious, but that he must not expect a conscious burden for every prayer, nor wait till he "feels moved to pray." He knows that to see a need for prayer is sufficient call for prayer, and if he waits for "feeling" that he can pray when he has vision to pray it is sin. He understands, too, in the sphere of the universal, the oneness of the whole Body of Christ, and that in that sphere of union, he can say "Amen" to the prayers of the whole Church, so far as they are of the Holy Spirit, in the will of God.

All this but touches the fringe of the war by prayer which could be waged upon the forces of darkness, for the deliverance of God's people, which is the true objective of Revival.

CHAPTER 12
Revival Dawn & the Baptism of the Spirit

We have seen that the period in the believer's life wherein he receives the Baptism of the Holy Spirit is the special time of danger from the evil supernatural world, and the Baptism of the Spirit is THE ESSENCE OF REVIVAL. Revival dawn, is, therefore, the great moment for deceiving spirits to find entrance into the believer by deception through counterfeits, resulting sometimes in the possession dealt with in preceding pages.

The hour of Revival is a time of crisis and possible catastrophe. A crisis in the history of every individual, as well as in the history of a country, a church, or a district. A crisis for the unregenerate man, wherein he settles his eternal destiny, as he accepts, or rejects conversion to God; a crisis to those who receive the fulness of the Holy Spirit, and to those who reject Him; for to the believer who bends and receives the Holy Spirit, it is the day of the visitation of the Most High, but to others it means the decision whether they will become spiritual men or remain carnal (1 Cor. 3: 1); whether they will elect to remain in defeat in the personal life, or determine to press on as overcomers.

Few go through the crisis without deception by the enemy in more or less degree, and only those who cling to the use of their reasoning faculties at this time, can hope to be saved from the catastrophe of becoming a victim to the subtle workings of evil supernatural powers.

If the believer does become deceived by evil spirits at the time that he is baptised with the Spirit, almost immediately after the highest point of his experience, he begins through deception to descend into a pit which ultimately means depth of darkness, bondage and misery, until he is undeceived and returns to the normal path. Those who do not discover the deceptions, sink into deeper deception, and become practically useless to God and to the Church.

REVIVAL THE HOUR AND POWER OF GOD

Revival is the hour and power of God, and of the devil, for the descent of the Divine power brings the accompanying onslaught of evil supernatural powers. It means MOVEMENT IN THE SPIRITUAL REALM. Revival itself is the hour of God, when heaven is opened, and the power of God works among men, but when the Divine power appears to pass away, and evil supernatural powers manifest their workings in a man, or a church, or a country, then men marvel that the devil's work should be where God had been so manifest, not knowing that the devil was planting his seeds, and DOING HIS WORK, FROM THE DAWN OF REVIVAL.

Revival ebb began with its flow, but all unseen. In the hour and power of God in Revival, the "Tempter" appears to be absent, but he is present as the Counterfeiter. Men say there is "no devil," and yet it is his greatest harvest time. He is netting his victims, mixing his workings with the workings of God, and beguiling the saints more effectively than he was ever able to do with his temptations to sin.

As a counterfeiter, and deceiver, the ever watchful foe uses his old methods of deception and guile on new converts, who, having victory over known sin, think the Tempter has left them, not knowing his new ways. His absence is only apparent, and not real. Satan was never more active among the sons of God.

WHY REVIVAL STOPS

The Devil's great purpose is to stop the Revival power of God, and every Revival that has been given of God to awaken His people, has ceased after a time, more or less short, because of (1) the Church's ignorance of the laws of the spirit for co-working with God; and (2) the insidious creeping on of the powers of darkness, unrecognised, and yielded to by the people of God through ignorance.

Those who are born of the Spirit at such a period of the manifested power of the Holy Spirit emerge into a spiritual world, where they come into contact with spirit-beings of evil, OF WHOSE EXISTENCE THEY HAVE NO EXPERIMENTAL KNOWLEDGE. They become conscious of spiritual forces and things which they think must be of God, and they do not know of the possibility of workings mingled by wicked spirits with the things of God.

This is the reason why Revival, which quickens the Church, and for a period manifests to the world the regenerating, uplifting power of God, produces as an aftermath a number of genuine Spirit-born believers who are said to have "religious mania," or are called "cranks." And this is why "Revival" is sooner or later checked and discredited, the testimony to the world destroyed, the sober section of the Church dismayed, and made fearful of its effects..

To put it in bluntest language, the Revival hour is the occasion for evil spirits to obtain "possession" of spiritual believers, and REVIVAL CEASES BECAUSE OF SUCH POSSESSION. The most spiritual believers, baptised with the Holy Spirit, and most fitted to be used of God in Revival service, may become deceived and possessed by evil spirits in their outer being THROUGH ACCEPTING THE COUNTERFEITS OF SATAN.

Believers who are not so abandoned to the Spirit escape the

acute "possession, " but in their contact with hitherto unknown workings from the spiritual realm, are equally open to deception which is manifested in a less recognisable way.

What is called the "fanatical" spirit, which in some degree, follows Revival, is purely the work of evil spirits. At Revival dawn the ignorant are teachable, but through their "spiritual experiences," later on they become unteachable. Pre-Revival simplicity gives place to Satanic "infallibility," or an unteachable spirit. Dogged, stubborn obstinacy in a believer after Revival is not from the source of the man himself, but from evil spirits deceiving his mind, holding his spirit in their grip, and making him unbending and unreasonable.

The scheme of the powers of darkness in Revival dawn, is to drive, or push to extreme, what is true. Their "push" is very slight and imperceptible at the beginning, in suggesting thoughts, or impelling to actions a very little contrary to reason, but as the "push" is yielded to, and the use of the reason is silenced, those who are thus deceived in due course become fanatical. The judgment of those believers impelled to unreasonable actions, may be against, and even resisting the things they are supernaturally urged to do, yet they are unable to stand against the supernatural power driving them, which they think and believe is from God.

REVIVAL AND WAR ON SATAN

All this, and much else already dealt with in preceding pages, together with the after history of all Revivals of the past, shows that REVIVAL MINUS WAR ON SATAN AND HIS WICKED SPIRITS, must always appear to end in partial failure through the mixed results, consequent upon Satanic counterfeits of the working of the Holy Spirit.

The Church, therefore, sorely needs believers equipped with knowledge and discernment, to meet the Satanic counterfeits which invariably follow the advent of Revival, knowing the symptoms of Satanic deception and possession, and able to resist the powers of darkness, and teach the children of God the way of victory over them, as well as the aggressive warfare upon them.

War upon the attacking spirits of evil is indispensable for maintaining the health, sanity and spiritual power of those who are revived. A PURE REVIVAL--free from the usual aftermath--IS POSSIBLE if the Church understood the truth about the powers of darkness, as well as the way of co-operation with the Holy Spirit. Apart from this same knowledge of the workings of Satan and his wicked spirits, so as to be able to recognise their presence under any guise, no one can with safety accept all the supernatural manifestations which accompany Revival, or believe all seeming "Pentecostal power" to be of God.

A PURE Revival is Divine power in full operation, minus sin

and Satan. It is not cold "belief," but life, and it has to do with the spirit, not the intellect.

PRAYER FOR REVIVAL

Apart from this same knowledge, those who pray for Revival do not clearly understand what they pray for, nor how to act when their prayers are answered; for they are not prepared to meet the Satanic opposition to their prayers; nor even the dangers attendant upon prayer for Revival.

Why is there not yet world-wide Revival in answer to world-wide prayer? For the same reason that Revival subsides when it has begun, and that prayer meetings for Revival may end in catastrophe, or powerlessness. The check to Revival, both when it has begun, and in the prayer preceding its advent, is caused by the spirits of evil deceiving or hindering the praying ones.

The hindrance to Revival, at the present time lies, not only in this opposition of the powers of darkness, but in the PRESENT CONDITION OF THE MOST SPIRITUAL SECTION OF THE CHURCH, through whom alone God can work in Revival power. These are the believers who know the Baptism of the Holy Spirit, and were liberated in spirit in the Revivals of the last decade, but who are now driven back into themselves by the pressure of the enemy in the atmosphere, or else are in captivity to the foe through his counterfeits.

Let these quenched or deceived believers be liberated once more, and THOSE WHO ARE NOW USELESS WILL BE PRICELESS IN VALUE for teaching and strengthening others when Revival is once more given.

INSTRUMENTS FOR REVIVAL

The Holy Spirit is still in those who were baptised with the Spirit, during the last Revivals. The mistake at the time of the Revival in Wales in 1904 was to become occupied with the effects of Revival, and not to watch and pray in protecting and guarding the cause of Revival.

The Spirit baptised souls, at present locked up in spirit, or sidetracked through Satanic deceptions, are still those who would be the instruments through whom God could work, were they but set free. Useless now, but priceless in maturity, and experience and knowledge for the guiding and guarding of a Revived Church, when they are once more liberated for true co-working with the Holy Spirit of God.

How, then, should the Lord's praying ones pray at the present time? They should pray

(1) Against evil spirits now blocking and hindering Revival.

(2) For the cleansing and delivering of those who became possessed through deception during the time of later Revivals.

(3) That when Revival is once more given it may be kept pure, and

(4) For the preparation of instruments for Revival, trained and taught of God to guard against further inroads of the powers of darkness.

In brief, let all who pray for Revival, pray for light to reach those who HAVE BEEN ENSNARED INTO BONDAGE TO THE DECEIVING POWERS OF DARKNESS, that they may be set free, and once more become usable in Revival service; then will the forces of evil be beaten back from the ground they have regained, which still belongs to God.

The Baptism of the Holy Spirit is the essence of Revival, for Revival comes from a knowledge of the Holy Spirit, and the way of co-working with Him which enables Him to work in Revival power.

The primary condition for Revival is, therefore, that believers should individually know the Baptism of the Holy Ghost. This term being used as a convenient expression for describing a definite influx of the Holy Spirit which thousands of believers throughout the Church of Christ have received as a definite experience. Such an infilling of the Spirit was the cause not only of the Revival in Wales in 1904-5, but of all other Revivals in wreld history.

The fact that the counterfeiting work of Satan follows Revival through such an opening of the spiritual world as enables the evil spirit-beings to find access to believers under the guise of the Divine Spirit, must not hold back the children of God from seeking the true flood tide of the Spirit, for the bringing about of pure Revival, and the emancipation of the Church of Christ from the bonds of sin and Satan.

WHAT IS A TRUE BAPTISM OF THE SPIRIT

It is of primary importance to understand what is a true Baptism of the Spirit, the conditions for its reception, and the effects of obtaining it. Previous chapters will have thrown much light upon what it is not, and the dangers to be avoided in seeking it.

It is not an influence coming upon the body, nor, according to the records in the Acts of the Apostles, does it result in physical manifestations, such as convulsions, twitchings and writhings of the human frame; nor does it rob a man of the full intelligent action of the mind, or ever make him irresponsible for his speech and actions.

In brief, the place of the indwelling of the Spirit of God in man, gives the key to all the true manifestations connected with the Baptism of the Spirit, as well as the conditions for receiving it, and the results in personal experience and service. THAT PLACE IS THE HUMAN SPIRIT. Once let the believer understand that his SPIRIT is the organ through which the Holy Spirit carries out all His operations in and through him, he will be able to discern the true meaning of being filled with the Holy Ghost, and how to detect the counterfeit workings of Satan in the realm of the senses.

The Baptism of the Holy Spirit may be described as an influx, sudden or gradual, of the Spirit of God into a man's spirit, which liberates it from the vessel of the soul, and raises it into a place of dominance over soul and body. The freed spirit then becomes an open channel for the Spirit of God to pour through it an outflow of Divine power.

The mind receives, at the same time, a clarifying quickening, and the "eye of the understanding" is filled with light (Eph. 1: 18). The body becomes entirely under the man's complete control, as the result of the dominance of the spirit, and often receives a quickening in strength for endurance in the warfare service he finds he has emerged into. That the Spirit of God OPERATES THROUGH THE ORGAN OF A MAN'S SPIRIT, as shown in the epistles of Paul, needs to be kept in mind in reading the records of the working of the Holy Spirit in the Acts of the Apostles.

THE INFLUX OF THE HOLY SPIRIT AT PENTECOST

On the day of Pentecost, the 120 disciples--men and women-- were filled in the spirit, as the Spirit of God filled the atmosphere, and their tongues were liberated, so that THEY THEMSELVES as intelligent personalities, could speak of the mighty works of God as the Spirit gave utterance, i.e., gave them power to speak.

The record gives no hint that they became automatons, or that the Spirit spoke HIMSELF through them, or INSTEAD of them.

From a spirit under the clothing of, and the afflatus of the Spirit of God, they themselves were given intelligent insight into, and utterance about, the wonderful things of God, as they were "moved" in spirit by Him.

This influx of the Divine Spirit into their spirits, not only left their mental powers in full action, but clarified them, and increased their keenness of discernment and power of thought, as seen in the action and the words of Peter, who spoke with such convincing power that through his words-inspired by the Spirit, but spoken by him in intelligent clearness of mind--three thousand were convicted and saved, the true influence of God the Holy Spirit being manifested through him, not in "control" of those who heard him, but in a deep conviction in their consciences which turned them to God, not conquered by terror of God, but by a godly awe, which led them to godly sorrow and repentance.

The "falling upon" of the Spirit (Acts 2: 15), is therefore upon the spirit, clothing it with Divine light and power, and raising it into union of spirit with the glorified Lord in heaven; at the same time, baptising the believer into one spirit with every other member of the mystical Body of Christ, joined to the Head in heaven. All who are thus liberated and clothed in spirit are "made to drink of one Spirit" (1 Cor. 12:13)--the Holy Spirit--Who then, through the spirit capacity of each member of the Body, is able to distribute to each the gifts of the Spirit, for effective witness to the Risen Head, "dividing to each one severally even as He will." (See 1 Cor. 12: 4-11).

THE HOLY SPIRIT REVEALING CHRIST IN HEAVEN

Another aspect of the true Baptism of the Spirit, having an important bearing upon the experiences of believers today, is to be found in the words of Peter on the Day of Pentecost, showing that the revelation of Christ given by the Holy Spirit at such a time, was of Christ as the glorified Man in heaven (Acts 2: 33, 34), and not in any vision or manifestation as a Person within.

The same attitude to Christ as seated on the right hand of God, is uniformly to be seen in all the later records of the work of the Spirit in the Acts of the Apostles. The martyr Stephen sees the "Son of Man, standing on the right hand of God" (Acts 7: 56), and Paul on the road to Damascus is arrested by a light from heaven (Acts 9: 3; 22: 6; 26: 13), out of which clothing of light the Ascended Lord spoke to him, saying, "I am Jesus . . . "

The Holy Spirit fills the human spirit of the believer, and communicates to him the very Spirit of Jesus, joining him in one spirit to the Spirit of the glorified Lord, imparting to him the life and nature of Christ for the building up of a new creation in His likeness (Rom. 8: 29; Heb. 2: 2-13). Instead of being turned inward to a self-centred apprehension of Christ, he is, by the influx of the Spirit of God into his spirit, lifted, so to speak, out of the narrow limit of himself, into a spiritual sphere where he finds himself one spirit with others who are joined to the Living Head forming one Body-or spirit organism--for the influx and outflow of the Spirit of the Lord.

REVIVAL DEPENDS UPON TRUE UNDERSTANDING OF THE BAPTISM OF THE SPIRIT

This aspect of the true meaning of the Baptism of the Spirit and its spiritual effect, has an important bearing upon Revival, and the reason why Revival does not come.

Revival is an OUTFLOW OF THE SPIRIT OF GOD THROUGH THE ORGAN OF THE HUMAN SPIRIT LIBERATED FOR HIS USE.

When the influx of the Spirit takes place into the spirits of many believers, and finds outlet through all, the unity which was so marked in the early Church is seen, and the united power becomes strong enough to overflow through all these liberated ones to others.

But if the believer turns INWARD, either (1) through the pressure of opposition, (2) powers of darkness in the atmosphere, or (3) to worship and pray in a self-centred way; or is occupied in any degree with an inward experience, THE OUTFLOW OF THE HOLY SPIRIT IS HINDERED; the unity with other liberated believers is checked by an invisible barrier, which has come between, and the released spirit, which was kept dominant over soul and body so long as the man turned outward as a channel for the inflow and outflow of the Holy Spirit, sinks down into the soul-vessel, a "spirit in prison," so to speak, once more.

"Revival" is then checked at its very birth, because believers who seek, and obtain a Baptism of the Spirit, do not clearly understand the conditions upon which the inflow was given, nor how to cooperate with the Holy Spirit in the purpose of His coming; which is to make them channels for the OUTFLOW of rivers of living water.

THE TRUE REVELATION OF CHRIST

The influx of the Spirit of God to a man's spirit, means love, joy, and liberty, buoyancy, light and power. It means a revelation of Christ as the Risen and Ascended Lord, which brings joy unspeakable and full of glory; and an intimate sense of His nearness in fellowship and communion, which makes the "I in you" a living power. It is at this time that ignorance is dangerous. If the believer does not understand that all this is an EFFECT WHICH IS INWARD AS A RESULT OF THE UNION WITH CHRIST

IN HEAVEN, and an effect which will continue only so long as he abides in the right attitude toward the glorified Christ in heaven, he will turn into and sink down into the soul, i.e., into himself; and then the deceiving spirits will counterfeit in the sense-sphere the true experiences which he had IN SPIRIT through the incoming of the Holy Ghost.

These "experiences" then have little result beyond the circumference of the believer. When the true influx of the Holy Spirit to the spirit took place, there was (1) unity with others in the same spirit, (2) joy, (3) liberty of utterance, (4) power to witness to Christ, (5) effective and permanent results in the lives of others, and a heavenly "fire" from God in a burning, consuming white heat intensity of SPIRIT (Rom. 12: 11) in service to God.

But when the sense counterfeit takes place, supernatural "experiences" frequently occur at the very same time that a wrong spirit is discernible, such as harshness, bitterness, pride, presumption, disunion, etc., showing either (1) that the "experiences" are not from the spirit, or (2) that the spirit is out of co-working with the Holy Spirit, and (3) the Holy Spirit is no longer able to bring forth the pure fruit of the Spirit through the believer's spirit and life.

The after counterfeit of the true is also marked by, (1) inability to recognise and unite with the Spirit of God in others, this being contrary to the pattern of the oneness of the Body shown in 1 Cor. 12, where the same Spirit in each member is in harmony with the Spirit in the other; (2) the spirit of separation and division on account of not seeing eye to eye in non-essential matters, for union of spirit, where the Holy Spirit is ruling and working, is possible apart from unity of faith, which can only be according to the degree of knowledge.

WHY BELIEVERS DO NOT OBTAIN THE BAPTISM OF THE SPIRIT

Believers who know that a Baptism of the Spirit is possible, and obtainable by them, may not receive that Baptism because of many misconceptions about experiences.

The reception of the Holy Spirit, and the Pentecostal measure of the enduement, or clothing, of the Spirit, vary in manifestation and result according to the preparation of, and the knowledge of the believer. Many do not receive the Baptism of the Spirit, because they have misconceptions which hinder them from co-operation with the Spirit of God in His workings, on account of these varying facts in connection with it, and the consequent apparent contradictions of teaching about it.

THE RECEPTION OF THE GIFT OF THE HOLY SPIRIT

After the manner of the Lord's dealing with His disciples, and borne out in the experience of many to-day, it is clear that there is a reception of the Holy Spirit answering to the experience of the Easter Day, as the initial stage of the manifestation of the Holy Spirit in enduement of power, by an influx of the Spirit of God into the human spirit, which liberates the man for utterance and witness bearing. The reception of the Holy Spirit in its initial form requires certain conditions which the believer should be able to quickly and simply fulfill. The (1) putting away of every known sin in the life; (2) definite trust in the power of the Blood of Christ to cleanse from all unrighteousness (1 John 1: 9); (3) obedience right up to the edge of light through the Word of God; (4) full surrender to God as His entirely, with not one thing clung to and withheld from Him; (5) the act of faith in which the believer, fulfilling these conditions, takes the Gift of the Holy Spirit, as simply as he received the gift of eternal life through Christ.

Believers should understand that these simple conditions can be carried out by the action of the will alone, with no conscious feeling of any kind. Once the transaction is made, it should be held to persistently and steadily, without question or deviation from a fixed volition. In some cases the entry of the Holy Spirit into the renewed spirit in the manifestation of the fruit of the Spirit (Gal. 5: 22) very quickly follows the fulfillment of the conditions. But the believer should be on guard not to turn to any experience as the basis of continued faith, or it will quickly pass away. The transaction with God upon His Word stands good, whether manifested in spirit-consciousness of the Holy Spirit's presence or not. Once made, the transaction should be held to, experience or no experience, by the surrendered believer.

It is from this stage that the Spirit of God now works to discipline and lead the believer on into knowledge of the greater influx of His power which is the enduement for service, and for aggressive warfare against the principalities and powers of Satan.

THE ENDUEMENT FOR SERVICE AND THE CONDITIONS

Some say they have prayed for hours for this needed equipment, to no purpose; others have spent weeks or months in waiting upon God for some experience they think accompanies this Baptism, with very grave results in a counterfeit power breaking forth upon them, with manifestations afterwards acknowledged to have come from the deceiving spirits of Satan. Others have received a true influx of the Spirit, but through ignorance and misconceptions have given place at the same time to the workings of evil spirits in the physical frame. This we have already dealt with in earlier chapters, and need only now set forth the conditions for knowing the enduement for service, and the effects which follow.

THE AWAKENED SENSE OF NEED

In the first place there must be a definite assurance that such an enduement of power is possible, and a deep conviction of, and sense of need. This may come about in the believer by his discovering that he has no effectiveness in his life and service, although he may have known for years the Holy Spirit in His indwelling power. Especially, the sense of need may be acute in lack of utterance and power to witness for God; and almost complete absence of the aggressive power against the forces of darkness so marked in the early church.

Sometimes those who are thus being moved by the Spirit to the sense of need, which precedes the greater influx of His power, are diverted or hindered from pressing on by others who are not at the same stage of the spiritual life, and who say this enduement is not obtainable. A believer in such a case should put aside the voices of men, and dealing with God direct, PUT TO THE PROOF FOR HIMSELF whether God will meet his awakened need.

This means a definite transaction with God, that, (1) He will give to the supplicant what HE MEANS by a "Baptism of the Holy Ghost"; and (2) in His own way grant to His redeemed one the liberty of utterance and, power for effective service, which he should have for fulfilling his part as a member of the Body of Christ.

This should be a transaction with God in a deliberate act of the will, which must not be departed from, whatever the after experience may be. This is taking the enduement of the Spirit by faith, on the ground of the Word of God. "Christ redeemed . . . having become a curse for us . . . that we might receive the promise of the Spirit through faith... " (Gal. 3: 13- 14).

As we have seen there is no command given to the Church after Pentecost to "wait" for a personal enduement for service. The Spirit of the Lord fell upon those in the house of Cornelius without any "waiting," and He will do so still upon any believer directly he is in the right attitude, and fulfilling the conditions for the Spirit of God to flood his spirit with His power. The waiting on the part of the believer, is really a patient waiting for the Spirit of God to do the work in him that is required, after he has definitely dealt with God for such an enduement of His Spirit. A "waiting" which is consistent with the faithful discharge of the duties of ordinary life, wherein he learns the minute obedience to all the known will of God, which is necessary when he is given more definite service later on.

THE OBSTACLES TO THE BAPTISM OF THE SPIRIT

During this period the believer's faith-dealing with God must continue to be active, trusting the Spirit of God to prepare him for the enduement required for his sphere of service. The danger now is the using of excuses to cover up lack of power, or else shrinking from the examination of points in the life which the Spirit of God is dealing with, or even quenching the Spirit by refusing to yield up to God what He claims, or quailing from some sacrifice, upon which turns the liberation of the spirit of the seeker for the influx of the greater measure of power.

In the initial reception of the Spirit, the conditions necessary, dealt with a narrow sphere. It meant just the centre of the man dealt with, in will and heart, the former in surrender to God, and the latter cleansed from the love of sin. But in the enduement of power the scope of God's dealings widens. The man's SPIRIT has to be separated from the entanglements of the soul, and the lawful things belonging to the natural, or soul-man, have to be surrendered, so that he may become a spiritual man, governed only by his spirit. He must have every trace of an unbending spirit removed, that his spirit may co-operate with the Holy Spirit with pliability; he must lose every degree of an unforgiving spirit, so as to give no inlet to evil spirits, when, by the moving of the Holy Spirit, he may be charged to rebuke sin, or suffer rejection for Christ's sake; and be freed from a narrow grasping spirit, if he is to be a wide channel for the outflow of the gracious life-giving Spirit of God.

Moreover, the man who seeks an enduement of power must be willing for the Spirit of God thoroughly to deal with his life, and remove out of it every obstacle to his immediate readiness to fulfil all the will of God; he must be searched in motive, and taught the principles of righteousness, for the enduement of the Spirit which he seeks to know, means an AGGRESSIVE WARFARE AGAINST SIN, and the powers of evil, and how can the Holy Spirit convict of sin by the preaching of righteousness, if the man He equips as a messenger of God is ignorant of the law of righteousness? He must learn what GOD'S ATTITUDE TO SIN IS IN HIS OWN LIFE, ere he can be God's witness against sin in others.

WHY DELAY IN THE BAPTISM OF THE HOLY GHOST

If a believer has made the transaction with God for the Baptism of the Spirit, and taken it by faith, and for a prolonged period there is no evidence in experience, he should renew his prayer to God for the removal of all obstacles as quickly as possible, and be on the alert to co-operate with God in every trace of light given him. Misconceptions as to the way the Spirit will work may prevent the believer recognising the evidence that his prayer has been answered. He may be expecting an experience similar to some other believer, or have some thought in his mind governed by his wishes or prayers, blinds him to the working of the Holy Spirit in an opposite manner.

It is here that advantage is given to the spirits of evil. If the believer is bent upon some special mark as evidence of the Baptism, the deceiving spirits use every possible means to give the seeker the counterfeit. The influx of the Spirit of God into the believer's spirit bears its own evidence, in the release of the spirit into light, liberty and power, resulting in liberty of utterance for witness bearing, and the co-working conviction of others by the Holy Spirit, which is the ultimate purpose of His coming.

Believers who are being disciplined and trained by the Holy Spirit for the enduement of power, should continue in present service for Christ, in the keenest faithfulness up to light, using to the full the measure of grace already received, for it is in the path of faithful service that the assurance of the enduement of power may be given. It is God's law that His children use all He has given them ere He gives more. The believer must DEMONSTRATE HIS OBEDIENCE TO GOD to the utmost extent of his present knowledge, learning to heed the sense of his spirit, and using his mind and judgment in reliance upon the illuminating of the Spirit of God, as he seeks to know the mind of God in His Word.

THE SPEAKING IN TONGUES

A question arises here as to whether believers may now speak in unknown tongues, as the disciples did at the time of the Holy Spirit's infilling at Pentecost. There are those that say, Yes, but the truths set forth in preceding chapters, show that until the spiritual section of the Church of Christ are more acquainted with the counterfeiting methods of the spirits of evil, and the laws which give them power of working, any testimony to such experience as true, cannot be safely relied upon.

Let it be said again: REVIVAL IS AN OUTFLOW OF THE SPIRIT OF GOD THROUGH THE ORGAN OF THE HUMAN SPIRIT, and the Baptism of the Spirit is the influx of the Spirit of God into the man's spirit, whereby it is released from all obstacles and bonds which oppress or hold it down, and closes or reduces its capacity as an outlet for the Holy Spirit. These obstacles may return through the deceptive workings of the Adversary, and the believer become locked up in spirit again, or rendered practically useless to God and His people.

THE OBJECTIVES OF THE TRUTHS ABOUT THE POWERS OF DARKNESS

There are two objectives to the truths which have been set forth in preceding pages. The first is, the removal of these obstacles, so that the Revival power which is lying locked up in many, may break forth once more, and the Church of Christ press on into maturity and power, victorious over the powers of darkness hindering her progress. These have gained their purpose of checking Revival through the ignorance of God's people, but they can be defeated and driven back from the ground they have gained, by knowledge of their workings, and by aggressive prayer against them. The truths about them, when put into operation, will not only set free individual believers, but disperse the block in the atmosphere in a church, or a town, or a country.

If it is proved that one evil spirit can be rendered powerless by prayer, then all the hosts of Satan in their onslaught on the Church can be conquered, if the children of God would use the weapons of victory. IF ALL HELL HAS BEEN CONQUERED BY CHRIST, THE FORCES OF SATAN CAN BE TURNED BACK, AND THE CHURCH OF CHRIST DELIVERED FROM THEIR POWER.

WHY GOD PERMITS SATAN'S ATTACKS

The hindrance to aggressive warfare against the foe lies in the unwillingness of the Church to face the truth; not in the lack of weapons for victory. Believers are content because they are ignorant of their state. The good they have, blinds them to the greater good, and the greater need of the Church. Therefore, to arouse them from their self-satisfied condition, God has permitted Satan to sift His people, for Satan cannot go one shade beyond the permission of God. Believers will be taught the truth about themselves only by experience, therefore God permits experience. The Church of Christ must be matured, and prepared for the Lord's appearing, therefore God permits the onslaught of the foe, for only through the fire of sifting will the people of God be urged forward to the battle and victory which will drive the forces of Satan from their place in the heavenlies, making way for the Church to ascend to her place of triumph with the Lord.

Wrong conceptions of Divine things can only be destroyed by experience. Many of the children of God are deceived whilst they think they are protected by God. They comply with the conditions for God to work, apart from intelligent understanding of why He does so, and they do not realise that it is just as possible to IGNORANTLY COMPLY WITH THE CONDITIONS FOR EVIL SPIRITS TO WORK, through ignorance of the laws governing both Divine and Satanic workings.

The supernatural manifestations of the present time, are being forced upon the notice of the Church of Christ, by the wreckage of work for God, and of devoted individual believers. Other children of God go into the midst of such manifestations in a blind confidence that God will protect, yet often they are not protected, because they do not understand the conditions for such protection. Sometimes their confidence covers a wrong condition in themselves, which is hidden from their knowledge, i.e., (1) they have a secret self-confidence that they are capable of judging what they see and hear, which has no basis of true reliance upon God through a deep consciousness of their ignorance; (2) a secret spirit of curiosity, of desiring to see what is "wonderful" ; (3) a secret wanting to go to such gatherings, without first seeking, with unbiased mind, a clear knowledge of the will of the Lord; or they may have (4) a real purpose of obtaining more blessing from God, which covers a deeply hidden pride, or self-ambition to be among the first in the Kingdom of God. Any of these hidden causes can frustrate God's protection, but where there is a true, pure, single-eyed reliance upon God to protect from the wiles of Satan, with a keen watching unto prayer, and a ready mind open to truth as God gives it, together with an unbiased faithfulness to the will of God--even though, for purposes greater than the personal good, the far seeing wisdom of God may allow the believer to discover by sore experience the deceptive workings of the Counterfeiter--such an one will be able to say, "out of them all the Lord delivered me." (2 Tim. 3: 11).

SATAN'S VICTIMS MADE VICTORS

The second, and greatest, ultimate result of the operation of the truths concerning the deceptive workings of Satan and the way of victory, is in connection with the dispensational position of the Church, in view of the closing days of the age, and the Millennial Appearing of the Ascended Lord. That Millennial Appearing of the Glorified Christ means to Satan and his hierarchy of powers, the triumph of his erstwhile victims, and their ascension to the throne of Christ, where, in reigning with their Lord, they will "judge angels" (1 Cor. 6: 2, 3). It means to the fallen archangel the deepest cup of humiliation he has yet had to drink, when redeemed man, who was for a little while made lower than the angels (Heb. 2: 7), and cast down, by his fall, near the level of the beast, is lifted up again, and made to sit among princes; lifted up above the high position which Satan once occupied as a great archangel of God; lifted up to one nature, and one life and position with the Son of God, as an heir of God, and joint-heir with Christ (Rom. 8: 17; Heb. 2: 11-12); lifted up with the Redeeming Lord, far above all principality and power and every name that is named in heaven or on earth, or below the earth; lifted up to the very side of the Triumphant Lord, to the place of judgment of the foe. For Satan, there awaits the abyss--the bottomless pit--the lake of fire. For his victims--the sharing of the throne of the Son of God, above the angels and archangels of God.

THE NAME OF THE CALVARY VICTOR AND ITS POWER

Is it a marvel, then, that at the close of the Age, and on the eve of the Millennial triumph of the Church, the whole hierarchy of evil powers endeavour to submerge the future judges of the fallen hosts of Satan? Is it any marvel that GOD PERMITS THE ONSLAUGHT, for it has been His way throughout the Ages to use this planet as the battle ground and training school of His people? The Son of God Himself had to become obedient unto death, even the death of the Cross, ere He was given the NAME which is above every name; that NAME which now speaks to every fallen angel, and every evil spirit among the dregs of the Spirit world, of the CONQUEST OF CALVARY. And every member of the Christ, who will reign with Him, and share in His judgment of the fallen angels, must individually, whilst on the planet of earth, learn first in person, not only to walk in victory over sin, but to trample under foot the viper brood of hell, in the Name of the Conqueror. They must overcome "As HE OVERCAME," if they are to share His throne and conquest. He led the way. They must follow. He passed through the hour and power of darkness on Calvary, and passed through it to the place of victory. United to Him in spirit, they pass through the same dark atmosphere, filled with the hosts of evil, to their place of triumph in Him.

That closing onslaught from the hosts of darkness is upon the Church. Not one living member of the Risen Head can escape attack if he is a true "joint" in the Body (Ephes. 4: 16). Some will know it before others, according to their place in the Body. "If the whole Body were an eye, where were the hearing?" They who are of the "feet" will know it latest, but know it they will, for they who are of the "feet" must also ascend, though the foot be the last part to move heavenward, and is nearest earth of the ascending Body. Some of the "elect" of the Body--yea, many--may "fall" victims to the deceptive wiles of Satan, but though they may seem submerged for a time, and--to their own vision--rendered useless to their Lord, if they but see how all the deceits of Satan can be turned into steps of victory, and equipment for the deliverance of others from his power, they can arise again, and become as it were "eyes" to the Body of Christ, in its advance through the aerial hosts of darkness contesting the way. They can arise again when they discover that what was meant by Satan to overwhelm them, can be changed by the light of truth into a glorious liberation from the enemy's power, and thus make them witnesses, not only to men, but to the principalities and powers in the heavenly regions (Ephes. 3: 10) of the manifold wisdom of God.

The hierarchy of Satanic power may hope to delay their judgment for a season, but the purposes of God must ultimately come to pass. He will draw His Church through to join the Risen

Head in due season, even though the hour and power of darkness now surrounds her. The ULTIMATE OF THE CALL TO WAR AGAINST THE POWERS OF DARKNESS IS REVIVAL! But the ultimate of that Revival which will come as the result of victory over Satan is ASCENSION TRIUMPH: THE MILLENNIAL APPEARING OF THE CHRIST, AND THE CASTING OF SATAN AND HIS EVIL POWERS TO THE ABYSS.

Even so, come Lord Jesus.

SUPPLEMENTARY NOTES

The True Workings of God, and Counterfeits of Satan.

"Knowledge and all discernment; so that ye may prove the things that differ, that ye may be sincere and void of offence. . . ." Phil. 1: 9,10, m.

True
1. The Baptism, or Fullness of the Spirit: An influx of the Spirit of God into the human spirit, which liberates the spirit from the soul (Heb. 4: 12), so as to become a pliable organ or channel for the outflow of the Spirit through the believer, manifested in witness to Christ and in aggressive prayer service against the powers of darkness.
It is a true baptiSing into the Body of Christ, and oneness with all the members of the Body. Its special mark and result is known in power to witness for Christ, and in conviction of sin in others, and their turning to God.
The highest manifestation of the Fullness of the Spirit is co-existent with the use of the faculties and self-control.
There is but one reception of the Holy Spirit: with many succeeding experiences, developments, or new crises, resultant on fresh acts of faith, or apprehension of truth; various believers having varied degrees of the same Infilling of the Spirit, according to individual conditions. The enduement of power for service is often a definite experience in many lives.

Counterfeit
1. Counterfeit workings of evil spirits may accompany a true reception of the Fullness of the Holy Spirit, if the believer "lets go" his mind into "blankness," and yields his body up passively to supernatural power. As a "blank mind" and "passive body" is contrary to the condition for use required by the Holy Spirit, and is the primary condition necessary for evil spirits to work, the anomaly is found in the Holy Spirit responding to the law of faith, and filling the man's spirit, at the same time that evil supernatural powers respond to the law of passivity fulfilled in mind and body. They then can produce in the senses manifestations, which seem to be the outcome of the Holy Spirit's entry to the spirit.
The results of the counterfeit manifestations are varied, and wide in their ramifications, according to individual conditions. The abstract result is great "manifestations" with little real fruit; "possession" by evil spirits of the mind and body in varied degrees; a spirit of division from others, instead of unity, etc., etc.

True

2. The Presence of God: Known in and by the human spirit, through the Holy Spirit. When He fills the atmosphere of a room the spirit of the man is conscious of it, not his senses. The faculties of those present are alert and clear, and they retain freedom of action. The spirit is made tender (Psa. 34: 18), and the will pliable to the will of God. All the actions of a person moved by the true and pure Presence of God are in accord with the highest ideal of harmony and grace.

Counterfeit

2. The counterfeit of the Presence of God is mainly felt upon the body, and by the physical senses, in conscious "fire," "thrills," etc. The counterfeit of the "Presence" in the atmosphere is felt by the senses of the body, as "breath," "wind," etc., whilst the mind is passive or inactive. The person affected by this counterfeit "presence" will be moved almost automatically to actions he would not perform of his own will, and with all his faculties in operation. He may not even remember what he has done when under the "power" of this "presence," just as a sleep-walker knows nothing of his actions when in that state. The inaction of the mind can often be seen by the vacant look in the eyes.

True

3. God in and with man in the spirit: John 14: 23. The Father in heaven is realized to be a real Father (Gal. 4: 6), the Son a real Saviour, the Holy Spirit a real Person; manifested as One in the spirit of the believer, by the Holy Spirit: with resulting effects as in Rom. 8: 9-11.

Counterfeit

3. Evil spirit's counterfeit, as the occasion serves them, each Person of the Trinity, and can thus obtain access, and become in and with a man in manifestations given to the senses, in which the real spirit-sense may have no part.

True

4. Christ manifested in the believer by His Spirit, so that He is known as a Living Person on the Throne in heaven, and the believer joined in spirit to Him there, with the result that Christ's life and nature is imparted to him, forming and building up in him a "new creation," (Gal. 1: 16; 4: 19. Col. 1: 27), the believer growing up into Him in all things

Counterfeit

4. Christ apparently manifested inwardly as a "Person," to whom the soul prays, or with whom he holds communion, yet there is no real evidence of the expression of the Divine nature, or true

growth of the Christ life, with a deepening fellowship with the Christ in heaven. On the contrary the Christ in heaven seems far away. The counterfeit centres and ends in an "experience" which keeps the person introverted or self-centred (spiritually).

True
5. Consciousness of God: Felt in the spirit, and not by the physical sense

Counterfeit
5. "Consciousness" of "God" in bodily sensations, which feed the "flesh" and overpower the true spirit-sense.

True
6. The Holiness of God: when realized by the believer produces worship and godly awe, with a hatred of sin. On the ground of the Blood of Calvary God draws near to men, seeking their love, but His presence does not terrorize.

Counterfeit
6. Evil spirits counterfeit this by giving a terror of God, which drives men away from Him, or forces them into actions of slavish fear, apart from the use of the mind, and volition, in glad voluntary obedience to Him.

True
7. Surrender to God: Of spirit, soul and body, is a simple yielding or committal to Him of the whole man, to do His will and be at His service. God asks the full co-operation of the man in the intelligent use of all his faculties. Rom. 6: 13

Counterfeit
7. Passive yielding of spirit, soul and body to supernatural power, to be moved automatically, in passive, blind obedience, apart from the use of volition or mind. Evil spirits desire "control" of a man, and his passive submission to them.

True
8. Fellowship with the sufferings of Christ: The result of faithful witness for Him, and in such "suffering," the joy of the Spirit breaks forth in spirit. (Acts 5: 41). The fruit of true conformity to Christ's death in the "fellowship of His sufferings" is seen in life to others, and growth in tenderness of spirit, and Christ-likeness in character. 2 Cor. 4: 10-12.

Counterfeit
8. "Suffering" caused by evil spirits is characterized by a fiendish acuteness, and is fruitless in result--the victim being hardened

instead of mellowed by it. The demons can cause anguished suffering in spirit, soul or body. "Possession" manifested in abnormal suffering, may be the fruit of (unconscious) acceptance of sufferings caused by evil spirits, often under the name of the "will of God."

True
9. Trusting God: A true faith given of God in the spirit, having its origin in Him, without effort reckoning upon Him to fulfil His written Word. Co-existent with the full use of every faculty in intelligent action. "Faith" is a fruit of the Spirit and cannot be forced. Gal. 5: 22. 2 Cor. 4: 13.

Counterfeit
9. "Trusting evil spirits" comes about through trusting blindly some supernatural words, or revelations, supposed to come from God, which produces a forced "faith," or faith beyond the believer's true measure, the result being actions which lead into paths of trial never planned by God.

True
10. Reliance upon God: An attitude of the will, of trust and dependence upon God, taking Him at His word, and depending upon His character of faithfulness.

Counterfeit
10. Reliance upon evil spirits means a passive leaning upon supernatural help and experience, which draws the person away from faith in God Himself, and from active co-action with Him.

True
11. Communion with God: Fellowship in the Spirit with Christ in the glory as one spirit with Him. The consciousness of this is in the spirit (John 4: 24) only, and not in "feelings" in the senses. See for conditions of true communion with God, 1 John 1: 5-7.

Counterfeit
11. "Communion" with evil spirits may take place by retiring within to enjoy sense communion, in "exquisite feelings" which absorbs and renders the soul incapable of the duties of life. The "flesh" is fed by this spurious spiritual "communion" as really as in grosser ways.

True
12. Waiting on God: The spirit in restful co-operation with the Holy spirit, waiting God's time to act, and a waiting for Him to fulfil His promises. The true waiting upon God can be co-existent with the keenest activity of mind and service.

Counterfeit

12. A "waiting for the Spirit to come," in hours of prayer, which brings those who "wait" into passivity, which at last reaches a point of "séance" conditions, followed by an influx of lying spirits in manifestations.

True

13. Praying to God: Having access to the Holiest of all, on the ground of the Blood (Heb. 10: 19). Penetrating in spirit through the lower heavens to the Throne of Grace. Heb 4: 14-16. True "prayer" is not directed toward God as within the believer, but to a Father in heaven, in the Name of the Son, by the Holy Spirit.

Counterfeit

13. Praying to evil spirits comes about by praying to "God" in the atmosphere, or within, or possibly to "pictures" of God in the mind; instead of approaching the Throne of Grace according to Heb. 10: 19.

True

14. Asking God: An act of the will in simple faith, making a transaction with God in heaven, on the ground of His written Word. "Answers to prayer" from God are usually so unsensational and so unobtrusive that the petitioner often does not recognise the answer.

Counterfeit

14. "Asking" evil spirits, by speaking to some supernatural presence in, or around the person. The "answers" are generally "dramatic," sensational, calculated to over-awe the person, and make him feel he is a wonderful recipient of favour from on high. By this means the demons gain control over him.

True

15. God speaking: Through His Word, by His Spirit, in the spirit and conscience of the man, illuminating the mind to understand the will of the Lord.

Counterfeit

15. Evil spirits speaking, wither puffing up, accusing, condemning or confusing the person, so that the is bewildered or distracted and cannot exercise his reason or judgment. The "speaking" of accusing spirits resembles the "thinking," or speaking to oneself, when the words are not uttered audibly.

True

16. The voice of God: Is heard and known in the spirit of man, wherein the Spirit of God dwells. God also speaks through the

conscience, and through the written Word (see "Texts"), never confusing or dulling the faculties of the man, or perplexing him, so as to hinder clearness of judgment and reason. The true voice of God does not make a demand of unreasoning obedience to it, irrespective of the man's free volition.

Counterfeit
16. The counterfeit "voice" of God is usually loud and comes from outside the person. It can come from within, when the person is deeply possessed. It is frequently imperative and persistent, urging to sudden action. Confusing and clamorous, or subtle in suggestion; producing fear through its insistent demands, making the man a slave to supernatural power. May also be distinguished from the voice of God by its sometimes, trivial objective, and fruitless results when obeyed.

True
17. Divine guidance: Through the spirit and mind; i.e., "drawing" in spirit, light in the mind: spirit and mind brought into one accord in harmony with the principles of the Word of God (Ephes. 5: 17; Phil. 1: 9-11 A.V. m.)

Counterfeit
17. Satanic guidance by supernatural voices, visions, leadings, drawings, are all dependent upon the passivity of the mind and reason, and take place in the sense-realm as a counterfeit of the true in the spirit.

True
18. Divine "Leadings": Are in the spirit; demand co-operation of the man in every faculty of mind, and spiritual intelligence in correctly rending the monitions of the Spirit. The will is always left free to choose and act. The true "leading of the Spirit" is never out of accord with principles of God's Word.

Counterfeit
18. Satanic "leadings" and impulses, demand passive surrender of mind and body. They are compulsory in effect, and all "compelling" and "compulsion" from the supernatural realm indicates the work of deceiving spirits.

True
19. Divine "Visions": When given, come (1) without seeking for them, (2) with definite purpose, (3) are never abortive, and (4) are co-existent with active use of the mind and faculties.

Counterfeit
19. Satanic visions, (1) demand a passive state, (2) are broken by

mental action, (3) are frequently contrary to truth, and (4) fruitless in result. Destroy all faith reliance on God.

True

20. Obedience to God: An act of deliberate will, choosing to do the will of God, when made known to the believer. A full examination of the source of the command preceding intelligent decision to obey, is co-existent with true obedience..

Counterfeit

20. Counterfeit of "obedience" is a passive, automatic, blind yielding to supernatural power or voices, apart from intelligent apprehension of results or consequences. The person fears to question or examine the source of the command.

True

21. God giving power: By the Holy Spirit in the man's spirit, strengthening him in spirit, so as to energise his mind and every faculty of his being to their fullest use, and enabling him to endure and accomplish what he would not bear or do apart from God. (Ephes. 3: 16)

Counterfeit

21. Evil spirits give power in a supernatural energy--generally spasmodic and unreliable--dependent upon the man being passive in spirit, soul and body. This "power," when it ceases, leaves the man dull and exhausted, the effect generally being attributed to natural causes.

True

22. God giving influence: Means that the believer draws others to God, not to himself. True Divine "influence" does not "control" others automatically, but constrains them to turn to God

Counterfeit

22. Evil spirits giving "influence," means a control or power over other which causes them to act apart from their volition, or reason. This "power" may be exercised unknowingly by persons the demons can use in this way.

True

23. God giving "impressions": Means a gentle movement in the spirit, which leaves the person free to act of his own volition, and does not compel him to action. "impressions from God" are within in the shrine of the spirit; and not from a "power" outside, e.g., in "touches" on the body, or an exterior compelling force.

Counterfeit

23. Evil spirits' "impressions" are from outside, upon the person, and require certain conditions for the "impressions" to be given-- i.e., a sitting still and waiting, etc. These conditions can also be fulfilled unconsciously by cultivating passivity of the whole being.

True

24. Divine life from God: Is known, not by "consciousness," but results, enabling the believer to bear and suffer what he could not bear or suffer humanly. There is rarely any "feeling" of strength or life, because consciousness of Divine life would draw the man from the path of faith to rely upon his experience.

Counterfeit

24. "Life" in thrills, etc., given by evil spirits, is known by its being in the senses, giving pleasant sensations, rather than true power. When it passes away, the person is dulled or weakened, and may go into spiritual darkness through numbness of the sensibilities, e.g., he says he is "like a stone."

True

25. Divine love: Shed abroad in the heart by the Holy Spirit, is co-existent with keen and faithful dealing with sin; with acute hatred to sin and Satan, and all that is contrary to righteousness.

God's love does not dull, but energizes every faculty to fulfil the action for which it was intended in creation. It has no "craving" in it, nor does it weaken those to whom it flows out.

Counterfeit

25. Counterfeit of the "love of God" makes the recipient cover over sin, compromise with it; dulls him to keen-edged righteousness; makes him incapable of true hatred to the things that God hates, for the faculty which "loves" is the faculty which hates.

The counterfeit of love, whether human or Divine, given by evil spirits, grips the sensibilities with an overmastering and painful "craving" for its object.

True

26. Fire from God: Is a purifying through suffering (Matt. 3: 11,12), or a consuming zeal in spirit, which deepens into white heat intensity to do the will and work of God, which no trials or opposition can quench. Fire from God is spiritual, not literal, and therefore falls upon the spirit, not the body.

Counterfeit

26. "Fire" caused by evil spirits is generally a glow in the body, which the believer thinks is a manifestation of "God" in

"possession" of the body, but afterwards results in darkness, dullness and weakness with no reasonable cause; or else it continues deceiving the believer into counterfeit experiences.

True
27. Texts from God: These are given through the organ of the spirit to the mind, when the spirit is (1) calm, (2) unstrained, (3) at liberty, (4) open to the Spirit of God. They do not confuse, and when acted upon are found to be confirmed in Providence, and are always in accord with the keen use of the faculties. Intelligent knowledge of the broad principles of Scripture is needed for the true interpretation of "texts" which arise in the spirit, lest they be misused through human conceptions of Divine things, e.g., the mind may take literally what God means spiritually.

Counterfeit
27. Texts from evil spirits "flash" into the mind: rush with force; come from without (audibly), or in the mental sphere. They elate or crush, condemn or puff up; confuse or turn out fruitless, leading those who obey them into vain actions, or into wreckage of circumstances. Evil spirits give a false "experience," and then "texts to confirm it," whereas true experience confirms the truth of the statements of the written Word. Evil spirits make use of all misconceptions of truth.

True
28. Sin from the fallen nature: Is from within, carries the will with it, or else forces the will by its pressure. The man knows the movement to sin is sin, and yet yields to it. Rom. 6: 6,11,12 is God's way of dealing with the fallen nature, and its workings, as the believer stands on the ground of the Cross, and wields Christ's finished Calvary work as a weapon for victory. The Holy Spirit bears witness to the Cross in setting free from sin, when it is the outcome of the evil nature.

Counterfeit
28. Sin caused by e.s., apart from temptation, is also within, but is forced into the spirit, mind or body, against the desire of the man, and should be recognised as distinctly not of, or from himself, e.g., blasphemous thoughts and unexplainable "feelings." If the "sin" infused by demons is dealt with as from the evil nature, although the person stands on Rom. 6: 6,11, and refuses it, no deliverance comes, but when it is recognised as the work of demons, and resisted on the ground of the Cross, freedom is quickly given.

True
29. Self-examination in the light of God: A discrimination of his

own actions exercised by the spiritual man, which does not produce "despair," "disappointment," a "crushed feeling," etc., but leads to rapid decision of action, and a joyous faith in the co-operating work of the Spirit in deliverance from all that does not bear the verdict of the light of God. John 3: 21.

Counterfeit
29. Self-introspection, is made use of by evil spirits to throw the believer into self-accusation and despair. This dries the person inward and downward to crushed impotence and faithlessness. God never crushes His children. He convicts only to reveal the remedy. Evil spirits seek to turn souls into self-centred absorption whereas God moves in them to live and care for others.

True
30. Conviction of sin: Comes from the Word of God, or by the direct action of the Holy Spirit, to the conscience, in times of quiet prayer or reading. It is never "vague" or confusing, and ceases directly the man decides to obey the Word, or go to God for cleansing in the Blood of Christ. True conviction is also a deepening experience, as the light of God shines into the conscience and life.

Counterfeit
30. Evil spirits' accusations, which are a counterfeit of conviction, are from without, in the ear (audibly), or to the mind, in a "nagging," persistent, confusing kind of "speaking," often without definite purpose or specific reason. No "confessing" or "step of obedience" affects these accusations, and they come again and again over the same things Many live under a perpetual cloud through the attacks of accusing spirits. They are under the shadow of being "always wrong."

True
31. Confession of sin: To God and man, should be the deliberate act of the will in obedience to the Word of God, and conscience. It should be followed by sincere repentance and putting away of the confessed sin, and have the witness of the Spirit to the conscience that the sin has been put away through the efficacy of the Blood of Christ.

Counterfeit
31. Compulsory confessions, by the driving power of evil spirits upon the mind in accusation, or from remorse; or, to silence the accusing voices, the man is sometimes impelled to "confess" "sins" which have no actual existence.

Notes

Without exception the manifestation of the Holy Spirit is marked by (

a) a Christ-like spirit of love,
b) soberness of spirit vision,
c) keenness of vision,
d) deep humility of heart and meekness of spirit, with lion-courage against sin and Satan, and
e) clearness of the mental faculties with a "sound mind." 2 Timothy 1: 7.
f) "Wherefore be ye not foolish, but understand what the will of the Lord is . . ."--Ephes. 5: 17, R.V.

***

Speaking generally, proof of "sense-manifestations" being from deceiving spirits may be found in the spirit being wrong alongside of "manifestations," e.g.,

1. Condemning spirit and judging spirit.
2. Spirit-vision dulled; cannot see marks of God at work in other ways.
3. Absence of true Spirit-power in (a) conviction of sin, (b) deliverance of souls, or (c) salvation of souls.
4. Or the spirit is "sweet" in a weak sense, with mind dulled, and unable to work with clearness.

Summary of "Ground"

Evil spirits must have ground.
- Degree of ground for possession cannot be defined.
- Ground can be deepened.
- Cannot interfere with faculties unless ground given.
- They deceive and attack to obtain ground.

The ground given to e.s. for access:
| mind | | | spirit, | soul, and | body |

Every thought accepted from them.
- Wrong conceptions suggested by them, of spirit things.
- Wrong interpretation of their workings, by believing their lies.
- Passivity of spirit, soul or body
- Accepting of counterfeits.

Note:
(a) The fallen nature is permanent ground, needing to be dealt with perpetually on the basis of Rom. 6.
(b) Acts of sin may also give ground.

Results of ground given:
Faculties dulled, rendered inoperative, etc.

How ground is given to e.s.:
By CONSENT, i.e., act of will consciously; deliberately given, or obtained by guile.

How ground has to be dealt with:
- Must be found out and given up, i.e., give up "thought," or "passivity," etc. Light on ground obtained by prayer.
- Knowledge of ground, and ground given up
- Must face truth about ground.
- Ground must be discovered in detail for full dis-possession from e.s.
- Ground given up specifically on points wherein deceived.
- Ground traced to radical cause, i.e., thought and belief.
- N.B. "Ground" cannot be cast out.

How ground is removed or given up:
- By revoking consent given in the past, knowingly or unknowingly, i.e., by steady refusal.
- Persistent refusal needed until liberty is obtained.
- Ground may pass away gradually.
- Ground may pass away unknowingly by standing on Rom.6.

Why ground does not pass away when given up.

How dispossession takes place:
- As ground is removed the e.s. depart, or lose hold.
- Believer dispossessed as ground passes away, i.e., wrong thoughts, passivity, etc.
- Faculties gradually released as ground is given up.

Ground refused to e.s. is ground retaken for God, e.g., faculties surrendered to e.s. when released are recovered for God.

Need of watching lest fresh ground given.

In conflict, because of e.s. reattempt to deceive, and re-enter, need of watchful and exhaustive refusal.

EXPLANATIONS

- Ground to be given up: e.g., a thought or belief discovered as deception, and "given up."
- Ground which admits e.s. keeps e.s. in possession: e.g., e.s. works on passivity which is ground for them to work upon.
- If not removed keeps e.s. in possession.
- Ground to be re-taken from the foe: e.g., the faculties recovered for use.
- Ground newly given: e.g., a new deception through believing one of e.s. lies.
- Notes. All supernatural manifestations by e.s. in believer denote that there is ground for their workings. The believer fighting to freedom, must watch lest new ground is given by wrong interpretation of manifestations of e.s.
- Need of watchfulness against "excuses" suggested by e.s. to cover ground, or divert dealing with it.

Seeking radical cause in ground
In seeking for radical cause of e.s. possession, the believer must look to the opposite to discover the ground of access, e.g., as in the following instances.

Believer thought he opened to God to obtain Knowledge Strength Truth Guidance Life Fire Healing Help Conviction Love All these things supernaturally given in counterfeit, the true objective and result being

N.B.--If believer takes all in Col. 1 from e.s., he is sure to get the results names in Col. 2.

Believer opened to e.s., which actually resulted in Ignorance

Weakness Lies Blunders Death Cold Infirmity Hindrance Accusation Suffering Example.--Believer troubled with e.s., speaking to, and accusing him. The true cause lies in the fact that he-

1. Opened, as he thought, to God Himself speaking of His own initiative, making communications to the man, apart from his asking for them, and he opened to and listened to what he thought was God speaking.

2. Or he thought God spoke to him in answer to prayer, and he listened. The cause therefore of e.s. speaking and accusing, is that the ground was given in the opposite, i.e., supposed listening to God.

Further Examples:

Believer conscious of "cold"--really supernatural trembling. Root cause in the past was the acceptance of "fire" from e.s. under belief it was fire from God. The cause of one extreme is the cause of the other. The two results come from same cause, e.g., the cause of the cold, or trembling, is the cause of the heat, etc.

If hindered by e.s. now, the believer accepted help from them in the past; that accepted help giving them access to hinder now. If no initiative now, then the believer ceased to act in the past, waiting for e.s. prompting, that prompting and waiting for it, giving them power to prevent initiatory action now If sudden stoppage of mind now, with result in mechanical words, the cause is a mediumistic attitude taken to God in the past, which produced the habit of cessation of action for supernatural action.

BRIEF NOTES

Thoughts of impatience,
i.e. directly physical, not moral, and result of d.p. Remedy is regaining of normal condition, and refusal of d.p. as cause.
Rom. 6: 11 must be kept as spiritual basis in all cases.

Daydreams in meetings,
Resist by active refusal of e.s. interference, and choosing to concentrate in attention.

Assurance of safety may be deception,
How then can a believer become sure? Only by seeking light from God, persistently, on all things, and definite reliance on Him apart from experiences.

Weakness,
Weakness is not given by e.s., but produced by them, by their counteracting man's own strength or force coming into action.

Terror of God;
slavish fear, "Awe" and terror are distinct. God inspires reverence and awe, as well as filial fear, but no terror.

The purpose of assertion,
The believer must counteract lies with truth and he says a thing aloud to counteract impressions on his own mind.

"Craving,"
It may be said generally that all cravings whether they be in the physical realm, i.e., for drink, or in the soul-realm, i.e., for love, fellowship, etc., are not from God.

Self-discrimination,
Every believer should discriminate or "judge" himself; the true "self," or person, must come to the bar of the man's judgment. The basis of judgment must not only be the purpose of the will, or the desires of the heart, but ACTIONS and life. Perpetual discrimination, or self judgment, is not introspection.

Cessation of action,
The believer must never stop action for "God to act," i.e., stop the memory for God to remind. Men stop for e.s. to work, but never for God, who energises the man to act. Sudden stoppage of mind is followed by mechanical words, caused by the interference of e.s., misnamed sometimes as "absentmindedness."

Burdens,
False burdens may be the result of d.p. and will not pass away as long as looked upon as pure spirit-burdens. They will, on the contrary, develop and grow, especially if the man prides himself on his "burdens," proving the evil of their character. If relief comes after getting rid of a burden, the inference cannot always be drawn that the burden was of God, because the enemy can give burdens, and when obedience is yielded to the purport of the burden, it goes.

Identity of e.s. with believer's personality

A letter speaks of a Christian worker with a "peculiar sense of not realising her own identity, but feels like one in a dream." At times she would be thrown into "convulsions," yet is a devoted worker for Christ.

Those who have this sense of no "identity," should definitely assert their personal experience. The e.s. in possession move such persons to constantly say "we" instead of "I". They should refuse temptation to plurality in thought and word. This sense of loss of personal identity can come about by constantly saying "not I" but Christ, until such a believer finds it difficult to use the personal pronoun at all.

The suppression of personality in thought and language, gives place to e.s. to identify themselves with the person, since God does not identify Himself with believers in such a way as to make them automatons.

Symptoms of insanity and d.p. indistinguishable,
On account of this the person may be constantly accused by e.s. of "going mad." He must refuse such a thought at all costs. If there is natural ground, there is hope of its removal if e.s. are resisted in their attempts to drive the person to accept--or practically, by acceptance, give consent to their suggestion. The same may be said in regard to temptation to suicide.

Healing by "suggestion,"
What is cured by suggestion was caused by suggestion. Fear in casting out, The refusal of all fear of evil spirits is absolutely essential for victory over them. There is no cause for true fear in view of the complete victory of Christ on Calvary, and His authority over all the emissaries of Satan. Any fear which cannot be got rid of is the result of obsession or possession. Keeping under the body, In some cases of d.p. "soul" manifestations dominate, and in others bodily ones. One form expresses every form of indulgence of the flesh, the other the utmost austerity and abstemiousness in food, sleep, and ordinary bodily comfort. Even in these cases the man is deceived in thinking all is under control, because the

spiritual manifestations feed the senses in another form. Talkativeness, Dumbness or evil silence is a symptom of d.p. with the effect of periodical lack of control of speech, caused by passivity of the human speaking in order for God to speak.

Counterfeit speaking of God,

How the lying spirits counterfeit the speaking of God, was seen in one child of God who was suffering from what was though a "breakdown in health," but what she and her family afterwards knew was possession. Praying one night to know God's will whether she was to recover, a soft and gentle voice said, "To-day, thou shalt be with me in Paradise." Answering so quickly her prayer, she took this as the "Voice of God" and yielded herself to it, when there came the suggestion to drink some poison at hand.

Under the supernatural power her judgment and conscience became passive, and she was found at the moment of drinking the poison, and restrained. This lady is now delivered.

Appendix Note.-

The page references in all cases refer to preceding chapters in "War on the Saints." The attitude of the Early Fathers to evil spirits.

"Tertullian says, in his Apology addressed to the Rulers of the roman Empire: . . Let a person be brought before your tribunals who is plainly under demoniacal possession. The wicked spirit, bidden to speak by a follower of Christ, will as readily make the truthful confession that he is a demon, as elsewhere he has falsely asserted that he is a god. Or, if you will, let there be produced one of the god-possessed, as they are supposed--if they do not confess, IN THEIR FEAR OF LYING TO A CHRISTIAN, that they are demons, then and there shed the blood of that most impudent follower of Christ. "ALL THE AUTHORITY AND POWER WE HAVE OVER THEM IS FROM OUR NAMING THE NAME OF CHIRST, AND RECALLING TO THEIR MEMORY THE WOES WITH WHICH GOD THREATENS THEM AT THE HAND OF CHIRST THEIR JUDGE, AND WHICH THEY EXPECT ONE DAY TO OVERTAKE THEM. FEARING CHRIST IN GOD AND GOD IN CHRIST, THEY BECOME SUBJECT TO THE SERVANTS OF GOD AND CHRIST. SO AT ONE TOUCH AND BREATHING, OVERWHELMED BY THE THOUGHT AND REALISATION OF THOSE JUDGEMENT FIRES, THEY LEAVE AT OUR COMMAND THE BODIES THEY HAVE ENTERED, UNWILLING AND DISTRESSED, AND BEFORE YOUR VERY EYES, PUT TO AN OPEN SHAME . . ."

Justin Martyr, in his second Apology addressed to the Roman Senate, says: "Numberless demoniacs throughout the whole world and in your city, many of our Christian men--exorcising them in the name of Jesus Christ who was crucified under Pontus Pilate-- have healed and do heal, rendering helpless, and driving the possessing demon out of the men, though they could not be cured by all other exorcists, and those who use incantations and drugs."

CYPRIAN expressed himself with equal confidence. After having said that they are evil spirits that inspire the false prophets of the Gentiles, and deliver oracles by always mixing truth with falsehood to prove what they say, he adds: "Nevertheless these evil spirits adjured by the living God IMMEDIATELY OBEY US, SUBMIT TO US, OWN OUR POWER, and are forced to come out of the bodies they possess. . . ." Symptoms of Demon Possession. pp 38, 96. Gleanings from "Demon Possession," by Dr. J.L. Nevius.

The one under demon-power is an involuntary victim. (The willing soul is known as a medium).

The chief characteristic of demonomania is a distinct "other personality" within. (This is different to demon-influence, for in this men follow their own wills, and retain their own personality.)

The demons have a longing for a body to possess (Matt. 12: 43, 8: 31), as it seems to give them some relief, and they enter the bodies of animals as well as men. There are distinctly individual peculiarities of the spirits.

They converse through the organs of speech, and give evidence of personality, desire, fear. They give evidence of knowledge and power not possessed by the subject.

In Germany, Pastor Blumhardt gives instances of demons speaking in all the European languages, and in some languages unrecognisable

.In France there were some cases having the "gift of tongues," speaking in German, Latin, Arabic. 6. The demon in possession of the body, entirely changes the moral character of those they enter, compelling them to act entirely contrary to their normal behaviour. Reserved, reticent men will weep, sing, laugh, talk, meek souls will rage, ordinarily pure-tongued men and women will speak of things not to be named among children of God, and act in manner and conduct contrary to their normal dignity and behaviour--all of which they are not responsible for whilst under "control" of this other personality within them.

In brief, they will exhibit traits of character utterly different from those which belong to them normally.

There are also nervous and muscular symptoms peculiar to demon possession in the body.

There is also an afflatus of the breast, which is a special mark of demon possession, and Oracular utterances are given in jerks and sentences, quite unlike the calm coherent sequence of language seen in the utterances of the apostles at Pentecost.

There is "levitation" of the body --well known by spiritists--when the subject will say he is quite unconscious of possessing a body--and there is invariably a passive mind. There is often a distinct voice which speaks through the lips of the subject expressing thoughts, and words unintentionally.

Demoniacal activity in later times. pp 12, 25. From "Spirit Manifestations." By Sir Robert Anderson.

"The Gospels testify to the activity of demons during the ministry of Christ on earth; and the Epistles warn us of a RENEWAL OF DEMONIACAL ACTIVITY in the "latter times," before His return. "All Scripture is God-breathed"; but it would seem that sometimes the revelation was made with special definiteness, and this particular warning is prefaced by the words; "the Spirit saith expressly." And it relates not to any new development of moral evil in the world, but to a new apostasy in the professing Church, a cult promoted by "seducing spirits" of a highly sensitive spirituality, and a more fastidious morality than

Christianity itself will sanction (1 Tim. 4)

The Gospel narrative indicates that some demons were base and filthy spirits that exercised a brutalising influence upon their victims. But the Lord plainly indicated that these were a class apart ("this kind" Mark 9: 29). They were all "unclean spirits," but in Jewish use the word akatharios connoted spiritual defilement. That it did not imply moral pollution is proved by the fact that the Lord Jesus was charged with having a demon, though not even His most malignant enemies ever accused Him of moral evil. It was only by prayer that these filthy spirits could be cast out; whereas pious demons acknowledged Christ, and came out when His disciples commanded them to do so in His Name . . ."

The physiology of the spirit. pp 214-223. Gleanings from "Primeval Man unveiled." By James Gall.

"The natural body has its senses, the spirit also has its senses . . ."

"There are busy senses within, examining and judging, approving and condemning, joying and grieving, hoping and fearing, after a fashion of their own, which no bodily sense can imitate . . ."

"There is a spirit within which we call ourselves, and it is perfectly distinct from the body in which we dwell..."

"If our spirits, which are generated in or with our bodies, are elaborated from immaterial substances into separate existences, constituting individual spirits . . . these individual spirits must be presumed to be composed of spirit substance or substances, and possessed of different faculties . . ."

"Our very language implies that the human spirit is an organism composed of parts mutually related, which, though individually different, are generically the same . . ."

"It is a well established doctrine of Scripture, that the body is animated by an intelligent and immortal spirit, that feels and acts by means of its material mechanism, without being itself material . . ."

Demon Possession among Christians.

The Case of a Christian Lady.

Extracts from private letters, by an Evangelist of repute in Germany.

". . . In the Spring of this year (1912) [this servant of God] who was possessed, came here, and the spirits possessing her spoke through her in voices utterly unlike her own. They would utter through her the most awful blasphemies against God, and against our Lord Jesus Christ, and would prophecy concerning the Church . . .

"Much prayer has been made for her, and with her. When the frenzy comes upon her, she is fearfully shaken, dashes about the room, made to howl like a dog, and her hands clenched, her face drawn with horrible contortions, etc., etc. But the marvel to everyone is that, although the frenzy is upon her every day, and sometimes once, twice, or more in one day, her health is perfect, she sleeps well, and in the interval is the MOST LOVELY SPIRITED CHRISTIAN WOMAN . . ."

". . . This sister is not one who has not got faith. She is well grounded in the same faith, and has the same light as we have; but we have here to do with a demon, the like of which I have never met before, nor read about . . . .

"It would also be an error if one were to think that PRAYER AND COMMANDING had not been of any use, for in these last three weeks God has done great and glorious things, so that we are full of adoration. The demon is still there, it is true, but he has broken down mightily, so that he cannot any more torment the sister. He is quite powerless in her, and she looks so radiantly happy with a heavenly gladness, fresh and strong. Also the demon has been divested of all power over her lips. Instead of the blasphemies and ravings, there is only a desperate and plaintive howling . . and that lasts all the time we pray."

Later... "For about a fortnight now the demon has been silent. For eight days he did not speak a single word, only he cried out twice: 'THE AUTHORITY CASTS ME OUT!' The only thing he does is howling and gnashing of teeth. Some days ago we prayed for about one-and-a-half hours. In this way it goes on now for ten or fourteen days--there is only this terrible crying, as if in great fear. There is not any blasphemy, nor cursing God, no more asserting threatenings, and all the sayings that he would not depart, that it would not suit him--all this has ceased. Instead of the dreadful ravings and outbursts of rage, there is now the desperate howling, often a dreadful screaming as if of fear, and the sister is almost free from his tormenting her . . . .

"The demon must have received a terrible blow from God, so that his blasphemies have been silenced. It was so last evening;

when we prayed, the desperate cry began at once, and I felt once more the impulse to command the demon in the Name of the Lord Jesus to depart. He then gave a great start, he trembled, howled, stretched out both hands as if imploring mercy, and begging us not to do that, but he was not allowed to utter a single word . But there followed strong reaction and vomiting, and this was repeated as often as I spoke the command in the Name of the Lord Jesus to depart. Of course we have to go on praying just as earnestly, but as God has done such great things, and if we go on praying, also the last blow will be given. The demon will have to depart."

Note: Further particulars of this case are given in "The Strong Man Spoiled," by A.R. Habershon. (id. Morgan & Scott, London).

The lady is now quite set free, and has been able to return to her mission work. It is stated clearly that her mental faculties were unimpaired, and she was able to prepare all the accounts and balance sheet of the mission she was engaged in, not long before the attacks became manifested. In this book, the demon's acknowledgment of the power and authority granted to those who commanded him, and the other spirits to depart, is striking. The spirit in possession said: "Oh, this authority, this authority which they have now recognised, is an awful thing for hell!" Pleading for mercy at another time the e.s. said, "Do leave off your commanding. For three weeks I have suffered unbearable torments because of it. Do not tell anybody that we had to yield to the authority . . . . Oh, these prayers of believers . . . they always pray, they are no longer afraid . . . ."

THE WORKING OF EVIL SPIRITS IN CHRISTIAN GATHERINGS

1. Supposed "conviction of sin" by deceiving spirits.

". . . I united with a number of brethren and sisters one whole week every month, in prayer to God to pour out more of His Spirit, gifts and power. After having done this for some time with great earnestness, such powerful and wonderful manifestations of God and His Holy Spirit (apparently) took place, that we no longer doubted God had heard our prayer, and His Spirit had descended into our midst, and on our gathering.

Amongst other things this spirit, which we thought to be the Holy Spirit, used a 15-year-old girl as his instrument, through whom everyone belonging to our gathering, and having any sin or burden of conscience, had it revealed to the gathering. Nobody could remain in the meeting with any burden of conscience without it being revealed to the meeting by this spirit.

"For example: A gentleman of esteem and respect from the neighbourhood came to the meeting, and all his sins were exposed in the presence of the gathering by the 15-year-old girl. Thereupon he took me into an adjoining room, so broken down, and admitted to me, with tears, that he had committed all these sins which the girl had exposed. He confessed this and all other sins known to him. Then he came again into the meeting, but hardly had he entered when the same voice said to him, 'Ha! You have not confessed all yet, you have stolen 10 gulden, that you have not confessed.' In consequence, he took me again into the adjoining room and said, 'It is true, I have also done this . . . 'This man had never seen this 15-year-old girl in his life, neither she him. With such events, was it astonishing that a spirit of holy awe came over all at the meeting, and there was one controlling note which can only be expressed in the words, 'Who among us shall dwell with the devouring fire? Who among us shall dwell with everlasting burnings?'

"Fearfulness hath surprised the hypocrites. There was a most earnest spirit of adoration, and who could doubt when even the strong were broken down, and nobody dared remain in the meeting if they were a hindrance. And, yet we had to unmask this spirit which had brought about these things--and which we took to be the Holy Ghost--as a terrible power of darkness. I had such an uneasy feeling of distrust which could not be overcome . . .

"As I made this known for the first time to an older brother and friend . . . he said, 'Brother Seitz, if you continue to foster unbelief, you can commit the sin against the Holy Ghost which will never be forgiven.'

"These were terrible days and hours for me, because I did not know whether we had to do with the power of God or a disguised spirit of Satan, and one thing only was clear to me, viz., that I and this meeting should not let ourselves be led by a spirit when we did not have clear light, and confirmation whether this power was from above or below. Thereupon I took the leading brethren and sisters to the uppermost room of the house, and made known to them my position, and said we must all cry and pray that we may be able to prove whether it was a power of light or darkness.

"As we came downstairs the voice of this power said, using the 15-year-old girl as his instrument, 'What is this rebellion in your midst? You will be sorely punished for your unbelief.' I told this voice that it was true we did not know with whom we had dealings. But we wanted to be in that attitude, that if it was an angel of God, or the Spirit of God, we would not sin against Him, but if it was a devil we would not be deceived by him. 'If you are the power of God, you will be in accord as we handle the Word of God.' 'Try the spirits whether they be of God.'

"We all knelt down and cried and prayed to God in such earnestness, that He would have mercy upon us, and reveal to us in some manner, whom we had dealings with. Then the power had to reveal itself on its own accord. Through the person which he had been using as his instrument he made such abominable and terrible grimaces, and shrieked in such a piercing tone, 'Now I am found out, now I am found out."

2. Supposed unity for "Revival."

For some time now it has been on my mind to try to put into language some of the things which it has been my painful experience to witness, and pass through, in connection with the workings of Satan as an "angel of light," but everything seemed so complicated and confused...

First, his attacks seem to be made upon the most spiritual souls--those who have made the fullest surrender to God, and who recognise a spiritual affinity, which they believe if broken, mars the whole purpose of God (1 Cor. 1: 10). The lying spirit insists on one mind, and judgment, and one expression. These souls thus "joined" form the "Assembly," so called, and claim Psalm 89: 7. Everything is brought into the "Assembly" for decision, the assertion being that no individual soul can get the mind of the Lord, based on Prov. 11: 14, 5: 22, and 20: 18. Hours were spent in bringing the tiniest details of daily life before the Lord. The leader spread each matter, asking that all might be brought to one mind. The response was then given by each one in some word of Scripture. The attitude taken to receive the supposed "word of the Lord," was the RESISTANCE OF ANY THOUGHT OR REASON, and LETTING THE MIND BECOME A PERFECT BLANK. If anyone ventured to give an opinion--or any judgment--they were ruled out of fellowship; the fact of reasoning being the proof of the "flesh-life." The discipline ministered to such was severe indeed. They were not allowed to speak to anyone, or to do any kind of work. In some cases this lasted for weeks, and even months.

The effect upon the mind was very terrible. The only way back was by making a statement in the "Assembly" which satisfied them that there was true repentance. Prov. 21: 4, and Isaiah 59: 3, are the words given for not working, and Rom. 8: 8. Prayer and reading the word--all adds to sin--consequently the soul is shut up in torment and despair, being excluded from all meetings. Second. The "manifestation of the Spirit" in prophecy, prayer and travail. One person would often pray for an hour, and sometimes two hours, without a break. Messages, too, would often last for two hours, and the whole meeting for eight or nine hours. Anyone yielding to sleep or exhaustion, was at once pronounced "in the flesh," and a hindrance to the meeting. "Travail" was manifested by tears, groans and twisting of the body; and with some it was exactly like hysterics, and would last for hours. This was greatly encouraged as the means whereby God would work for the deliverance of souls--and those who did not come under this manifestation, were judged as preserving their own life, not willing to "let go"--lovers of themselves; and it was believed that when the whole company were unitedly under the so-called "manifestation of the Spirit" then God would break through in Revival. I might say here, that all this began with a nightly prayer meeting for Revival, with no limit as to time. The paralysing fear of resisting God by any lack of submission, and evading the Cross by an unwillingness to suffer, just sways the soul; and it dare not yield to one thought contrary to the "mind of Christ" in the "Assembly . . ."

From a book recently published, said to contain the very words of the Lord Jesus, spoken THROUGH some of His children, and written down as spoken in the first person, the following brief extract is taken, showing the extract of the mediumistic control by deceiving spirits, which some are believed to be the work of the Holy Spirit. The Lord Jesus is supposed to have said:-"The manifestations of the Spirit, in some things, are very strange. Sometimes He will twist the body this way, and that, and the meaning is dark to you. I want you to know some things about this part of the Spirit's work. I want you to see that they are not useless. If you had spoken in your own tongue, when the Spirit came in, it would have graciously blessed you; but perhaps you might have thought it was yourself , as many have. So the Spirit comes in and speaks in an unknown tongue to you, that you might know that it was NOT YOURSELF SPEAKING . . . Your hands He has often lifted up, and again He has raised your fingers in various ways. Your eyes open and shut by the Spirit now, as they did not before. Your very head has been shaken by the Spirit, and you have not known why He did this. You have thought sometimes, it was just to show He was living there, and that is true, but there is more in it than that, and He will show you as well as He can, in a few words, what some of these things are . . .

Some things in the manifestations are very peculiar to you. You have gone on wondering about them. Don't think it strange that the Spirit works in you in many ways. His work is more than a twofold work. It is manifold. This is puzzling many minds. They see the Spirit shaking. They hear Him singing. They FEEL HIM LAUGHING, and they are sometimes tried with His various twistings and jerkings, as though He would tear them to pieces. Sometimes it seems He is imitating the animals in various sounds and doings. This has been all a mystery to the saints. His work, I say, is manifold. He seeks, in some, to show them that they are all one with each other, in the whole creation . . . If He shows you, by making a noise as of some wild animal, and that you are like that, you must not despise His way of working, for the Holy Spirit knows why He does it. He makes these noises in the animals, can't He make them in you?